The
Complete
Fisherman

For Lynette

The Complete Fisherman

by

Ian Ball

Typeset in 10pt Times by One And A Half Graphics, 4 Linkfield Corner, Redhill, Surrey.
Printed and bound in Great Britain by Cox & Wyman Ltd., Reading, Berkshire.

Clarion: published from behind no. 80 Brighton Road, Tadworth, Surrey, England.

Contents

Part 1

Freshwater Fishing

1
Freshwater Fishing

Freshwater fishing is the sporting pursuit with rod and line of
fishes that live in fresh water: still or flowing water, which is
more-or-less drinkable, not salt water.

An angler

As you see from fig 1, fishing is all angles. The name "angler"
has been used in the U.K. for several hundred years and perhaps
it is because when we fish, our rod and line forms an angle. We
are "angling" for fish. The name *angler* also shows we are not
fishermen using nets.

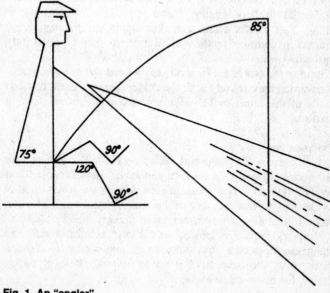

Fig. 1 An "angler".

Coarse fishermen

Some people who fish with rod and line prefer to call themselves fishermen. A *coarse* angler or fisherman fishes for coarse fish. All freshwater fish except salmon and trout are "coarse" fish. Salmon and trout are called *game* fish because they are wise and strong fighting fish, offering us good "game" or sport.

Nobody knows for sure why most freshwater fish are called coarse fish. Some say the reason is their coarse flavour when cooked; others believe the name comes from the coarse, rough scales on the skin of many freshwater fish, compared to the smoother scales of the game fish – salmon and trout. In America, "coarse" fish are called "rough" fish.

Your guess is as good as anyone's. Angler, coarse angler, freshwater fisherman/woman/person; call yourself what you will. Americans who fish for pleasure with rod and line call themselves *sport fishers*.

Tackle dealers

Get to know your local specialist tackle dealer; visit the shop and have a good look round. Chat, ask for advice and guidance on all fishing matters. Your friendly tackle dealer will help select the right tackle; provide the correct freshwater *rod licence* – essential to fish legally – and recommend waters worth fishing. Your tackle dealer can also supply any *fishing permit* required in addition to the rod licence, to fish a particularly worthwhile water.

Support the tackle dealer with *your* valued custom, and you'll be rewarded handsomely with the dealer's expert hints, tips and details of the latest tackle developments and "secret" fishing hotspots.

Close seasons

In most parts of England and Wales no fishing is allowed for *coarse fish* between March 15th and June 15th inclusive (their breeding season). The close season for *brown trout* is from 1st October to the last day of February, inclusive. The close season for *salmon* is November 1st to January 31st inclusive.

Scotland, Northern Ireland and Eire, each have different arrangements, which may vary from one water to another. Check with the respective Tourist Boards, or local tackle dealers, for up-to-date details.

Outwit the fish

To catch fish think one step ahead. Big fish stay unhooked because foolish anglers can't outwit them. Let Nature remind you how to hunt – be animal cunning from the start. Wear drab-colour clothes that blend with the background; wear nothing bright or flashy. Put tackle together away from the waterside and approach quietly; tread softly. Creep from one bank edge hiding-place to another (bush, tree etc). Scan the water for promising spots to fish. Be aware that alert fishes can see images of natural food and angler's baits reflected downwards from the surface of *calm water* (which acts as a mirror) and can at the same time, watch the bankside for motion betraying the presence of prowling anglers.

Never feel self-conscious about crouching or crawling towards open bankside areas devoid of cover. Nobody will think you silly when you land the BIG fish others can't catch!

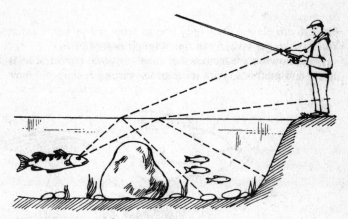

Fig. 2 Fish's eye view of water and bankside.

Relax to succeed

This book tells all you need know to locate the right spots to fish, and the best ways to present tempting hookbait. The rest is up to you. When you're certain you've found a stretch of water that holds fish, apply the knowledge you've learned and fish your way to success. Relax, be confident you know enough to hook that Big one... And when it seizes your hookbait, don't panic. Remain calm and in control. Reel-in line, and land your fish.

2
Superfish

Fish have learned a lot about us over the last couple of million years. Prehistoric man, Ancient Egyptians, Greeks and Romans have painted pictures of themselves fishing. We've all shared the same problems: where are the big fish; how can we get near them undetected; what's the best bait to use, and how should we land our fish once hooked?

More fish get off the hook than are caught. We have much to learn.

Big brainy fish
Big fish are clever. They only live to grow big by being smart. You have to get up early in the morning to fool them.

Fish know we are hunters and keep an eye on our latest baits, tackle and methods. With more of us starting fishing for sport,

Fig. 3 Superfish.

14

fish have extra practice avoiding our hooks.

Modern research has shown that big fish educate baby fish and we have to think of new ways to catch them. Wise fish outwit us; grow huge (for their species) and pass their secrets to young fish. This is what we are up against – big brainy fish.

Fish ears

Beware! Fish have ears. Sound is clearer in water than in air. Fish have ears inside the head and hear us coming from as far away as 12m (40 ft) in any direction. We must sneak down on them.

Fishy smell

Fish have a highly-developed sense of smell. They track food for long distances in muddy water and at night. Fish are also able to detect tiny traces of chemicals in water and are upset by the slightest pollution.

Fish eyes

Fish have all round, full-colour daytime sight. They see everything happening around them without moving their bodies. At night and in murky water fish switch to black and white vision. Fish have no eyelids and sleep with their eyes open.

Water acts like a mirror and fish see any movement in the water reflected on the underneath of the surface. Fish also spot motion on the bank and at the water's edge.

Touch and taste

A fish knows when the water temperature alters by a fraction of a degree.

Fish do not need to take food into their mouths to taste. Fish can taste food just by touching it with their lips. Hooks in bait may be felt and the bait rejected, or simply sucked off the hook.

Fish wear combat jackets

Fish are camouflaged by colour patterns which blend in with their surroundings – just as we wear clothes for fishing that make us difficult for fish to see. Fish are hard to find by glancing into the water, because they swim in "camouflaged combat jackets". Fish are white underneath and invisible to an enemy below, who can't see them because the fish's belly matches the sky. The white belly gives a flashing effect when hooked fish roll to dislodge a hook.

Fish speak

Yes, fish talk to each other in "fishese". They pass information and gossip though the water in secret code about food, natural enemies and fishermen, by moving their bodies and insides to make special sounds only they understand. And if the message to scoot is broadcast, fish move fast. A 457mm (18 inch) fish sprints at about 16 miles per hour and cruises at 10 miles per hour.

So, how can we hope to catch *Superfish?* Well, we can, read on...

3
Food Chain

Our hunt for fish begins with a look at the way their food develops in fresh water. Knowing what fish eat gives clues to help us catch big fish.

Life-giving plants
Plants of various sizes grow in fresh water. Some large plants root and rise from the bottom, while others grow and flourish

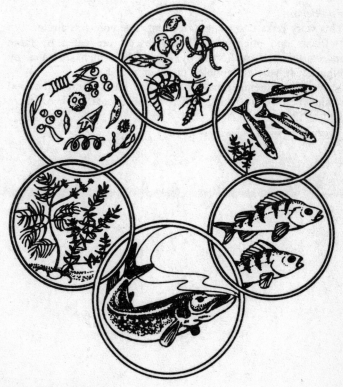

Fig. 4 The food chain.

near the surface. Microscopic plants float on top of water. Life in fresh water depends on plants.

Plants draw energy from the sun's rays and convert sunlight into life-giving oxygen, which they bubble into the water.

Plants clean water by filtering waste matter passed out by fish and insects, and convert the waste into nourishing nutrients like nitrogen and phosphates that help plants grow. All dead things are broken down by bacteria into nutrients to be used by plants.

Plants provide fish with food, supply shelter from strong sunlight and offer a hiding place from enemies – kingfishers, herons, otters and big fish who eat smaller fish. Plants also give fish somewhere to lay their eggs.

Fish, snails, shrimps, insects, worms and many other forms of freshwater life feed on plants.

All types of water life are eaten by fish.

Food chain
This story links into a chain of events that goes full circle.

Plants and microscopic water insects are eaten by large insects that are swallowed by small fish, which are eaten by bigger fish, who are gobbled up by great fish.

We must remember the importance of water plants to the food chain when we go fishing. Where we see plants, we know there will be fish!

4
Freshwater Fish

Soft-finned fish

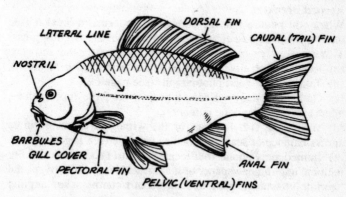

Fig. 5 General features of soft-finned fish.

The *dorsal* and *anal* fins enable the fish to balance; the *pectoral* and *pelvic* fins assist the fish's movements, and the *caudal* fin, combined with body movement, propels the fish through water. Some species of fish have sensitive *barbules* to feel and taste for food hidden from the fish's sight, at the water bottom. The *lateral line* is a series of scales with tiny holes, giving the appearance of a line. The "holes" are pores through which changes in pressure are communicated to the fish's brain. The lateral line of pores warns the fish of approaching objects; lurking predators, and hidden prey.

Spiny-finned fish, like perch and zander, have a spiny dorsal fin and a second, *posterior dorsal* fin on the back, close behind.

Fish file
Pick your fish before you go fishing. Study the "Fish file" on the next few pages; decide which fish you want to catch and then read on to find the top tackle and best methods for catching the big ones.

All our fish have English and Latin names. The Latin names are used by scientists of every nation. In the "Fish file", the Latin name of each fish is bracketed next to its English name.

Fish belong to families and fish belonging to the same family are related to each other, even though they may look very different.

REMEMBER: *to know your fish helps you plan how best to catch him.*

Record breakers

When you hook a fish big enough to be a record breaker (see current *Record rod-caught weight* reports in the angling press) TRY to:

(a) Keep the fish alive (an angler's fine-mesh *keep-net* is ideal).

(b) Take several good photographs (see page 60).

(c) Gather as many witnesses as you are able (note names, addresses and telephone numbers).

(d) Weigh the fish in front of the witnesses on an accurate spring-balance or scales as soon as possible (see page 60).

(e) Immediately phone your local specialist tackle dealer and/or national angling newspaper or magazine. Keep a note of special "hotline" telephone numbers for record claims – see angling press for details.

Politely ask a "witness" to phone on your behalf while you nurse the celebrity fish. Await advice and instructions from the experts contacted by telephone.

And support your local newspaper by contacting the editor with your front page "scoop" story.

But the fish comes first

Should the fish appear to be suffering, make do with your photographs and the names, addresses and phone numbers of witnesses, and release your fish to recover fully in the safe and secure atmosphere of its water.

Stop Press

Information given in your "Fish file" is correct at the moment of printing. Our knowledge of fish behaviour is constantly advanced by anglers' painstaking observation, reasoning and accurate record keeping (see Chapter 18) – enabling us to go out and catch big record breaking specimen fish!

Up-date facts about fish by regularly reading angling newspapers and magazines.

Sport****Star****Ratings

Each species of fish in your "Fish file" is star rated to give an idea of the fish's usual fighting and sporting qualities. You might disagree with my ratings after you've fought with the fish, in which case please amend the ratings and award or take away a *Star*.

BARBEL

Name: Barbel *(Barbus barbus).*

Family: Cyprinidae. Other members of family found in Europe, Africa and Asia.

Size we can expect to catch: Average weight about 1.81kg (4 lb).

Where barbel like to live: On the bottom of fast flowing streams and rivers. Found in many rivers, especially the Hampshire Avon, Dorset Stour, Kennet, Lea, Nidd, Severn, Swale, Thames, Trent, Welland, Ure and Yorkshire Ouse. Barbel are spreading fast, assisted by angling clubs introducing barbel to club waters.

Fig. 6 Barbel.

How to recognise barbel: Long snout with 4 barbules (feelers) on thick lipped, drooping mouth. Green-brown back, pink-orange fins and silver-white belly.

Sport "Star" rating: ******Excellent fighting fish******

Barbel's favourite natural food: Worms, insects, small fish and water plants.

Baits to catch barbel: Bread flake, bread paste, caddis grubs, cheese paste, hempseed, luncheon meat, maggots, sausage (lightly boiled), silkweed, slugs, wasp grubs, worms.

Barbel's peak sporting fitness: AUGUST/SEPTEMBER/OCTOBER/ NOVEMBER/DECEMBER/JANUARY/FEBRUARY.

Know your barbel: Barbel is known as "Old Whiskers" to his friends, who say barbel should visit the barbus for a shave. Barbel (*barbus barbus*) is a powerful fish who always gives us a fight to remember.

Barbel grow big and a few probably reach 9kg (20 lb). But such huge barbel are clever and have not been caught in the U.K. A barbel of 7kg 260g (16 lb 1 oz) was accidentally hooked in the fin and landed by C.H. Cassey in 1960 on the Hampshire Avon at Ibsley. Because the barbel was hooked in its fin and therefore not caught fairly (hooked in the lip) it was not counted as a record.

Barbel use the feelers on their mouths to find food amongst plants, stones, roots and mud.

Barbel swim in shoals, usually hugging the river bed. They hide in holes and deep pools beside weirs or dams and in water plants or submerged tree roots. Barbel are shy, moody fish and sometimes sulk for days without feeding. When barbel feed they hungrily wolf down food and stick to regular mealtimes. Some shoals of barbel feed only in one spot.

Big *Barbus barbus* is waiting for you!

Groundbait effective? YES – see Chapter 9.

Best fishing methods for BIG Barbel: Legering (see Chapter 13) and float fishing (see Chapter 12).

Right line strength for big barbel: At least 2.26kg (5 lb) breaking strain.

BREAM

Name: Bream, bronze (*Abramis brama*).

Family: Cyprinidae. Other members of family found in Europe, Africa and Asia.

Size we can expect to catch: Average weight about 1.36kg (3 lb).

Where bream like to live: On the bottom of deep, quiet, slow-moving or still waters. Common in canals, lakes, lochs, ponds, reservoirs and rivers across the U.K., notably: The Cheshire meres, Great Ouse, Nene, Norfolk Broads, Severn, Thames, Welland, Witham, Yorkshire Ouse etc.

How to recognise bream: When young silvery; adult bream bronze-brown; wide-bodied, hump-backed. Tail fin deep forked.

Sport "Star" rating ****Good fighting fish****

Bream's favourite natural food: Insects, shellfish, vegetable matter, worms.

Baits to catch bream: Bread flake, bread paste, maggots, worms.

Bream's peak sporting fitness: AUGUST/SEPTEMBER/OCTOBER/ NOVEMBER/JANUARY/FEBRUARY/MARCH.

Fig. 7 Bream.

Know your bream: Bream is a disciplined and orderly shoal fish. New born bream congregate in shoals 100's, sometimes 1,000's strong. Each shoal is gradually reduced in numbers by natural predators and normal death, until only a few big bream survive. Because bream shoal at birth and probably stay in the same shoal until they die, bream belonging to a particular shoal are all of roughly the same size. Spy one big bream rolling on the surface and you'll know other big bream aren't far away. Every shoal has a leader and he patrols an area of water to a carefully rehearsed time-table, followed closely by his shoal. The bream shoal's predictably regimented pattern of movement and behaviour gives observant fishermen the chance to catch many bream at precise times and locations – whole shoals can be caught by astute anglers. However, really big bream feed at night, or in the early morning hours (2 a.m. to 3 a.m.).

Bream feed at the water bottom; consume vast amounts of food and are caught mainly on stationary baits.

Bream are shy, cautious fish, who keep well away from the bank; sticking to the comparative safety of deep water. Bream feed voraciously in the summer months; eating less and diving deep during the cold winter weeks.

Bream are slow but determined fighters once hooked.

Groundbait effective? YES (exceptionally responsive to groundbaiting and "feeding") – see Chapter 9.

Best fishing methods for BIG Bream: Legering (see Chapter 13) and float fishing (see Chapter 12).

Right line strength for big bream: At least 1.81kg (4 lb) breaking strain.

CARP

Name: Carp, common *(Cyprinus carpio).*
Family: Cyprinidae. Other members of family found in Europe, Africa and Asia.
Size we can expect to catch: Average weight about 2.72kg (6 lb).
Where carp like to live: Mud-bottomed lakes, rivers, gravel pits and ponds. Carp like quiet, heavily weeded, sluggish water. Many of the really big carp can be found only in club and private syndicate waters.

Fig. 8 Carp.

How to recognise carp: Thick, deep body. Large, greenish-brown scales. Two barbules (feelers) on each side of its upper jaw.
Sport "Star" rating: ******Excellent fighting fish******
Carp's favourite natural food: Water plants and vegetable matter; worms, insects and shellfish.
Baits to catch carp: Earthworms, bread paste (mixed with honey or yeast extract spread); small potatoes (lightly boiled), green peas, maggots, wasp grubs, "casters"; cheese paste, cherries (stone removed); most types of grain; special commercially produced high protein baits; legered floating crust, sweetcorn.
Carp's peak sporting fitness: AUGUST/SEPTEMBER/OCTOBER/NOVEMBER/DECEMBER.
Know your carp: Carp is a native of Asia, where he is often bred in "stockponds" as a food fish; they grow huge very quickly. Carp were probably brought to Europe by the Romans, and

24

introduced to the U.K. in the fourteenth century by monks who kept carp in stockponds; fishing and catching them for the traditional religious Friday fish supper.

In European waters, carp of over 29.48kg (65 lb) are not uncommon. Carp live a long time. Some have, in captivity, lived to be over 40 years old!

They are shy, highly intelligent fish; wary of unfamiliar foods fished as bait, and notoriously difficult to catch.

Carp live alone, or in small groups. They are moody and fickle feeders; affected by light and water temperature; losing interest in particular foods or baits at a whim. Big carp feed mainly at night.

Warm weather brings the best sport; carp tend to become inactive on numerous waters during cold winter months, though they can still be caught.

Hooked carp pull away like trains and fight hard and furiously for their freedom.

Groundbait effective? YES – see Chapter 9.

Best fishing methods for big carp: Legering (see Chapter 13) and float fishing (see Chapter 12).

Right line strength for big carp: At least 3.62kg (8 lb) breaking strain.

CHUB

Name: Chub *(Leuciscus cephalus).*
Family: Cyprinidae. Other members of family found in Europe, Africa and Asia.

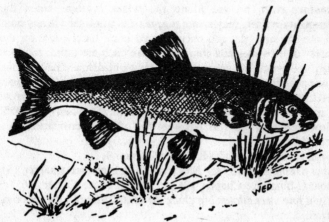

Fig 9. Chub.

Size we can expect to catch: Average weight about 680g (1½ lb).
Where chub like to live: Prefer flowing water – rivers and streams. Introduced to some stillwaters. Chub are fond of waters like the Dorset Stour, Great Ouse, Hampshire Avon, Kennet, Ribble, Severn, Thames, Trent, Welland and Wye. Chub are not found in most parts of north Scotland, west Wales, Devon or Cornwall.
How to recognise chub: Big head and mouth, with thick, pale lips. Dark back; large silver/bronze scales. Black edged tail; bright red lower fins.
Sport "Star" rating: ****Good fighting fish****
Chub's favourite natural food: Small fish, frogs, fruit, insects, shellfish, worms.
Baits to catch chub: Banana cubes, beetles, bluebottles, bread crust, cubes and paste; casters, caterpillars, cheese (particularly Danish blue or Gorgonzola), cherries (stone removed), elderberries, hempseed, luncheon meat, macaroni (boiled), maggots, sausage (lightly boiled), silkweed, slugs, snails, strawberries, sweetcorn, wasp grubs, worms.
Chub's peak sporting fitness: AUGUST/SEPTEMBER/OCTOBER/ NOVEMBER/DECEMBER/JANUARY/FEBRUARY.
Know your chub: Chub is a strong, bulky fish with a large appetite. He's a sociable shoal fish, but also inclined to be shy and independent; often leaving the shoal to hunt food on his own – big chub usually choose to live a solitary existence. Chub like underwater holes and hollows; submerged roots and overhanging bushes and trees. Chub feed at all depths; in cold weather chub browse along the water bottom; when the temperature rises, they cruise the surface. Chub feed at any hour of the day or night, and once hooked immediately dive for the safety of obstacles and snags. Because chub are timid, cautious fish, they must be approached extra carefully; or they'll soon disappear from the stretch of water you're fishing. Chub grow BIG. A chub of 4.76kg (10 lb 8 oz) was caught by Dr. J.A. Cameron while fishing the river Annan (Scotland) in 1955. However the chub was not kept for official verification as a record breaker.
Groundbait effective? YES – see Chapter 9.
Best fishing methods for BIG chub: Legering (see Chapter 13), float fishing (see Chapter 12) and spinning (see Chapter 16).
Right line strength for big chub: At least 2.26kg (5 lb) breaking strain.

DACE

Name: Dace *(Leuciscus leuciscus).*
Family: Cyprinidae. Other members of family found in Europe, Africa and Asia,
Size we can expect to catch: Average weight about 115g (4 oz).
Where dace like to live: Widespread in England and Wales. Dace like the fast running water of rivers and streams.

Fig. 10 Dace.

How to recognise dace: Slim, silvery fish. Dark brown or blue-green back. Lower fins yellowish, or soft pink.
Sport "Star" Rating: *****Very good fighting fish*****
Dace's favourite natural food: Insects, worms and water plants.
Baits to catch dace: Maggots, worms, silkweed, bread crust, flake, paste, hempseed, small berries (especially ripe elderberries).
Dace's peak sporting fitness: SEPTEMBER/OCTOBER/NOVEMBER/ DECEMBER/JANUARY/FEBRUARY/MARCH.
Know your dace: Dace is a gregarious shoal fish. He is always active, frisking, dashing and darting near the surface. Dace feed mainly at the surface and mid-water in warm weather, preferring the water bottom during cold periods. "Dainty" dace is a fun loving fish, who feeds steadily through summer, autumn and winter.
Groundbait effective? YES – see Chapter 9.
Best fishing methods for BIG dace: Float fishing (see Chapter 12), and legering (see Chapter 13).
Right line strength for big dace: At least 0.90kg (2 lb) breaking strain.

EEL

Name: Eel *(Anguilla anguilla).*

Family: Anguillidae (also called "Apodes"). There are over 500 related species of eel worldwide, including the conger eel and moray eel.

Size we can expect to catch: Average weight about 680g (1½ lb).

Where eels like to live: All waters; in holes and hollows at the bottom of rivers; deep pools in streams, and particularly lakes, lochs, reservoirs, gravel pits and snag-ridden ponds.

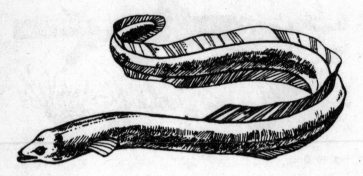

Fig. 11 Eel.

How to recognise eels: Dark brown or black with silver belly; snake-like appearance.

Sport "Star" rating: *****Very good fighting fish*****

Eel's favourite natural food: Small fish, frogs, insects, worms, shellfish etc.

Baits to catch eels: Earthworms, cheese paste, chunks of dead herring, sprat or mackerel.

Eel's peak sporting fitness: JUNE/JULY/AUGUST/SEPTEMBER/OCTOBER.

Know your eel: Eel is a mysterious fish. Much about his life is unknown. Freshwater eels are born in the Sargasso Sea, a vast mass of floating vegetation in the North Atlantic Ocean. Young eels drift in ocean currents for 3 years before entering European rivers and streams as "elvers" (tiny bootlace size eels). Some eels travel overland on damp nights to isolated ponds and remote land-locked waters (eels can live for long periods out of water); slithering adult eels have been seen climbing 1.8m (6 ft) high obstacles in their quest to find a new watery home. After reaching maturity, most eels return to the Sargasso Sea to breed;

then die. Eels don't breed in freshwater. Some adult eels prefer not to make the arduous journey back to the Sargasso Sea; stay put in their freshwater homes and grow huge. Eels of 9kg (20 lb) and above certainly exist, but have never been successfully landed on rod and line.

Eels have a highly developed sense of smell; feed mainly after dusk, especially at night and often track food for considerable distances.

Groundbait effective? YES – see Chapter 9 (include plenty of chopped worms or fish and a little grated cheese).

Best fishing methods for BIG eels: Legering (see Chapter 13).

Right line strength for big eels: At least 4.53kg (10 lb) breaking strain. Big eels have powerful jaws and small sharp teeth, which may sever line. Many anglers fish for big eels with special fishing *trace wire* attaching hook to line.

GRAYLING

Name: Grayling *(Thymallus thymallus)*.

Family: Salmonidae. Other members of family found in Europe, Asia and northern North America.

Size we can expect to catch: Average weight about 340g (12 oz).

Where grayling like to live: Sparkling-clear, fast flowing rivers and streams. Found in Scotland, northern England; the Midlands and southwest England, especially the chalk streams of Hampshire and Berkshire.

Fig. 12 Grayling.

How to recognise grayling: Attractive and elegant fish; silver, purple/blue colours flashing brightly from its scales. Large eyes and small mouth.

Sport "Star" rating: ******Excellent fighting fish******

29

Grayling's favourite natural food: Flies, insects, snails, worms and water plants.

Baits to catch grayling: Flies (real or artificial), worms, maggots, bread flake etc.

Grayling's peak sporting fitness: JUNE/JULY/AUGUST/SEPTEMBER/OCTOBER/NOVEMBER/DECEMBER/JANUARY/FEBRUARY.

Know your grayling: Related to the salmon and trout but officially classed as a "coarse" fish, graceful grayling is known as "Lady of the Stream". Grayling swim in small shoals; feed mostly near the water bottom and mid-water depth, but frequently rise to take flies and insects from the surface.

The shoals rove between holes and hollows at the edge of fast flowing water or streamy runs, and dense growths of weed in deep water.

Grayling feed enthusiastically throughout the year, and when hooked fight with sustained power and tenacity.

Groundbait effective? YES (very small amounts, mainly "feeding") – see Chapter 9.

Best fishing methods for BIG Grayling: Float fishing (see Chapter 12) and legering (see Chapter 13).

Right line strength for big grayling: At least 0.90kg (2 lb) breaking strain.

PERCH

Name: Perch *(Perca fluviatilis).*

Family: Percidae. Other members of family found in Europe, Asia and North America.

Fig. 13 Perch.

Size we can expect to catch: Average weight about 227g (8 oz).
Where perch like to live: Quiet ponds, lakes, lochs, canals, gravel pits, rivers and streams across U.K.
How to recognise perch: Handsome fish. Olive-green back shading into golden-brown, with 5-7 dark green stripes down each side. Spiky top fin; lower fins bright red or orange.
Sport "Star" rating: ****Good fighting fish****
Perch's favourite natural food: Small fish, worms, shellfish, insects etc.
Bait to catch perch: Worms, maggots, "casters"; small chunks of dead sprat or herring.
Perch's peak sporting fitness: JULY/AUGUST/SEPTEMBER/OCTOBER/ NOVEMBER/DECEMBER/JANUARY/FEBRUARY.
Know your perch: Perch's distinctive colouring has earned him names like, "sergeant fish" and 'freshwater tiger".

The perch is a predator – hunting and feeding on living or recently dead creatures. Small perch swim in shoals, adolescent perch hunt in packs and large adults live and feed alone; specializing in ambush techniques from hides in weed beds, reed and thick growths of underwater vegetation.

Perch hunt principally by sight and are attracted by movement. During the summer, they pursue shoals of fish fry in shallows and weeded bankside runs, fully prepared to track their prey over long distances. In winter, perch follow shoals of small fish into deep water and take position in holes and hollows at the water bottom. Perch get peckish all year, especially in winter, when surviving young fish are wiser and more difficult for perch to catch.

Groundbait effective? YES (very small amounts, mainly "cloud" to draw fish fry, which attract perch) – see Chapter 9.
Best fishing methods for BIG Perch: Legering (see Chapter 13), spinning (see Chapter 16) and float fishing (see Chapter 12).
Right line strength for big perch: At least 1.36kg (3 lb) breaking strain.

PIKE

Name: Pike *(Esox lucius).*
Family: Esocidae. Other members of family found in Europe, northern Asia and North America.
Size we can expect to catch: Average weight about 3.62kg (8 lb).
Where pike like to live: Flowing and still waters throughout Britain; lakes, lochs, ponds, gravel pits, reservoirs, rivers and streams. Among the best known haunts of monster pike are the

Norfolk Broads, Hampshire Avon and Loch Lomond.

How to recognise pike: Distinctive green and yellow camouflage markings, varying in shade and pattern from one water to another. Long body, forked tail; strong jaws and shark-like teeth!

Fig. 14 Pike.

Sport "Star" rating: *****Very good fighting fish*****

Pike's favourite natural food: Fish, frogs, frog spawn, water birds, rats, voles, worms, insects.

Baits to catch pike: Dead herring, sprat or mackerel; earthworms.

Pike's peak sporting fitness: JULY/AUGUST/SEPTEMBER/OCTOBER/NOVEMBER/DECEMBER/JANUARY.

Know your pike: Pike is an immensely powerful, awe-inspiring fish. His nickname – "freshwater shark" – describes the terror with which monster pike have always been regarded. Pike's mouth is equipped with hundreds of sharp, inward pointing teeth – once they snap shut on a victim, there's no escape!

Few baits are too large for big pike to swallow. Ducks are frequent prey and swans have been reported attacked. A pike of 32.65kg (72 lb) was caught on Loch Ken in 1774; an old and dying pike of 27.21 (60 lb) was found at Dowdeswell.

Pike lurk at the water bottom behind screening stones; in

holes, hollows and bank undercuts, and hide in weed, reed and lily beds. They hunt mostly by eyesight; feed mainly in daylight and make their kills by speedy acceleration to bushwhack unsuspecting fish.

Although pike prefer eating flesh, they do seize insects and in summertime sometimes bask near the surface; soaking up sun.

Pike feed in patterns – definite times and locations that alter after a period of days or weeks, seemingly related to weather, wind and temperature changes. In summer, pike often feed alone and at dawn; occasionally hunting in packs, making planned attacks on shoals of fish. Solitary hunting and pack attacks continue in winter. Mid-day can be a productive time to fish for pike on cold days.

Pike feed wherever fish congregate, and are caught in still or slow moving, deep water; also near shallows and fast flowing bankside runs.

Even small streams may hold pike of 3.62kg (8 lb) in weight. *Groundbait effective?* YES (small amounts of chopped fish and/or worms) – see Chapter 9.

Best fishing methods for BIG Pike: Legering (see Chapter 13) and spinning (see Chapter 16).

Right line strength for big pike: At least 5.44kg (12 lb) breaking strain. Because pike have sharp teeth that can easily cut through line, it's wise to fish with special fishing *trace wire* attaching hook to line.

NOTE: Remove hooks from pike with an angler's hook disgorger, forceps or pliers. To hold open big pike's jaws safely while removing your hook, gently fix an angler's *pike gag*.

ROACH
Name: Roach *(Rutilus rutilus).*
Family: Cyprinidae. Other members of family found in Europe, Africa and Asia.
Size we can expect to catch: Average size about 170g (6 oz).
Where roach like to live: Slow flowing rivers; canals, lakes, pits, ponds and reservoirs in most parts of Britain, except northern Scotland.
How to recognise roach: Dark green or blue-brown back; silvery sides and belly. Red eyes and reddish fins; small mouth with projecting upper lip.
Sport "Star" rating: *****Very good fighting fish*****
Roach's favourite natural food: Vegetable matter, insects etc.
Baits to catch roach: Sweetcorn, hempseed, pearl barley, tares,

bread flake or paste, maggots, "casters", cheese paste, worms, caddis grubs and silkweed.

Roach's peak sporting fitness: JULY/AUGUST/SEPTEMBER/OCTOBER/NOVEMBER/DECEMBER/JANUARY/FEBRUARY.

Fig. 15 Roach.

Know your roach: Roach is a sociable shoal fish. He has a healthy appetite and feeds contentedly in warm and cold weather. Smaller shoal roach sun themselves in shallow water in summer, ducking in and out of weed and lily roots. Large roach don't seem to like bright light and stay deep in hot weather, feeding in the cool of early morning or late evening.

Roach shoals patrol a regular beat; inspecting water plants, whirling eddies and edges of fast runs for food. But they hide out of sight; alter patrol times and occasionally vacate an area in moments, only to return a short while later.

Roach are basically bottom- or near-bottom feeding fish, although in summer they rise to seize insects on the water surface. During winter roach remain at the bottom of deep water.

Groundbait effective? YES – see Chapter 9.

Best fishing methods for BIG Roach: Float fishing (see Chapter 12) and legering (see Chapter 13).

Right line strength for big roach: At least 1.36kg (3 lb) breaking strain.

RUDD

Name: Rudd *(Scardinius erythrophthalmus).*
Family: Cyprinidae. Other members of family found in Europe, Africa and Asia.
Size we can expect to catch: Average weight about 141g (5 oz).
Where rudd like to live: Widespread in England, Wales and Ireland. Found in lakes, ponds, gravel pits and quiet stretches of rivers.

Fig. 16 Rudd.

How to recognise rudd: Beautiful fish, golden/yellow colour; yellow-orange eyes, reddish lips and rich red fins.
Sport "Star" rating: ****Good fighting fish****
Rudd's favourite natural food: Insects, water plants, worms and shellfish.
Baits to catch rudd: Worms, maggots, bread flake, cheese paste, caddis grubs etc.
Rudd's peak sporting fitness: JULY/AUGUST/SEPTEMBER/OCTOBER/NOVEMBER.
Know your rudd: Rudd is a summer surface-feeding shoal fish. He stays close to water plants, weed beds, reeds and lily pads. Shoals also make for bankside runs of water beneath overhanging bushes and trees to snap falling insects.

The shoal's surface sucking sounds are clearly audible on quiet summer's days.

Rudd reduce feeding in winter months and can be tricky to catch; they stay near the water bottom; take limited amounts of food at irregular intervals – livening up at noon on sunny-warm winter's days.

Big rudd occasionally snatch scraps of food from the water bottom summer and winter.

Groundbait effective? YES – see Chapter 9.

Best fishing methods for BIG Rudd: Float fishing (see Chapter 12) and legering (see Chapter 13).

Right line strength for big rudd: At least 0.90kg (2 lb) breaking strain.

TENCH

Name: Tench *(Tinca tinca).*

Family: Cyprinidae. Other members of family found in Europe, Africa and Asia.

Size we can expect to catch: Average weight about 1.36kg (3 lb).

Where tench like to live: On the bottom of heavily weeded lakes, ponds, canals, and slow flowing waters. Widely distributed throughout the U.K.

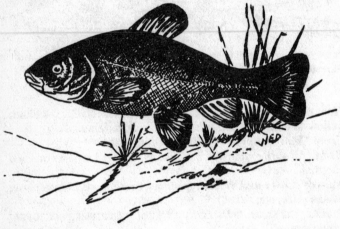

Fig. 17 Tench.

How to recognise tench: Smooth, dark olive/golden scales; small barbule (feeler) at each side of the upper lip. Large rounded fins and small red eyes.

Sport "Star" rating: ****Good fighting fish****

Tench's favourite natural food: Insects, shellfish, worms and vegetable matter.

Baits to catch tench: Bread flake, bread paste, maggots, sweetcorn, worms.

Tench's peak sporting fitness: JUNE/JULY/AUGUST/SEPTEMBER/ OCTOBER.

Know your tench: Tench is a handsome, shy shoal fish. Tench wander along the bottom of quiet, weedy and reedy waters in small groups; shovelling, grubbing and feeling for scraps of food with their barbules (feelers) and fins. Patches of bubbles bursting on the water surface may betray their presence. Tench feed enthusiastically only in warm, bright summer months; early morning and evening are the best times to catch tench. Summer early morning anglers see tench rolling lazily on the surface. Big tench frequently feed near the bank and sometimes investigate areas of the water bottom deliberately stirred or raked by tench anglers to release particles of appetizing food.

Although normally passive fish, tench are strong fighters when hooked.

A tench of 5kg (11 lb) was hooked and landed from a pit at Wraysbury, Middlesex in July, 1959 – but put back before being examined and accepted as a record breaker.

Groundbait effective? YES – see Chapter 9.

Best fishing methods for BIG Tench: Legering (see Chapter 13) and float fishing (see Chapter 12).

Right line strength for big tench: At least 2.26kg (5 lb) breaking strain.

TROUT

Name: Trout, brown *(Salmo trutta).*

Family: Salmonidae. Other members of family found in Europe, Asia and North America.

Size we can expect to catch: Average weight about 0.90kg (2 lb).

Where trout like to live: Lakes, lochs, pits, reservoirs, rivers and streams. All waters that are clear, clean and well oxygenated.

How to recognise trout: The "brown" trout can be various colours spanning yellow/brown with brightly coloured spots and rings, to silver, speckled with black spots.

Sport "Star" rating: ******Excellent fighting fish******

Trout's favourite natural food: Flies, insects, worms, small fish, shellfish etc.

Baits to catch trout: Flies (real or artificial) and worms.

Trout's peak sporting fitness: MARCH/APRIL/MAY/JUNE/JULY/ AUGUST/SEPTEMBER.

Know your trout: Trout is a great individualist; cunning, adaptable and robust, he lives and hunts alone; guarding his own water territory with courage and ferocity.

Fig. 18. Trout.

Rainbow trout (introduced to Europe from North America) are stocked with brown trout in many stillwaters. American brook trout are also stocked in some stillwaters. Sea trout (silvery in colour) are brown trout that have chosen to live in the sea; returning to rivers and streams to spawn.

All trout may be fished for successfully using similar tackle and methods.

Adult brown trout living in a narrow stream might be small, but trout can grow huge, depending upon size and depth of water and food supply.

Scotland is the home of monster brown trout and fish approaching 9kg (20 lb) are caught on some of the larger lochs. In 1866, W. Muir took 2½ hours to land a *foul hooked* (accidentally hooked in body or fin) brown trout from Loch Awe. The fish weighed 17.91kg (39 lb 8 oz)! The body was preserved and displayed in a case, but unfortunately this historic trophy was later destroyed by fire.

Good sport may be had fly-fishing for trout. However, big trout are often exclusively cannibal; eating only smaller fish and seldom, if ever, rise from deep water to take insects at the surface.

Hooked trout are wild and fierce fighters; jumping somersaulting and diving to dislodge your hook or smash the line. Even after being landed the fighting gymnastics continue.

Groundbait effective? NO.
Best fishing methods for BIG Trout: Spinning (see Chapter 16) and fly-fishing (see Chapters 19-27).
Right line strength for big trout: At least 2.26kg (5 lb) breaking strain.

ZANDER

Name: Zander, also known as Pikeperch *(Stizostedion lucioperca).*
Family: Percidae. Other members of family found in Europe and North America.
Size we can expect to catch: Average weight about 1.81kg (4 lb).
Where zander like to live: Lakes and rivers. Common in Europe, introduced to U.K. in 1878 at Woburn Abbey Lake. In 1963, 97 tiny zander were released into the Great Ouse Relief Channel. They bred and spread fast. Mainly found in East Anglia, also stocked in some club waters.

Fig. 19 Zander.

How to recognise zander: Long, perch-like body. Greenish-grey back and silvery belly. Large mouth and sharp teeth!
Sport "Star" rating: ****Good fighting fish****
Zander's favourite natural food: Small fish, worms, insects.
Baits to catch zander: Chunks of dead herring, sprat or mackerel, worms, maggots.
Zander's peak sporting fitness: JULY/AUGUST/SEPTEMBER/OCTOBER/NOVEMBER/DECEMBER/JANUARY/FEBRUARY.
Know your zander: Zander is cousin to the perch. He feeds deep down in water; hunting in packs that tear into shoals of small fish; often biting, ripping and spitting out its prey several times before swallowing the bits. Sometimes, in cat-and-mouse fashion, zander "plays" with its victim until, having made the

kill, zander loses interest and leaving the dead victim, moves on.

Zander can scent and track food across considerable distances; feeding happily in muddy and murky water.

Groundbait effective? YES – see Chapter 9 (include plenty of chopped worms or fish).

Best fishing methods for BIG Zander: legering (see Chapter 13) and spinning (see Chapter 16).

Right line strength for zander: At least 3.62 kg (8 lb) breaking strain. Big zander have sharp teeth, which can cut through line. Some anglers prefer to fish for big zander with special fishing *trace wire* attaching hook to line.

NOTE: Remove hooks from big zander with an angler's hook disgorger, forceps, or pliers.

5
Tackle

Good tackle helps catch big fish. Lots of tackle is on sale to today's angler, but the key to success is *your* ability to use tackle correctly and with confidence when hooking and landing fighting fish.

Buy best
Buy the best quality tackle you can afford. Buying cheap costs dear in the long run.

Quality tackle is produced by experts. You pay extra for their know-how and guarantee of excellence. Makers of quality tackle provide an after-sales maintenance and repair service. Their address is included in catalogues and with products.

Cheap tackle frequently doesn't work well, breaks; loses large fish and requires constant repair, or replacing.

Know your dealer
Get to know your local specialist tackle dealer. Visit his shop and view the huge amounts of tackle on display. Leaf through some catalogues; see the fishing newspapers, magazines and books offered for sale.

All tackle dealers are friendly and helpful fishing experts. Chat to your dealer; ask his advice about tackle, baits, local fishing clubs and contests.

Your tackle dealer is wise, buy all you need for fishing from him and have no worries.

Rods
Special rods are designed for:
Float fishing (see Chapter 12) to cast light lines long distances and give maximum float and line control; *legering* (see Chapter 13); to cast heavy weights and baits, and *spinning* (see chapter 16) to cast and rapidly retrieve strong lines and weighty artificial lures. *Pole fishing* (see Chapter 14) and *fly-fishing* (see Chapters 19-27) also need specialized rods. However most types

of fishing may be enjoyed successfully with a general purpose rod of 3m (10 ft) to 3.65m (12 ft) in length.

Selection of specialist rods is best discussed with your local tackle dealer, who'll let you try rods in his shop before you buy.

Reels
Reliable reels are vital to fishing success. Buy the best you can afford. Describe to your tackle dealer the sort of fishing you intend doing. He'll guide your choice. A reel suitable for general purpose fishing is unlike one made for competition match anglers; reels for heavy pike spinning, or gentle fly-fishing are highly individual in design and performance.

For effective casting always fill your reel fully with line.

Line
Your line connects you to the hooked fish. Poor quality line is the fish's friend. Don't be parted from your catch – buy good line!

Competition match anglers often fish fine lines of about 0.5kg (1 lb) breaking strain; some specimen hunters, chasing big fish, use lines of 2.26kg (5 lb) to 4.5kg (10 lb) breaking strain and sometimes stronger, depending on the species they're after (see suggested line strength for big fish in each fish's "Fish file", Chapter 4).

A good general purpose line should have a breaking strain of at least 1.36kg (3 lb).

Floats
There's a float for every fishing situation (see Chapter 12). Most of us collect too many floats and rarely use half of them! Buy a few carefully chosen floats and from experience find how to fish them correctly before adding more floats to your collection.

Landing net
A length-adjustable (telescopic) landing net is a must. The longer the handle when fully extended and larger the net, the better. Never let a surprise huge fish escape because you can't get your fish out of the water before it smashes the line.

Hooks
Your choice of hook size depends on the bait you want to fish (see Chapter 6). Hooks without a barb (sharp inward projecting piece of wire at hook point) penetrate better and are easier and

quicker to free from the fish's mouth; this may prove vital in competition match fishing (see Chapter 15). However, barbed hooks are better for wriggly baits like maggots or worms, which don't always want to stay on barbless hooks.

Odds and bits
All sorts of optional extras are on sale in your local tackle shop including: angler's thermal and waterproof clothing, bait and bait containers, bait aprons for match anglers, battery headlamps for night fishing, catapults for long distance ground-baiting, electronic bite alarms, eye shades, float caps, polarised sun glasses, reel pouches, rod bags, rod rests, scissors, swivels, tackle boxes, umbrellas, vacuum flasks, and weights.

Sound advice
Discuss tackle purchases with your specialist tackle dealer and *listen* to his sound advice. Aim to use the least amount of tackle necessary to catch fish; choose recommended tackle *you* like the feel and look of; buy the best you can afford, and remember that although good quality tackle helps catch big fish, there is no substitute for your intelligence, cunning and hunting skill.

D.I.Y.
Fancy making your own value-for-money "customized" tackle – rods, floats, fly-tying etc? Instruction books and tackle making kits are stocked by your dealer, or can be ordered for you.

Security
Watch out – there are thieves about!

Record serial numbers of your equipment: etch tackle with your own easily identifiable secret symbol; insure tackle against theft and damage. Glue or sew an address label to rucksacks, tackle bags or boxes. Don't forget to give your telephone number. Sometimes stolen or mislaid tackle turns up in the most unlikely places!

6
Baits and Breeding

Many baits can be bought from tackle dealers; some are ordinary foods available from food stores – a few baits you may choose to breed.

Baits similar to the natural foods found in the water you plan fishing are likely to be highly effective when fished with skill; easily fooling fish into accepting your bait as safely familiar, tasty food.

Finding bait the natural way
For an exciting and challenging way to fish, search the waterside for the fishes' normal food immediately before you begin fishing. Then you know your natural bait is fresh and eagerly sought by the fish.

Where to look
Under piles of rotting leaves, weed or rushes; fallen branches and rotten tree stumps for worms, woodlice, earwigs, grubs and beetles. Check chewed fresh leaves for caterpillars and watch for ripe berries growing near the water.

Wrigglies' Liberation Front
If you believe worms, maggots and other wrigglies need love and understanding and you are loth to spike them on a hook and drown them; stick to bread, cheese, fruit, grain, meat, vegetables, artificial spinning lures and artificial flies – these all attract big fish too!

Push the point
To make sure that fish taking your bait bite the hook point; push your hook through whatever bait you are using until the sharp hook point protrudes. Then the bait won't stop your hook penetrating the fish's lip when the line is tightened.

Get fresh
For best results leave buying or gathering and preparing your

baits until the last convenient moment before fishing.

The fresher your bait; the finer your catch!

Hook sizes: A word in your ear.

Choose a hook size to suit your bait. Suggested hook sizes are given for most baits detailed on the following pages of this chapter. However, these hook sizes are *suggestions* only. The bigger your bait, the bigger the hook and vice-versa.

Bread
Use your loaf to hook fish.

Crust
Suggested hook sizes: 12 or 14 or 16.

At the waterside; rinse your hands, then pluck a hunk of crust from the top of freshly baked, unsliced white bread. Some fluffy white bread attached to the crust is desirable.

Cubes
Suggested hook sizes: 8 or 10 or 12 or 14.

At home, cut a 6mm ($^1/_4$ inch) thick crust from the end of a freshly baked unsliced white loaf; lay the crust on a large *clean* cloth; cover crust with the cloth; place on a hard, flat surface and leave to press under a heavy weight (wooden board, heavy saucepan etc.) for 2 hours. Then cut into cubes.

Flake
Suggested hook sizes: 10 or 12 or 14.

At the waterside, use the fluffy bread plucked from the *inside* of an unsliced freshly baked white loaf.

Paste
Suggested hook sizes: 8 or 10 or 12.

At the waterside, rinse your hands; then – in a suitable bowl – mix some of the water with a little stale white bread several days old. Don't make too much at once. Knead until soft and tacky – a texture judged to be right for staying on your hook.

Appetizing extras sometimes add appeal to bread paste and bring spectacular success. Among popular titbits that can be popped into your paste mix are: bananas (ripe), cheese (grated), cheese (spready), chocolate powder (drinking), custard powder, fruit (soft), honey, meat pastes, soup powder, and yeast extract spreads.

Pellets

Suggested hook sizes: 14 or 16 or 18.

At the waterside, use a bread punch (available from your tackle dealer) to punch pellets from a freshly baked white loaf.

Maggots

Suggested hook sizes: three maggots on size 10 or 12; two maggots on size 14; one maggot on size 16.

Maggots are larvae hatched from flies' eggs. They're bred commercially on maggot farms and sold by many specialist tackle dealers. A maggot develops into a chrysalis (or "case") known to anglers as a *caster* before emerging as a fly.

Maggots and casters are valuable fish catching baits. To slow down your lively maggots' change into unmoving "casters", keep them somewhere shaded and cool before and during fishing.

Sympathetic womenfolk sometimes let us store fresh, securely bait-boxed, maggots for a day or three in the family fridge.

A water-tight container may be stood in a covered bowl, bucket or watering can partly filled with cold water and hidden in a shady spot.

The warmer your maggots are, the sooner they'll turn into casters.

Summer maggot breeding

To breed your own maggots when summer comes, buy a small piece of cheap meat (heart is ideal). Slash three deep cuts in the meat; then put the meat in a suitable container – bucket; box etc. Place container outside after dark; we're after the big, juicy maggots that hatch from eggs laid by the night-flying *callyphora erythrocephalia*. Fit a lid or covering allowing a small space for an adult fly to enter.

Watch out for marauding cats! Put the container somewhere safe.

Next morning look for white patches of flies' eggs. Each patch of eggs is called a "blow" and will produce *dozens* of maggots. Fasten an airtight lid during the daytime. Repeat the procedure for one or two more nights. Several "blows" supply sufficient maggots to last a few lengthy fishing trips.

If your meat is blessed with too many "blows", you can scrape off unwanted eggs with a knife.

Wrap the "blown" meat in a couple of sheets of clean

46

newspaper. Pour *bran* over the paper-wrapped blown meat to form a layer of about 25mm (1 inch) deep over the container base. Fasten a lid with *tiny* pricked or bored holes; alternatively, secure over the container top with string or elastic, a piece of cloth or nylon (stretched old tights, curtain etc.) or pin-pricked plastic sheeting.

Keep somewhere cool and dark for 7 days; then transfer hatched maggots into your bait box. Throw away decomposing meat and smelly bran. Add some fresh bran to your bait box to warm and nourish the maggots. Then store in cool. Your maggots are ready for use.

TIP

Always keep your "live" bait alive and wriggling by storing it in a bait container with tiny air holes pricked in the lid.

TIP

When hooking live "wriggling" bait, simply nick your hook point through the skin; leaving the bait maximum freedom of "natural" movement in the water. Deep hooking quickly kills your bait, which is then less tempting to fish.

Worms
Bloodworms
Suggested hook sizes: 18 or 22.
Larvae ("grub" stage) of the midge fly. Found in mud at the water bottom. Best bought from your specialist tackle dealer.

Brandlings
Suggested hook sizes: 18 or 22.
Red and yellow banded worm. Found in compost heaps, manure and among rotting leaves. Easily bred in home-made "wormery" – an old sink, aquarium etc. with a 25mm (1 inch) deep pebble base for drainage; covered with leaves and alternate layers of soil and old potato peelings, tea leaves, apple cores etc. Keep covered in a cool, dry place. Regularly water soil to dampness with collected rain water and feed worms with tiny scraps of leftover vegetable and fruit. Remove any diseased or dead brandlings you come across.

Earthworms (lobworms)
Suggested hook sizes: 6 or 8 or 10.
Found under large stones and in shaded, damp soil. Encourage

earthworms to a specific area of your garden by daily emptying tea leaves from the teapot or split tea bags. Keep soil rich and damp and you'll always be able to fork up a few worms for fishing.

Earthworms can also be collected above ground on close cut grass after rain, or at night. Tread quietly; after dark use a torch with beam dimmed by handkerchief or tissue.

For ace results aim to store earthworms for a couple of days in damp moss before fishing – a week is ideal. Moss makes worms lively, tough skinned (for staying on your hook) and doubly appealing to fish!

Remove any dead or sickly worms.

Fig. 20 The right way to hook a worm.

Taking worms fishing
When you take worms fishing, keep them in a bait container filled with moss or damp newspaper (not soil) and *never* mix worms with maggots. Why? Because maggots *eat* worms. Use separate containers.

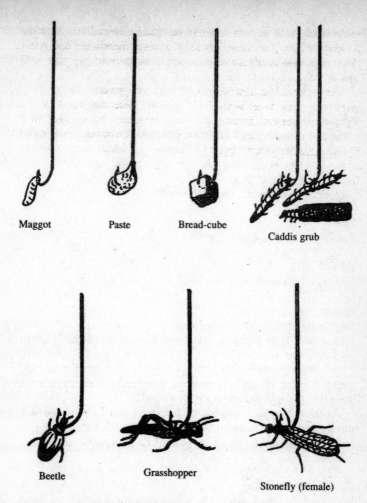

Maggot Paste Bread-cube

Caddis grub

Beetle Grasshopper

Stonefly (female)

Fig. 21 A selection of hooked baits.

Slugs
Suggested hook sizes: 6 or 8.
Gather slugs from their dark, damp hideouts, or sink slug traps (empty, unwanted plastic cartons/food containers) into soil before nightfall, with the open mouth at ground level; pour in a *small* quantity of beer. Slugs love home brew! Remove "merry" slugs in the morning.

For super slugs, store them a few days in a container lined

with damp soil; pop in some large chunks of melon, cover the container (don't seal air-tight) and place somewhere cool. After your luscious slugs have banqueted on melon, big fish will queue for a bite at them.

Grain
Prepare uncooked grain for fishing by gently simmering in a saucepan of water until soft (don't overcook); or put grain in hot water and leave to soak for 12 hours.

Hempseed
Suggested hook sizes: 18 or 16 or 14.

Tares
Suggested hook sizes: 16 or 14.

Wheat
Suggested hook sizes: 14 or 12.

Potato
Suggested hook size: 1/0 or 1 or 2.
Pick small, firm potatoes about the size of a golf ball. Don't peel. Simmer in a saucepan of water until just tender – not soft. Then immediately remove the potatoes and submerse in cold water to arrest the cooking process. When cold, pierce a hole for your line through the potato with a needle.

At the waterside, tie hook to line *after* you've threaded line through the hole. Break off a piece of peel before casting to reveal some inviting white potato flesh against the water bottom.

Give it a go!
Here are more baits to try. The list of successful baits is endless. New ones are found every day. Fish seem to like soft baits better than hard baits, but apart from this preference anything goes – experiment, experiment, experiment!

Where appropriate, suggested hook sizes are bracketed next to baits; choose a hook size to suit the size of bait you're fishing.

TIP
A combination of two different baits on one hook often draws special attention from greedy fish.

All-sorts

Bacon – fatty / baked bean (14 or 16) / banana chunk – ripe / beetroot – diced / berries – general (12 or 14 or 16) / blackberry (8) / blackcurrant (14) / bluebottle / caddis grub – in or out of its case / carrot – diced and lightly boiled / cheese – ripe and smelly / cherry – stone removed (12) / chocolate – soft centre (6) / currant (14 or 16) / herring – dead – hooked through eye sockets (2) / luncheon meat – chopped into chunks / macaroni – boiled – with a little grated cheese worked in as an appetizer / mussels – freshwater – removed from shell (8 or 6) / peas (14 or 16) / sausage – whole or part – lightly boiled (2 or 4 or 6) / silkweed – wrapped around hook (10 or 12 or 14) / spaghetti – boiled / sprat – dead – hooked through eye sockets (2) – sultana (14 or 16) / sweetcorn – two grains (10) / tomato – sliced / etc., etc.

7

Know Knot Sense

We must know and practise our knots. Big fish strain our line, and the weakest point in line is usually a wrongly tied or unsuitable knot. When we lose rod-bending fish through line parting from hooks or knotted joins, we have ourselves to blame. So know knot sense and get knotted right.

Knots are great fun to learn and always useful to know – once knotted, never forgotten!

Reel knot

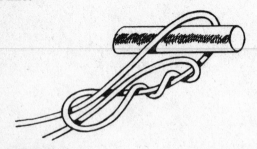

Fig. 22 Reel knot.
For attaching line to reel.

Tucked half blood knot

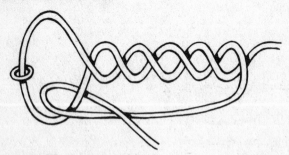

Fig. 23 Tucked half blood knot.
For tying eyed hooks, artificial flies, lures or swivels to line.

Loop knot

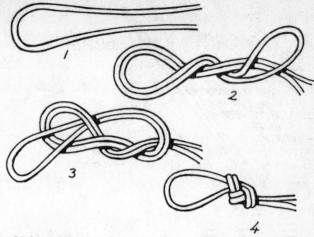

Fig. 24 Loop knot.

To make a loop for securing hooklength (see page 57).

Figure of 8 knot

Fig. 25 Figure of 8 knot.

To fasten line to hooklength (see page 57).

Double grinner knot

Fig. 26 Double grinner knot.

Strong knot for joining 2 lines of the same or different breaking strain.

Stop knot

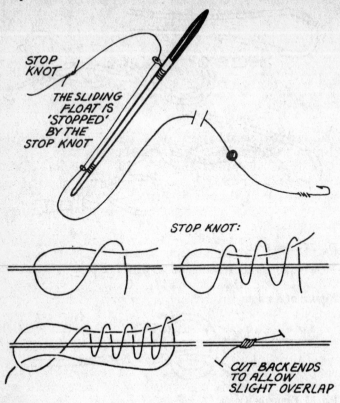

STOP KNOT

THE SLIDING FLOAT IS 'STOPPED' BY THE STOP KNOT

STOP KNOT:

CUT BACK ENDS TO ALLOW SLIGHT OVERLAP

Fig. 27 Stop knot.

For stopping a "sliding float" at pre-set depth when fishing deep water (see page 79).

8
Secrets of Success –
Think Fish

Once we understand how fish think, and why they behave as they do, we become more successful at catching them.

Study the "Fish file" (Chapter 4). Each species of fish has developed its own specialized technique for survival, incorporating cunning tricks and dodges.

Starting out
Outsmarting fish starts at home, before you go fishing. Leave brightly coloured clothes and flashy-white shirts in the drawer. Wear drab camouflage colours that blend with bankside vegetation. Pop a pair of polarised sun-glasses in your pocket and pack a peaked cap, or floppy wide-brimmed hat, or angler's eyeshade. Wearing hat or eyeshade and polarised glasses (even in dull weather) reduces water and background glare; hiding fish become visible!

Check you've got all your tackle. Don't forget to take a spare copy of this book and a notebook and pen or pencil (wrapped in a protective plastic bag) for handy waterside reference and important jottings (see Chapter 18).

Timing
Remember, many fish feed ravenously at dawn and dusk (often in the shallows) because at these quiet times the light is changing and fish have the edge over insects and other prey that can't re-focus vision as rapidly as fish can. After feasting, fish take about 12 hours to digest food completely, so may not seek another meal until much later in the day.

Fish are cold-blooded; their body temperature is dependent on the water temperature. The warmer water is, the more active fish become. Busy fish use energy fast and must feed to replenish energy reserves. Therefore, expect fish to feed more frequently in warm weather; less determinedly on cold days. Sudden drops in temperature usually put fish off their food –

sometimes for several days!

Reading water

Learn to "read" water. With practice you'll be able to look at any area of water and know whereabouts to fish for particular species. Sketches to help you read waters are included in this chapter.

Fig. 28 Fish haunts in a river:

1, 2 and 3: Roach are usually near weed beds.
4 and 5: Large perch like holes near bank.
6:   Mouths of inflowing streams are good for chub.
7:   Deep runs near and among weed are favoured by pike.
8:   Fast water is liked by dace and grayling.
9:   Eddies and runs near bankside rushes may hold chub, roach and dace.
10: Barbel like deep water.
11: Bream and tench prefer slow, sluggish water.

Waterside approach

Put your tackle together away from the waterside. Approach the water quietly; crouch low and move from cover to cover. Stay well back from the water; don't get close enough to admire your reflection, or cast a telltale shadow across the surface.

Plumbing

To find by "plumbing" the exact depth of the water you're going to fish:

a) Slip a movable float onto your rod line.
b) Tie an angler's *plummet* weight (or suitably heavy weight) to the end of your line.
c) Slide your float up the line to the approximate (guessed) depth of the water and fasten float in position.
d) Accurately cast line and plummet weight – soft entry into water, no splash.

You've gauged the depth when your float is bobbing upright on the water surface. Simply measure the length of line between plummet and float.

Establishing the precise depth of water can be important to all methods of fishing, especially float fishing (see Chapter 12) and spinning (see Chapter 16).

Thermometer

A special angler's thermometer, attached to your line in addition to (or in place of) a plummet weight, increases your knowledge of water conditions; supplies valuable figures for record keeping and may advance our appreciation of fish feeding patterns peculiar to particular species and waters.

Hooklength

Some anglers like to fish with a fine (low breaking strain) "hooklength" line securing hook to main reel line. For right knots, see Chapter 7.

A "hooklength" line should be between 304mm (12 inches) and 609mm (24 inches) long, cut from a spool of ordinary fishing line.

The advantages of fishing with a hooklength are:

Hooklength line is less visible to fish than the heavier main reel line.

If a big fish snags and breaks the hooklength line, your float (if any) and/or weights (if any), fixed to the main line, won't be lost.

The disadvantage is that an unexpectedly large hooked fish is likely to smash a hooklength line and escape.

Although a hooklength line can be any strength slightly below the main reel line strength, the most popular hooklength line strengths range from 453g (1 lb) to 1.36kg (3 lb) breaking strain depending on the species of fish angled for, and size of bait and hook used (see page 45). The smaller your bait and hook; the finer your hooklength.

Except when match fishing (see Chapter 15) many anglers

prefer to fish with main reel line tied direct to the hook.

Hooklengths are not recommended when fishing for eels, pike or zander (see Chapter 4).

Fig. 29 A carp lake showing likely fishing spots:

1. During daytime carp like to browse and bask among and near weed beds.
2. Deep water near shaded banks is a favourite place.
3. Near lily pads and bush-shaded banks are also favourites.
4. At night-time carp come close to shore to forage among weeds and rushes.

Landing net
Assemble your adjustable long-handled (telescopic) landing net and position the net nearby, preferably close to shallow water beneath the bank.

Hooked!
As soon as you've hooked a fish, begin recovering line. The fish's first instinct is to dive for cover and wrap your line round underwater obstacles 'til the line snaps or your hook is dislodged. Don't let it happen. Keep a tight line and reel-in. Your bending rod saps the fish's strength.

Try to remain out of sight; make no sudden movement. Stay cool, calm and in control. The instant your hooked fish sees you, he'll panic and surge away with line-snapping power! Ease the fish towards your landing net.

Fig. 30 An eddy beneath a weir attracts many species of fish, including barbel, chub, perch, pike, roach, trout and zander. Dace and grayling prefer the fast runs.

Using the landing net
When you've hooked a fish, slip your net into the water. A long handle reduces the distance you have to draw the fish before netting and landing – putting the odds in your favour.

As you reel in line, steer the hooked fish over the mouth of your net; then raise the net and land your fish.

Wet your hands
Because fish are cold blooded, the touch of our dry, hot hands burns their flesh just like hot pokers would burn ours. Dry hands also tear away fishes' protective scales – leaving skin exposed to possible infection. Always wet your hands in cooling water before touching a fish to remove your hook from the fish's mouth.

59

Weighing

Find your fish's weight without causing physical damage to the fish – use a spring-balance and specially designed fish weighing net.

Photographs

Preserve happy fishing memories; impress friends and confound cynics by taking waterside snaps of your best fishes before hurriedly returning them to the water.

To take first-class pictures:

a) Make sure something appears alongside your fish in the photograph that gives a true impression of size – item of tackle, or this book, ruler etc.

b) Get the focus right!

c) Hold the camera steady.

Returning fish

Speedily and gently return your fish to its water, a short distance from the stretch you're fishing. Hold the fish upright (facing into the current in flowing water) until the fish feels strong enough to swim away.

TO CATCH FISH – THINK FISH!

9
Best Groundbait Methods

Groundbaiting is a ploy to help us catch large numbers of particular fish. Refer to the "Groundbait" entry in each fish's "Fish file", starting on page 19, for details of the fish groundbaiting is most effective in attracting.

Groundbaiting applies to float fishing (see Chapter 12) and legering (see Chapter 13). Groundbaiting is not used when spinning or fly-fishing.

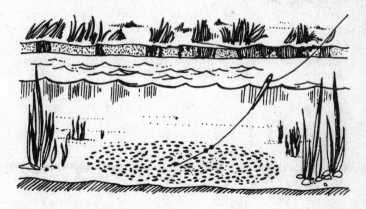

Fig. 31 Groundbait on the bottom.

Aims of groundbaiting
a) To attract fish to the area of water you are about to fish.
b) To whet the appetite of attracted fish.
c) To offer, mixed with groundbait, small or chopped samples of the larger bait fixed on your hook. This makes fish less suspicious of your hook bait.
d) To encourage attracted fish to stay and continue feeding in the area of water you are fishing.

Types of groundbait

Cloud

Fig. 32 "Cloud".

Light, "fluffy" particles designed to fall in a "mysterious", enticing rain through the water from surface to bottom, drawing inquisitive fish to investigate.

Heavy groundbait

Fig. 33 Heavy groundbait.

Heavier mix, to drop in a ball rapidly through the water and dissolve in a blanket of appetizing morsels on the bottom.

Cloud or heavy?

Cloud

Ideal for shoals of fish feeding close to the surface of clear flowing water and shallow still water.

Heavy

Best for bottom feeding large fish; fast flowing water and deep murky water.

Do's and don'ts

There are no definite do's and don'ts in groundbaiting. Experiment with mixes and methods. Use the ones that work for you!

Tackle dealers stock various groundbaits containing "secret" ingredients, together with full mixing instructions. These are worth trying, but you can also make your own.

Here are some guidelines:

Recipes

CLOUD

Ingredients: stale white bread; egg shells and dry powdered milk.

Method

The amount you make depends on how much cloud you intend using and the proportions of ingredients are variable; but most of the mix should be stale or lightly toasted (not browned or burned) powdered crumbs from white bread (no crust), 85%; a few dried crushed and powdered egg shells, 10%; and a pinch or two of dry powdered milk, 5%.

Save and store these items in an air-tight container as they become available. Then you'll have the mix ready whenever you need some.

Don't add water to the mix until you arrive at your fishing spot. Then tip some water and mix into a round mixing bowl about 127mm (5 inches) deep. Round bowls are best because no dry patches collect in corners.

Special collapsible bowls are sold by specialist tackle dealers.

At the water's edge

Quiet and crouching low; wash sweat, grease and human smell from your hands. Scoop water into your mixing bowl; sprinkle in some cloud mix. Add chopped or crushed samples of your hook bait (crushed or chopped grubs, maggots, worms or raw meat "bleed" scent and succulent flavour into the water to attract hungry fish). Gently mould into a fluffy *not stodgy* ball, about the size of a golf ball. Make a little at a time, so the mix doesn't dry out.

HEAVY GROUNDBAIT
Ingredients: Stale brown bread and / or toasted "browned" white bread, 75%; bran and / or broken biscuit crumbs, 10%; a small amount of freshly cooked, mashed potato, 10% and / or a pinch or two of semolina powder, 5%.

Method
The quantity you mix depends on the amount of heavy groundbait you want to use and the proportion of ingredients can be varied, but the bulk of mix should be bread (no crust).

Don't put the mix in water until you arrive at the waterside. Then pour some mix into a round mixing bowl about 127mm (5 inches) deep.

At the water's edge
Keeping quiet and out of the fishes' view; rinse your hands in the water; then scoop water into your mixing bowl; sprinkle in a little heavy groundbait mix. Add chopped or crushed samples of your hook bait. Mould into a *stiff*, "heavy" ball about the size of a tennis ball. For fast flowing water or water over 3.5m (12 ft) deep, add stones and / or a thin outer casing of mud. Moisten the outside of your heavy groundbait ball with water to seal cracks.

Hints
★ Where possible, do your waterside mixing a short way *downstream* (down current) from the spot you intend fishing.
★ Before you throw your mix, select a *target marker* in the water or on the opposite bank (lily pad, stick, tree or bush etc.) so you can cast your baited hook to the same position your groundbait ball entered the water.
★ Throw your ball of cloud or heavy groundbait gently and *low* across the water to avoid a big fish scaring splash!
★ When throwing groundbait or casting line into fast flowing water, reach the spot you want to fish by allowing for the current and throwing or casting slightly upstream (up current).

★ Allow time for your thrown ball of cloud or heavy groundbait to settle on the bottom before casting your baited hook.

★ Special angler's catapults are available for easy and accurate long distance groundbaiting and "feeding" (see below).

Feeding

Having drawn fish to your baited hook; *keep them interested* – there are plenty to catch! Toss a *few small* samples of your hook bait into the water with each fresh cast of your baited hook.

Every 20 to 30 minutes throw another ball of cloud or heavy groundbait, but *never* bigger than a large coin. Leave the fish hungry for your hook bait!

Remember, still shallow, or slow moving waters don't want as much groundbaiting as fast flowing or deep waters. You don't wish to build a mountain of groundbait. Please leave room in the water for fish!

10

Care for your Tackle

Love your tackle.

Take care of your tackle and it won't let you down when you hook the big one!

Badly maintained tackle may lose you the fish of a lifetime.

Listen to the maker
When you buy new equipment, look for the enclosed notes or booklets telling you how to care for the tackle. Read, remember and *do* as the maker advises. He knows best.

While fishing
Rods
Most serious damage to rods occurs when fishing. Don't accidentally tread on a rod section when you're piecing the rod together, or taking it apart.

When dismantling your rod, start by gripping the top end section at the joint (ferrule) and *pull* the rod sections apart. Twisting strains the ferrule fastening. Then work down to the bottom, butt section.

Line
If your line gets snagged, don't strain the rod by pulling; unravel snagged line within easy reach, or gently tug the line free with your hand.

On the move
When walking between trees or bushes with assembled tackle, point the rod behind you; keep the tip low and clear of the ground.

Water's edge
Keep equipment off soil when assembling and dismantling tackle. Protect rod joints (ferrules), rod rings and your reel from unnecessary contact with dirt and grit.

After fishing
As you carefully pack away your tackle at the water's edge, gently wipe the reel, rod sections and rod rings with a soft damp cloth. Check there is no grit or grime on the rod rings, especially the insides; then slip your rod sections into the rod bag.

At home
Examine your tackle for damage or signs of wear and tear. List lost, broken or worn tackle for replacement or repair.

Rods
Remove rod sections from bag; wipe with soft cloth soaked in warm soapy water to remove grease and stains; stand sections in warm to dry. Clean cork handles with a nylon brush or old toothbrush (kept for this purpose) dipped in warm water. When a cork handle gets wet, check it's dry before putting your rod back into the *dry* rod bag.

If rod joints (ferrules) fit too tightly for easy assembly or dismantling, lightly rub them with household soap or a white candle before storing them (unless the maker instructs differently).

Hang rods somewhere cool in rod bags, suspended by the loop provided for this purpose, or stand in a supportive rod rack, or store laid flat in a safe place.

Line
Wind the length of line you estimate you've used for fishing onto an empty bobbin or line spool and wipe the line with a damp cloth; then dry and wind back onto your reel. Check the end section of your line for nicks or cuts. If necessary, cut off and discard any length looking worn or limp, stretched and strained. Always cut line; never break off line by snapping, which weakens the line.

Landing nets and keep nets
Wipe landing net handle with damp, soapy cloth. Lightly grease any moving parts. Use special grease supplied for tackle. Check that nuts, bolts and screws tighten properly. Rinse and sponge netting in clean water and leave in warm to dry. Look for holes or tears in mesh. Repair by tying with fine fishing line where possible; replace with new net when badly torn.

Reel

Clean outside of reel with damp cloth; remove any unwanted grease with spirit or cleaning fluid, then dry. Lubricate exterior moving parts monthly with tiny drops of maker's recommended oil. Don't get oil on your line! Keep reel in reel bag, stored in a dry place, away from direct sunlight and extremes of temperature.

Floats

Wipe clean. Replace perished rubber "float caps" (new rubbers available from your tackle dealer).

Hooks

Sharpen used hooks on emery cloth, or special sharpening stone (sold by tackle dealers).

Clean and dry flies, lures, plugs or spinners used. Check that swivels work correctly.

Tackle box

Keep small items of tackle neatly stowed away in a tackle box.
"A place for everything and everything in its place."

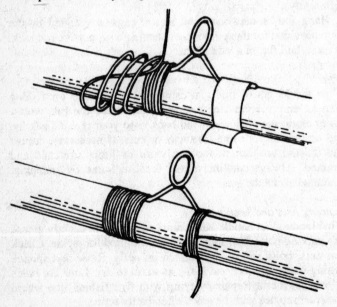

Fig. 34 Replacing rod rings; how to attach new ones.

Then you know where to find things quickly and without fuss and bother.

Season's end
At the end of your fishing season clean carefully, check and store your tackle, ready for the next fishing year.

Some anglers like to start each season with new line.

Resist the temptation to tinker with the inside parts of reels. If your reel needs attention, pack it securely and post to the maker's service centre. The address is included with your reel's instruction booklet. Don't forget to enclose a letter giving your name, address, telephone number and details of what is wrong with the reel.

Several seasons on
After several seasons your rod may require revarnishing. Use special rod varnish supplied by your tackle dealer.

Chipped or groove-worn rod rings damage lines and need replacing. Buy new rings, whipping thread and rod varnish.

To attach new rod rings
a) Remove damaged ring by carefully cutting along old whipping thread with small scissors or sharp tool. Discard old ring and thread.
b) Position new ring precisely and temporarily fasten one end of the ring to rod with sticky tape.
c) Whip the other end of ring onto the rod, as shown opposite in fig. 34. Pull thread right. Cut off loose end of thread. Cut away and discard sticky tape. Whip remaining end of rod ring to rod.
d) Paint thin layer of varnish on whippings with clean brush.
e) Smooth varnished whippings with clean piece of cloth.
f) Apply another coat of varnish; smooth with cloth; then put rod somewhere warm and dust-free to dry.

11

Personal Safety

Stay safe at the waterside or afloat in a boat, by following these basic guidelines.

Take a friend
Take a friend fishing. Apart from the cheering company, if one of you has an accident, the other can assist or go for help.

Learn to swim
All anglers should be proficient swimmers. Under qualified supervision, learn to swim *at least* 50m (55 yds), fully clothed.

Never go afloat in a boat until you can swim at least 50m (55 yds), fully clothed.

Should you decide to go afloat in a boat always fish with an experienced boat-handler; never fish from a boat on your own – tell someone ashore when to expect your return; wear a life-jacket at all times, and never stand up in the boat, you could capsize the boat and/or fall into the water.

Never wear waders or fishermen's thigh boots in a boat – if you fall overboard, they will quickly fill with water and sink you like a stone!

High-voltage overhead electricity cables
Keep well away from high-voltage overhead electricity cables. A back-cast fishing-line tangle with an overhead cable conducting electricity could kill you. Some cables are surprisingly close to the ground.

Be aware that electricity from an overhead cable can arc down and strike your fishing rod even if you have no direct fishing-line contact with the cable.

Thunderstorms
Do not fish during a thunderstorm.
Lightning can kill.
A strike by lightning could kill you.

Find a safe place to shelter **before** the thunderstorm begins *(breaks)*.

Do not go out in a boat if a thunderstorm is forecast.

If you are afloat in a boat, aim to get ashore before the thunderstorm begins *(breaks)*, and seek a safe place to shelter.

Do not shelter directly beneath a tree, lightning striking that tree could kill you.

Lightning does not always strike the highest point in the area where it flashes to earth. Lightning can strike anywhere.

When caught in the open during an overhead thunderstorm, put your fishing rod, landing-net, and any large metal objects you might be wearing or carrying (lightning is attracted to metal) in a neat pile; move well away from the pile and keep a low profile – kneel, or lie down flat on the ground, and remain in that position until the thunderstorm has passed.

You may get wet and muddy and think you look silly, but you will be alive!

Eyes

A peaked cap or floppy hat with spectacles or sunglasses help protect your eyes from the hooks of artificial flies airborne during a fly-line cast (your cast or the cast of someone else).

I always wear polarizing (anti-glare) sunglasses when fly-fishing, whatever the weather.

For extra safety, wear spectacles or sunglasses with frames that mould in a curve round the side of your eyes.

Keep safely clear of fly-fishers when they are casting.

Clothing

Be wise and always carry a set of heavy duty waterproofs (jacket with hood, and trousers) and pack a spare woollen pullover. A woollen scarf helps prevent icy wind and rain from funnelling down your neck, and in cold weather a pair of *fingerless* woollen or thermal fishing mitts keep your hands warm without interfering with your fly-fishing.

Never be without a peaked cap or floppy hat, and/or a woollen hat in cold weather; much of our valuable body heat is lost through a bare, unhatted head.

A cap or hat also helps protect your head from the hooks of artificial flies airborne during a fly-line cast (your cast or the cast of someone else).

Food

Always pack some warming and nourishing food; sandwiches, flask of hot soup and a couple of chocolate bars.

Apply standards of hygiene for handling food and drink at the waterside similar to the standards you would normally set at home.

Insect repellent

Always carry an adequate supply of insect repellent and apply liberally to escape the unwelcome attention of waterside insects that bite.

First aid notes

Be prepared: carry a basic first aid kit containing assorted waterproof plasters, roll of sterile bandage, safety pins, antiseptic cream and pain killing tablets.

NEVER allow an open cut, scratch or graze to come in contact with *untreated* water, or with any freshly caught fish.

Always wash immediately *(where possible)* any cut, scratch or graze in *treated* tap water; apply antiseptic cream and a waterproof plaster and/or a sterile dressing (bandage).

If the cut, scratch or graze does not heal, or you feel unwell, see your General Practitioner (Doctor), and explain that the accident occurred by the waterside while you were fishing. (Waterborne diseases, e.g. *Leptospirosis,* a form of leptospiral jaundice commonly known as Weil's disease, can be transmitted into the bloodstream through minor cuts and abrasions.)

In the event of serious injury seek *immediate* medical attention.

12

Float Fishing

Float fishing is skilful and exciting. Few sporting thrills compare to the heart-throbbing moment your float quivers with life as a fish bites your baited hook.

The right rod
A long rod between 3.35m (11 ft) to 4m (13 ft) is advisable for float fishing. The longer your rod: a) the more easily you may fish well back from the waterside – staying hidden from the fishes' sight; b) the further you can cast light lines and floats; c) the greater your control over the "natural" presentation of float fished bait; d) the quicker you can tighten and reel-in line when your float indicates you've hooked a fish.

Floats are for:
a) Indicating when a fish is investigating, nibbling or swallowing your bait.
b) Suspending your bait at the precise depth you expect the fish to be feeding.
c) Giving you delicate control over the drift, position and presentation of your baited hook.
d) Keeping your bait above muddy, leafy, weedy water bottoms; obstacles and snags.
e) Enabling you to float and present your bait, in a natural way, to fish-infested stretches of water beyond casting distance; overhung by branches or bushes, or otherwise inaccessible.

Types
Floats are made in many sizes, weights and styles. In general, floats with their main buoyancy ("fatness") near the top are designed for maximum effectiveness on fast and medium-fast flowing water; floats with their main buoyancy ("fatness") near the bottom are especially effective on slow moving and still water. Despite the numerous names, there are basically two types of float.

73

1. Stick floats and balsas

These floats are fastened to your line at the top and bottom ends and designed for fishing fast and medium-fast *flowing* waters.

TIME SAVER

For quick and easy float change (useful when competition match fishing, see Chapter 15); attach stick floats and balsas top and bottom to the line with *two* rubber rings (float caps). Then you don't have to thread line through the float's bottom eye, and "instant" float changes are possible.

2. Wagglers (including missiles, antennas, duckers etc.).

Specially designed to fish *still* and *slow moving* waters. These floats attach to your line through their bottom eye only and can be kept in place by weights fastened on the line at both sides of the float's eye (see below, fig 35).

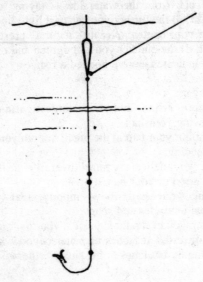

Fig 35. How to attach a waggler.

Pointers to success

To achieve maximum success float fishing, take note of these points:

a) Quietly and without undue disturbance, plumb the depth (see page 56) of the stretch of water you are about to fish.

74

b) Decide at what depth the fish you're after are probably feeding (see "Fish file", Chapter 4) and how much line to allow between your float and the hook to reach the correct "feeding" depth.

c) Always select the smallest and lightest float that suits the water you're fishing, so fish feel minimum resistance on the line when they examine your bait. Fast flowing waters, long casts, heavy baits and strong winds may dictate use of heavier floats.

d) Choose a float with its top painted a colour *you* can see best at a distance. Different colours stand out well against particular backgrounds and in different light conditions. But our eyes vary in the colours most readily picked up – you'll have to experiment.

Easily spotted float top colours include: black, orange, red, white and yellow.

Make sure the underside of your float is white or a drab, mottled camouflage colour. We don't want the fish dazzled!

e) Aim to fix as few weights as possible on your line when float fishing. Fish feel the unnatural pull of each weight when they tug your bait. Some weight is usually necessary to "cock" your float (make it float upright). When correctly cocked, only the tip of your float should be visible.

f) Sometimes the weight of your baited hook alone is sufficient to cock the float and addition of weights to your line may be unnecessary.

g) Self-cocking floats are marketed and give good casting performance without added weights.

h) Weights might be necessary to sink your bait quickly in fast flowing water. Never bunch weights too close together; space them out and decrease the size as you near the hook, then your bait rises and falls naturally in the current; offering minimal resistance to suspicious fish.

i) If your float instantly disappears under the water when cast, you've either hooked a fish or, more probably, put too many weights on your line. Remedy: take off some weights – or use a bigger float!

j) For long casts without excessive weighting of your line, mould mud or groundbait around one of the weights on the line, or your hook bait; then cast. The extra weight of mud or groundbait carries your bait the right distance and falls loose on impact with the water.

k) Don't cast long distances, or fish your float far away without good reason. The further your float from the rod tip, the less control you have over presentation of your bait, and the more delay tightening and reeling-in hooked fish. Any delay in landing a hooked fish favours the fish's chance of escape!

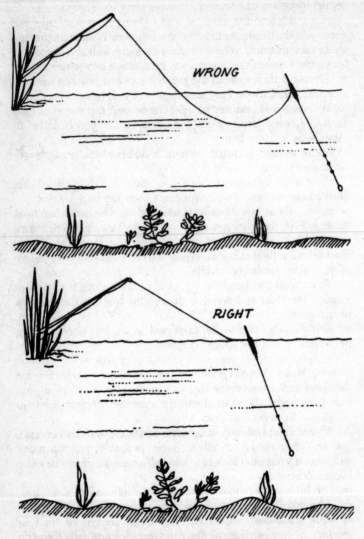

Fig. 36 Keep the line between rod tip and float taut.
(Above): The *wrong* way. The line between the rod tip and float is not taut.
(Below): The *right* way.

l) When fish fail to show interest in your float-fished bait:
1. Change the bait.
2. Alter the depth you're fishing by adjusting the float.
3. Remove, add or reposition the weights on your line.
4. Don't resort to your "lucky" float in moments of despair. Look, think, then adapt your tackle, bait and approach according to your *reasoned* assessment of the situation.

When all else fails... there's always your lucky float!

m) Keep the line between rod tip and float taut and *off* the water (see fig 36). *Unless*, the water is unusually choppy and you're float fishing with the line fixed only to the bottom eye of your float by two weights (see fig 35); in which case place the rod tip slightly *below* the water surface and reel the line tight. This action reduces the transmission of disturbing vibrations to your hook bait.

Bites

When a fish has taken your hook bait into its mouth and you have a "bite", you should straightaway tighten the line to drive your hook firmly into the fish's lip.

Your float indicates a "bite" by:
1. Not standing upright in the water after being cast (immediate bite by fish).
2. Quivering in the water.
3. Disappearing under the water.
4. Lifting out of the water.
5. Rising slightly, then laying flat on the water.
6. Moving across the water, against the current.
7. Travelling with the flow of water, but faster than the current could carry it.
8. Stopping still instead of moving with the current.

Your hunting instinct will tell you when your float shows a fish has taken the bait. There's no mistaking the way your float suddenly "comes to life" and your response – to tighten the line – is instantaneous.

A – Z Float fishing methods
Free-line surface fishing
Fishing a floating bait without using a float or weights! An exciting and challenging way to hook fish. Watch to see the fish seize your bait, then tighten the line. Grease your line (buy some fly-fishers' line grease, see page 143) for good results, and fish

Fig. 37 Free-line surface fishing.

baits like bread crust, floating maggot chrysalis ("caster", see page 46), housefly, grasshopper, beetle etc., or carefully cast your line so it drapes over a lily pad and daintily dangle the hook bait (any bait) slightly beneath the water surface. See fig 37.

Laying-on
Float fishing with your bait "laying on" the water bottom; held in position by a weight fixed firmly to the line. See fig 38. Refer also to float legering on page 85 (where the leger weight is attached but not "fixed" to the line – which is free to run through the leger weight).

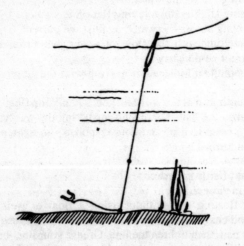

Fig. 38 Laying-on.

Off-bottom float fishing

Standard float fishing practice. Suspend your bait "off-bottom" at a pre-selected depth. See fig 39.

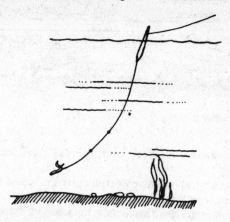

Fig. 39 Off-bottom float fishing.

Sliding float

When float fishing deep water, you may wish to fish your bait deeper than 3.65m (12 ft). Simply measure the length of line you want to fish beneath your float; tie a stop knot (see page 54) onto the reel line at the required depth setting; wind your line back on the reel; slip your float onto the line by threading line through the float's bottom eye, and leave the float free, so after casting the float slides up the line until it's held by the stop knot. Special "sliding floats" are marketed.

The sliding float indicates bites in the usual manner.

Stret-pegging

After plumbing the water depth, adjust your float to support enough line for your baited hook to reach the water bottom *and* allow an additional length of approximately 305mm (12 inches). Cast your line. Keeping the rod tip low and pointing towards the water, hold your float stationary. Make sure that when the line between rod tip and float is taut the line's off the water surface. Your baited hook rises, falls and wavers in the current fractionally above the water bottom (see overleaf, fig 40).

When you want to fish a different stretch of water; reel-in and re-cast.

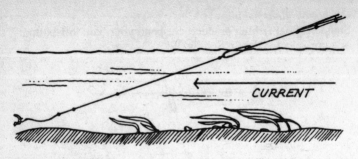

Fig. 40 Stret-pegging.

Trotting (also known as "long-trotting" and "swimming the stream").

Feeding out line, allow your float to carry the baited hook in natural fashion with the flow of the current for distances up to 30m (98 ft) or until the float can't be seen, or fairly swift tightening of the line becomes impractical. Useful method for fishing otherwise inaccessible spots, and tempting shy or suspicious fish, while staying hidden beyond their sight and hopefully, hearing.

13

Legering

Legering is fishing with your bait anchored in position on or near the bottom of the water by a weight or weights.

Some advantages
a) You can cast far from the bank with a heavily weighted line. The heavier the weight, the further out you may fish. A 15g (¹/₂ oz) weight carries your baited hook up to 55m (60 yds); a 21g (³/₄ oz) weight to 73m (80 yds).
b) A bait anchored at the bottom of fast flowing water often fascinates fish and proves a sure way to make big catches.
c) Large fish frequently lie in hiding at the bottom of deep water and are easily reached by legering.
d) Clear patches at the bottom of heavily weeded, reeded, branch- or root-cluttered water can be fished with precision, without worrying too much about getting your line snagged on submerged obstacles.

Leger tackle
A sturdy rod 2.75m (9 ft) or 3m (10 ft) in length is ideal. Use a slightly stronger line than you would normally, to allow for shock and strain caused by casting a heavy leger weight. The heavier the weight, the stronger your line must be.

Tackling up
1. Always use the lightest leger weight necessary to:
a) Cast the distance you want to achieve.
b) Keep your baited hook on or near the bottom.
2. When fishing stillwaters without below surface currents, you probably need no leger weight whatever; simply allow your bait to sink naturally and settle life-like on the bottom.
3. The closer a weight to your bait, the less rise and fall of the baited hook in any current, and the more obviously a trap to clever fish. Try to leave about 152mm (6 inches) to 457mm (18 inches) of unweighted free-drifting line between hook bait

and the nearest weight.

To hold your baited hook on or near the water bottom in strong currents, the leger weight should be close to the bait.

Handy hints
Before fishing
a) Select the stretch of water likely to hold the best fish; choose the exact spot you want to place your baited hook.

b) Scan water for visible signs of submerged obstacles; note position of weed beds.

c) Check the depth of the area of water you intend fishing by plumbing (see page 56). Gently reel in line; feeling for sudden tautness, indicating underwater snags. Look for pieces of weed caught around the plumbing weight – warning of the presence of heavy weed.

d) Expect gradual drift in leger weight and bait position when fishing in a strong current. A leger wait of 42g (1½ oz) might be required to anchor your baited hook in very fast flowing water.

TIP
Groundbait (see Chapter 9) firmly balled around your leger weight gives added distance to your cast and supplies a bonus attraction for fish as it fans out and settles seductively close to your baited hook.

Detecting bites
To detect bites when leger fishing without a float, you can buy easily-attached sensitive rod tip or rod butt swinging bite indicators that fit most rods.

Super-sensitive electronic bite indicators, fitted onto bank sticks (rod rest supports) are useful for daytime and night-time legering.

Also effective as a bite indicator is a lump of bread paste or piece of silver paper (or white painted cork, split down the

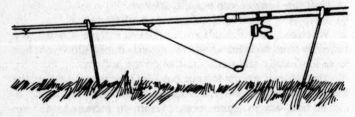

Fig. 41 An effective home-made bite indicator.

centre) pinched onto loose hung line (see fig 41). Movement of the paste or paper shows a bite.

A float may be used as a bite indicator when legering (see fig 43 and fig 45). Pick the smallest, slimmest float you can see without straining your eyes.

Touch legering is a sensitive, thrilling and skilful way of detecting bites. Keep your rod pointing steadily downwards towards the bait. With line taut; grip the line in front of your reel gently between thumb and forefinger, and wait to feel unmistakable sharp tugs, snatches, twitches or tremors that telegraph the fish's bite through your line preceding a run with the bait; tighten... and the fight is on!

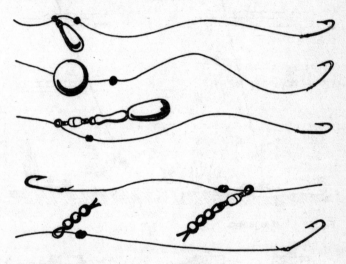

Fig. 42 Five ways of setting up a line for legering.

a) Bomb or pear shape leger weight.
b) Pierced ball or "bullet" shape leger weight.
c) Bomb or pear shape leger weight clipped onto link swivel.
d) Link leger – easily made (see page 85), attached to swivel on line.
e) Link leger – easily made (see page 85), attached direct to line.

Leger weight guide-lines

Here are some examples of successful ways to set up lines for legering. These are guides; your own experimental and tested adaptations and modifications should work just as well.

The tiny "stop" weight, placed in front of the heavier free-running leger weight, prevents the leger moving too near your hook; at the same time allowing curious and suspicious fish to examine and swim away with your baited hook without immediately feeling resistance from the heavy leger weight. Another small "stop" weight may be attached about 457mm (18 inches) above the leger weight to prevent the leger weight working its way too far up the line in a rolling current.

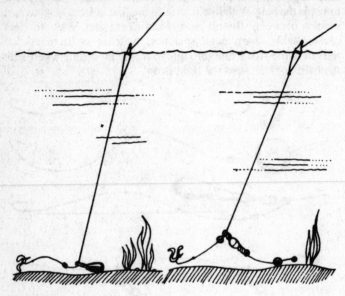

Fig. 43 Float legering.

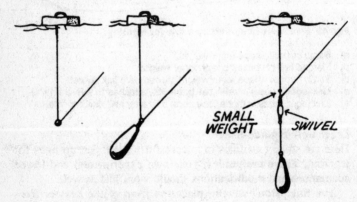

SMALL
WEIGHT

SWIVEL

Fig. 44 A legered floating bait.

A – Z legering methods

Float legering

Attach a small, slender float to your line; keep your line tight and off the water, unless the surface is especially choppy (see page 77, letter (m)). Bites are usually indicated by your float quivering and/or disappearing under the water, but watch also for other unexpected or "unnatural" movements of your float, which might show a bite.

Free-line legering

Allow the baited hook to sink slowly and naturally without any weight or float attached. Ideal in still or slow moving water. Move rod tip to influence direction of bait's "natural" drift.

Legered floating bait

A light, naturally floating bait (like bread crust) may be held in position by a leger weight (see fig 44).

Link legering

Convenient, speedily adjustable and effective form of legering, see fig 42. The "link leger" is made by fixing weights on a short length of looped line. This is an inexpensive way of making your own leger weights at home or on the bankside.

The total weight may be altered by adding or removing single weights of similar or different size.

Paternoster

Can be fished with or without a float, see fig 45.

Keeps your bait stationary above weed beds and underwater snags. Fix a 3 way swivel. An easily attached and adjustable smooth split ring "stop" saves tying unnecessary line-weakening knots to fasten the swivel to your rod line.

Swimfeeder

A swimfeeder does the job of a leger weight *and* deposits an attracting stream of groundbait or feed (see Chapter 9) near your hook bait.

Simply fill the swimfeeder with tasty scraps and cast.

Regular 10 to 20 minute rewinding of the swimfeeder; refilling and recasting keeps shoals of fish feeding keenly and can lead to large catches.

Swimfeeders come in various designs, weights and sizes, and may be set up in different ways. Experiment to find your

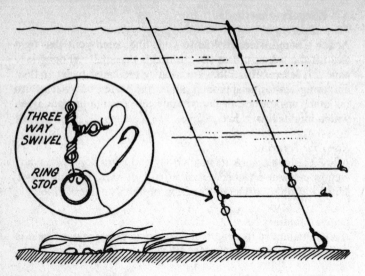

Fig. 45 A paternoster.

Fig. 46 A swimfeeder.

favourite design and style of use.

Extra weight can be added to the line when fishing fast flowing water or where an especially long cast is desired.

Upstream legering

Very effective in shallow water running with strong currents.

The link leger (see fig 42) is best for this type of fishing. Cast the baited hook upstream (up current) and let the current slowly roll the legered bait to your feet. Then repeat the action. Encourage continuous motion of the bait by occasional reeling-in. Don't pull your bait out of the water the minute it reaches you – careful fish follow awhile, then snatch and run at the last moment!

14

Up the Pole

The increasingly popular pole is no newcomer to the U.K. Although now mainly associated with Continental fishermen, the pole was fished in parts of England many years past, and only slipped out of use in the early 1900's.

Fully extended, today's poles range in length from round 3m (10 ft) to 9.5m (31 ft). Given ideal conditions, the splendid pole can catch far more small fish at close range than could rod and line.

The pole often proves a match winner!

The pole's many attractive features include:

*Line attached directly to pole end, therefore no reel or reeling-in to bother you and eat up valuable match fishing time. Simply swing hooked small fish into your hand, or large fish into a long-handled landing net.

*Line shock absorbers built in and/or attached to the pole mean you may fish almost invisibly fine lines of 227g (8 oz) breaking strain and land fish of 1kg (2¼ lb) in weight.

*Your pole can be extended to drop a lightly weighted line and hook bait gently, without splash or scary noise – up to 9.5m (31 ft) away.

*From safe cover far back on the bankside, you can thoroughly fish the water in front of you, before approaching the water's edge and fishing across towards the opposite bank.

*Because your float may be fished less than a metre (3 ft) from the pole end, you have total control over the "natural" presentation of the hook bait and should really fool fish.

*No casting necessary, so no more nasty tangles!

*You have direct contact with hooked fish, which don't have slack line to run with and can't escape by snagging your line in weed or submerged obstacles.

*Replacement lines, complete with pre-selected float, weights and hook, are wound on clearly labelled special line winders by you at home and neatly connected to the pole end when fishing.

This saves fiddling, time-consuming water's edge tackle changes.

*You can fish into strong winds that would make conventional rod and reel float fishing extremely difficult.

Disadvantages
1. You can't fish much beyond 9.5m (31 ft).
2. You'll get "smashed" by BIG fish.
3. You'll soon tire of holding the pole, *unless* you hold it properly.

Pole holding

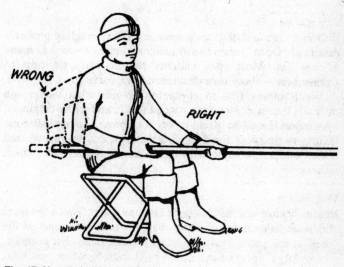

Fig. 47 How to hold the pole.
Left: Wrong. Body muscles not relaxed.
Right: Correct. Weight of pole balanced by left arm. Knee acting as a pole-rest and pivot. Body relaxed.

15
Win Matches

To *win* matches you must acquire knowledge, experience and skill; develop confidence and be highly competitive. You must will yourself to win. Firstly, you *need* the help, support and encouragement of a good fishing club.

Join a club
Fish in a club and club team matches. Check angling press for details of "Open" (open to all) matches; enter or watch as many as you can. Most open matches require early payment of entrance fee – check date deadlines; book early.

Watch others fish in competitions, see what tackle and methods they use. Note any special tackle and tricks employed by winners. Don't be afraid to ask for tips and advice, *after* the fishing is finished! Read angling newspapers, magazines and books. Keep up-to-date with tackle developments and fishing techniques.

Visit venues
Before fishing in a match, try to visit the water. Watch the local club team fish; chat to club members – watch, listen and get the "feel" of the water. Study the water – make notes. For instance: which "pegs" (pegged and numbered bankside match positions, see fig 48) are likely to produce which species and size of fish? What special snags and advantages does each peg offer? Which baits usually produce best results in what particular weather and water conditions? Should you try for a winning weight of small fish, or win with fewer heavy fish?

Specialize
Specialize in your local waters. You can easily practise and perfect your methods and you should aim to become unbeatable in your "home" matches.

Before the match
Plan your strategy: what weight of fish will you probably need

Fig. 48 Match fishing "peg".

to win? Which species will you catch to make this weight? What methods and tackle should produce winning results? Check match rules for banned baits – wasp grubs, hempseed etc.

Sort out your tactics: what breaking strain line/lines, hook baits, groundbait, hooks and floats will you use? And in what order of precedence?

Aim to keep time-consuming changes to a minimum. Time cost is fish lost!

Practise your match methods.

Be prepared to scrap ideas and re-think your approach. Never get stuck in a rut. The right method is the one that wins!

Day before match find out what probable weather and water conditions. If necessary, amend plans accordingly.

Check all tackle is in A1 condition. Put new line on reel if necessary; sharpen hooks; securely tie hooks to hooklength line (see page 57).

Get a good night's sleep.

On match day collect bait; keep bait cool and fresh. RELAX. Remain cool, calm and confident. Your careful preparation should win the match.

Fingers crossed for a little luck at the peg draw. Be prepared for a long hike to your peg – never pack unnecessary equipment. Don't let spectators affect your calm, confident approach. You are there to enjoy yourself.

At your peg, lay out assembled tackle and bait *neatly* and within easy reach. Take your time, "more haste, less speed". When permitted, plumb depths; pick best spots to begin fishing. It's often best to begin by *lightly* groundbaiting near the bank; fish caught can be quickly unhooked and keep-netted. If you've no bite within 5 minutes, change your hook bait. Lightly groundbait at 10 to 15 minute intervals; reduce groundbaiting as bites increase. Reduce groundbaiting further as bites become less frequent – the fish are stuffing themselves with your groundbait!

Concentrate on drawing fish into a small, easily fished area. Allow an unfished "safe zone" to develop at a convenient spot in your stretch of water where frightened fish feel secure. Don't scare them into your neighbour's peg! You can catch all the "safe zone" fish near the end of the match.

Expect nearby experienced competitors to try tricking you into making foolish moves that could cost you the match. Watch for feigned heavy groundbaiting or "feeding" (see page 65); mock hook baiting (is that large container of maggots or sweetcorn really being used, or merely a blind?). Keep an eye on anglers doing well, but don't be panicked into changing your plans and copying their temporarily successful techniques. In an hour they'll be copying you!

Don't dwell on mistakes; be positive and believe in yourself. Your painstaking practice rewards you with an automatic skill that coasts you to victory.

After the match has finished *check* your catch weight on the scales at weigh-in, then immediately and gently return fish to their water.

Keep smiling. You could be the next World Champion!

16
Spinning Sport

Thrill to the hunt for bream, chub, grayling, perch, pike, roach, trout and zander by luring them to snap at spinning or diving artificial baits; enjoy the exciting feel of the fish's fierce strike, and the exhilaration of playing and landing the fish.

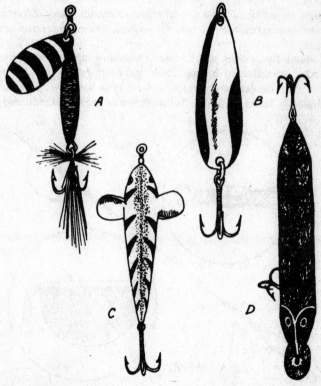

Fig. 49 Artificial baits.
(A) Fly spoon.
(B) Spoon.
(C) Devon minnow.
(D) Plug.

Balance tackle

Light and powerful specialized spinning rods range in length
from about 1.82m (6 ft) to 2.74m (9 ft); for maximum comfort
and ease of casting, carefully balance your tackle by selecting
reel and line that suit the rod. Your specialist tackle dealer will
be pleased to advise you.

On the move

Spinning offers great sport. Travelling light; constantly moving
from one likely spot to another keeps us active, athletic and
warm in winter. And you can cover a lot of water in a short time.

Lures

Lures, or artificial baits for spinning, come in many different
shapes and sizes; they include fly spoons, spoons, minnows and
plugs.

Small fly spoons and ordinary wobbling spoons are often
deadly attractive to bream, chub, grayling, perch and roach;
trout and zander rarely resist a well spun minnow: pike are
frequently taken on plugs. But there are no rules and enticingly

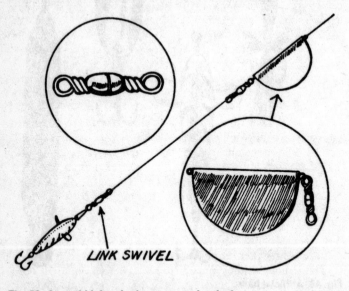

LINK SWIVEL

Fig. 50 An anti-kink spinning vane and swivel.
Use either or both along your line. The link swivel (to clip a change of
lure onto your line quickly) is optional; you may tie the lure direct to the
line.

presented lures attract cannibal fish of all species.

The size of the water you fish suggests your choice of lure. Big waters hide the biggest fish. So choose small spinners for streams and larger lures for rivers, ponds, lakes and lochs.

Swivel and anti-kink
To be sure of preventing kinks and tangles sometimes caused in your line by your lure's spinning, attach a swivel and/or an anti-kink vane (or anti-kink weight) to the line, see fig 50.

Selective spinning
Carefully select the spot you spin. Look for large fishes' likely hideaways; quietly plumb the water or guess the depth. Eye water for weeds and underwater obstructions which could snag your spinner or plug and snap the line. The more hooks attached to your lure the greater your chance of losing the lure. Cast low over the water and accurately, to avoid excessive fish-scaring splash. Begin rewinding line as the lure slips into the water; keep line tight – skilfully vary speed of reeling; alter rod tip and angle. Breathe life into your lure through the connecting line by making the lure rise, weave, dip and dive like a wounded fish – just off bottom and temptingly close to the monster fish's lurking place. Bring your line to the bank's edge before removing the lure from the water: often a cannibal fish follows, strikes and seizes its prey at the very last second.

So fierce is the fish's seizure of a lure that tightening the line to drive hooks home is unnecessary and you'll have no doubt your fish is hooked by the strain on your rod and line.

Spin each promising stretch of water at varying depths in criss-cross patterns until satisfied there is no big feeding fish present, then move on. If you're sure a large fish is lying low, change the lure and carry on until you've caught him.

Persistent spinning usually pays.

****TIPS****
1. To cast a longer distance, attach a heavier lure and/or anti-kink weight.
2. Lures spin better retrieved *against* the current.
3. Dark coloured lures generally catch most fish. Bright lures can be extremely effective on dull days when the water is clouded.
4. Don't spin water close to other people fishing, or you'll ruin their sport.

Sink and draw

Big pike and zander can be caught by fishing a dead sprat, mackerel or herring fixed to *two treble* hooks and line, as shown in fig 51.

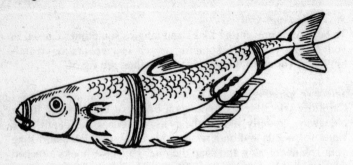

Fig. 51 Preparing a dead sprat, mackerel or herring for sink and draw.

Bind or sew the mouth shut. Puncture the fish with a sharp knife before casting, to be certain it sinks; then slowly reel back the line as you would when spinning; raise and lower the rod tip to sink your bait to the water bottom; then draw the bait towards the surface in a series of jerky movements; make the dead fish appear frantic and distressed. Pull the line tight when you feel the bait seized, then the fight is on...

17

How to Hunt BIG Fish

Anyone can hunt big fish, few catch them.

Qualities you need
Wide practical experience of fishing; knowledge and understanding of traditional and modern theory and practice, and, more important, a sympathetic awareness of how and why fish behave as they do, combined with an ability to predict correctly fish movement and feeding patterns.

You must be keen, skilful, confident, dedicated and patient. Above all, you need luck!

Secret service
Start your own secret service agency today. Gathering fish intelligence is vital for catching BIG fish.

Keep a separate file on each species of fish you are interested in pursuing. Record details of waters where big fish have been, and are being, caught. Note date, baits and tackle used by captor; time of day or night fished; weather conditions and water temperature (if known). Was groundbait used? If so, what mix? Trawl information from fishing papers, magazines and books; T.V. and local radio.

Check maps for likely locations of "secret" waters yielding big fish referred to by fishermen or the media. Listen to anglers' gossip – jot down stories about monster fish sighted or hooked and lost. Trace the water's owner – individual, club, syndicate or "free" – and, if applicable, ask for details of licence and/or ticket fees, membership application, water rules and regulations.

Method is a must
Work begins once you've found a water holding big fish of the species you are hunting.

Methodical approach and preparation is essential to success. Before you dip baited hook in water check, record and map (with the aid of polarised sun-glasses, line and plummet weight and thermometer) the following:

a) Depths.
b) Underwater holes and hollows.
c) Water temperatures.
d) Weed beds.
e) Sunken obstacles/fish cover.
f) Approximate wind speeds (strong, medium, light etc.) and direction.
g) Natural food sources (overhanging trees, bushes, in-flowing streams etc.).
h) Natural food types.
i) Natural cover for *you* to hide behind.
j) Baits most often used by anglers (with which fish will be most familiar) listed in probable order of popularity with anglers *and* fish.

Think big
For big fish use:
1. Big bait.
2. Big, *sharp* hook.
3. Strong tackle, in perfect condition.

TIPS
a) Each season, concentrate on catching big fish of one particular species.
b) Join, or set up, a specimen (big fish) hunter's club in your locality. The exchange of information, help, encouragement and advice is invaluable.
c) Fish when few people are likely to be about. The presence of noisy humans scares away shy big fish.
d) Be prepared to fish at whatever "unsocial" hours big fish feed (water rules permitting).
e) Fish as close to the bank and your landing net as possible. The nearer your net to the big fish, the less chance the fish has to escape.
f) Expect to spend days and/or nights at the waterside without catching fish.
g) When night fishing, fish "blind"; use no light (except for *occasional* safety reasons); make no sound. Listen, touch and feel. Close your eyes and concentrate instincts and senses you didn't know you have. Learn to "see" in the world of the blind – it's a fascinating and useful accomplishment once achieved!
h) Be inventive, look out for new ideas, tackle and methods to adapt to *your* requirements.

i) Aim to learn something new each trip.

j) Don't spend all your time reading about fishing; get out there and do it!

18

How to Keep Records

As soon as you get home from fishing; have cleaned, dried, packed and put away your tackle – record the outing's events.

We learn from mistakes and success. Our records jog the memory, making bigger and better catches of fish possible in the future.

Your records should be a joy to read; store valuable information; build your knowledge and understanding of fish, fishing, wild life and natural surroundings.

Put as much information as possible in your records.

Take pride in presentation. Others might like to read and learn from your records. And one day you may have them published!

Style choice
The type of record you keep suggests the style of recording. For instance, should you want to keep brief records, you can make notes on plain postcards – stored in a plastic or cardboard box; or write in an inexpensive, paper-covered exercise book.

For posh, permanent records, use a large, hard-covered notebook with lined or blank pages; or a ring binder and loose-leaf file paper.

Design
Organise the layout of your records so important information is sensibly arranged and easily found.

Things to include
Note all details you think might be useful to remember next time you go fishing. Anything that could help you catch more and bigger fish. If you have time, record interesting sights and sketch or paint pretty flowers and memorable scenes. Keen photographers add snaps of places visited and fish caught.

Make the effort and turn your fishing knowledge and memories into special records you are pleased to read and proud to show.

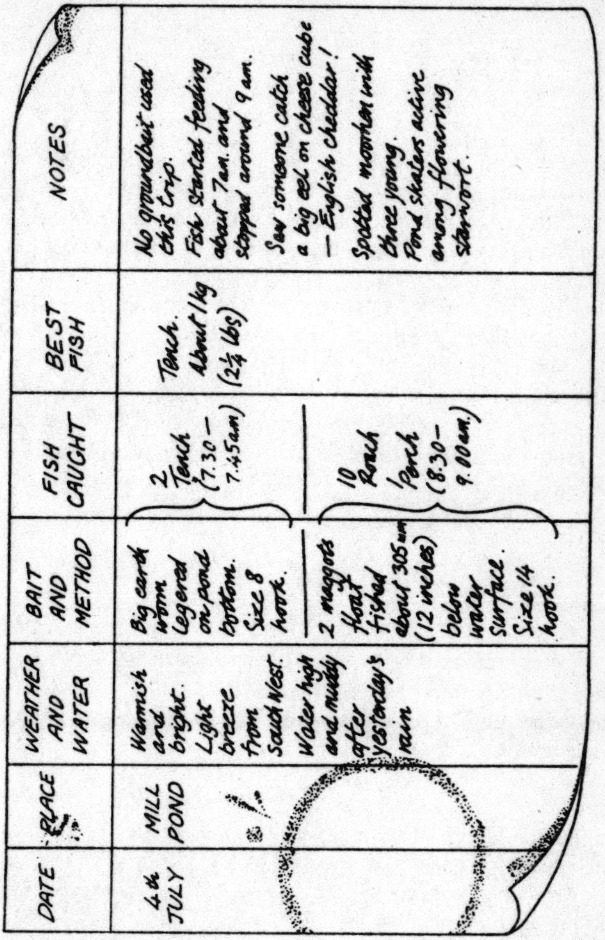

DATE	PLACE	WEATHER AND WATER	BAIT AND METHOD	FISH CAUGHT	BEST FISH	NOTES
4th JULY	MILL POND	Warmish and bright. Light breeze from South West. Water high and muddy after yesterday's rain.	Big earth worm. Legered on pond bottom. Size 8 hook.	2 Tench (7.30 – 7.45 am)	Tench. About 1 kg (2½ lbs)	No groundbait used this trip. Fish started feeding about 7 a.m. and stopped around 9 a.m. Saw someone catch a big eel on cheese cube — English cheddar! Spotted moorhen with three young. Pond skaters active among flowering starwort.
			2 maggots float fished about 305 mm (12 inches) below water surface. Size 14 hook.	10 Roach 1 Perch (8.30 – 9.00 am.)		

Fig. 52 Record sheet.

Part 2

Fly-Fishing For Trout

19
Secrets of
Fly-Fishing for Trout

Part Two of this book explores the wonderful and exciting underwater world of the trout; teaches how best to locate and catch large trout using the right tackle, artificial flies and fly-fishing techniques, and gives priceless information, hints and tips to help *you* catch more and even bigger trout in the months and years ahead!

It provides an excellent introduction to the sporting pursuit of trout living in the flowing waters of rivers and streams; the still-waters of small natural lakes; man-made fisheries; ponds, pits, lakes; and the still-waters of reservoirs, large natural lakes, Scottish lochs and Irish loughs.

Also included are extremely helpful and informative reference sections, which should prove valuable and beneficial throughout your fly-fishing lifetime.

Where to fly-fish?
Begin with a visit to your local fishing tackle dealer.

Tackle dealers
For accurate, knowledgeable, up-to-date information about the availability of inexpensive fly-fishing in your locality, visit the local fishing tackle dealer, who will be delighted to furnish details of the licence/permit/ticket required to fly-fish for trout on local waters, give tips on the best artificial flies to use for bonus catches of big trout, and supply any item of fly-fishing tackle you may require.

Magazines and newspapers
Read fly-fishing magazines and the fly-fishing sections of angling newspapers for information about the latest exciting developments on different trout waters; details of new tackle, techniques and innovative patterns of artificial trout-flies to buy or tie, and try for yourself.

Angling clubs

To make the finest possible start in the thrilling sport of fly-fishing for trout, join an angling club which offers expert instruction in fly-fishing, and organizes regular fly-fishing trips to top trout waters.

To succeed

To achieve consistent fly-fishing success, *specialize* in fly-fishing on one or two trout waters each year; learn the best spots to locate trout and the most successful techniques and artificial flies to use.

Aim to learn something new each outing.

Keep detailed notes in a fly-fishing diary or logbook, which fast becomes a personal gold mine of trout-hooking hints, tips and wisdom to help increase your catch rate of specimen trout.

ABOVE ALL: BE PATIENT AND PERSISTENT TO SUCCEED.

Personal safety

Before fly-fishing be sure to read Chapter 11 on "Personal Safety".

20

The Trout's Anatomy and Senses

Trout are powerful and athletic fish, able to thrive in fast-flowing or still-waters.

Trout can live in vigorous water currents flowing at speeds of up to 24.14km (15 miles) per hour.

Trout are streamlined for action.

The trout's body from gills to tail is power-packed muscle.

Trout have supreme eye-body-fin co-ordination.

The trout's mouth is lined with tiny inward-pointing sharp teeth, so prey once seized, can't escape.

TROUT ARE PERFECT PREDATORS.

Anatomy of the trout

All members of the salmon *(Salmonidae)* family can be distinguished by the presence of the fatty, small *adipose* fin on the back, between dorsal fin and caudal fin (tail).

The *dorsal* and *anal* fins enable trout to balance. The *pectoral* and *pelvic* fins assist movement. The *caudal fin* (tail), combined with body movement, propels the trout through water.

The *air bladder* controls air pressure inside the trout, empowering the trout to rise or sink in water and maintain the desired depth.

The *lateral line* is a series of tiny holes (pores), giving the appearance of a line. The pores communicate changes in pressure to the trout's brain, supplying a special sense of *feeling* (see page 111).

An adult trout can swim at 8.05km (5 miles) per hour for hours, reaching a comfortable sprint speed of 16.09km (10 miles) per hour, and accelerate to a speed of 24.14km (15 miles) per hour in short bursts.

A hooked trout, racing from an angler for its life, can touch 32.18km (20 miles) per hour.

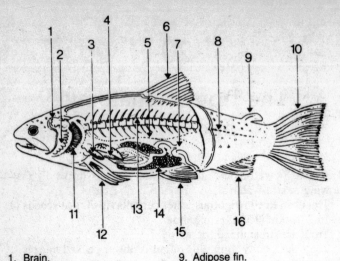

1. Brain.
2. Gill rakers.
3. Heart.
4. Liver.
5. Air bladder.
6. Dorsal fin.
7. Intestines.
8. Lateral line sensor.
9. Adipose fin.
10. Caudal fin.
11. Gill filaments.
12. Pectoral fin.
13. Vertebrae.
14. Ovary.
15. Pelvic or ventral fin.
16. Anal fin.

Fig. 53 Anatomy of the trout.

A wary feeding trout snatches food fast and jets to safety.

A hooked trout's rapid acceleration puts a huge strain on an angler's line. The trout's sudden explosion of energy can break a strong line.

An accelerating trout weighing 227g ($\frac{1}{2}$ lb) can snap fishing line tested to 1.13kg ($2\frac{1}{2}$ lb) breaking strain.

The trout's senses
The trout has highly developed senses of sight, hearing, feeling, smell and taste.

Sight
Trout have *binocular* (focusing with both eyes) vision of what lies before them – to pinpoint prey – and independent *monocular* (one eye only) vision of 180° on each side.

In clear water, trout can see objects up to 4.57m (15 ft) away, and discern different colours; in murky water and at night, trout switch to black and white vision.

Trout have, in effect, all round colour and black and white vision.

The trout's eyes are sensitive to bright light. (Fish have no eyelids to protect their eyes from bright light.) Trout prefer to avoid bright light by diving deep or swimming into shaded areas of water.

Trout's eyes are slow to adjust to *rapid* changes in light and trout can have trouble focusing when day dawns, suddenly brightens or darkens, or when dusk falls quickly.

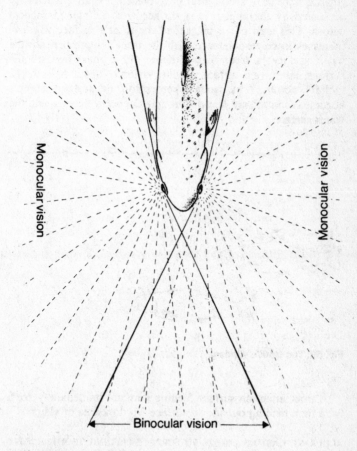

Fig. 54 The trout's vision.

Be aware that a *calm water* surface acts as a mirror for trout.
When the water is calm, trout can see an angler's above water
movements, monitor water surface insect activity, and
simultaneously view images of below water natural food and the
movement of anglers' artificial imitations: images *mirrored
downwards* from the surface of calm water.

The trout's area of *surface vision* is affected by the trout's
depth in the water. A trout lying 127mm (5 inches) beneath the
surface may only see natural prey present, or an artificial fly
presented by the angler, in a surface area 127mm (5 inches)
across. This area of vision, called the trout's surface *window,*
increases in correspondence with the trout's depth beneath the
water surface: a trout lying 305mm (12 inches) beneath the
surface will have a surface window vision of about 305mm (12
inches) across. The trout's perception of surface objects
becomes dimmer and less distinct the deeper it lies beneath the
water surface.

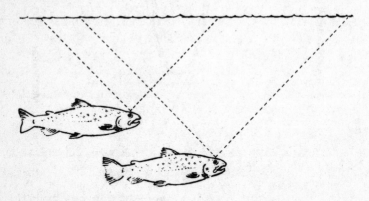

Fig. 55 The trout's window.

A trout intent on surface feeding may not immediately *see* a
food item landing outside its surface window area of vision.

ACCURATE CASTING DIRECT TO SURFACE FEEDING TROUT IS VERY
IMPORTANT.

Trout have well developed night vision, and, once their sight becomes accustomed to the dark, can locate food by sight.

Trout also employ their other senses.

Hearing

The trout has two sensitive ears inside its head and can hear sound vibrations transmitted through water 12m (40 ft) from the sound's source.

Sound travels $4\frac{1}{2}$ times faster through water (approximately 1 mile or 1.61km per second) than through air. Sound is also clearer in water than in air.

WE MUST APPROACH THE WATERSIDE QUIETLY, TREADING SOFTLY.

Feeling

The trout's *lateral line* (see fig 53) of tiny pores along its sides *feels* underwater vibrations (pressure waves), alerting the trout to the presence of objects and minute movements in the water up to 7.62 (25 ft) distant.

Information passed to the trout's brain from the lateral line enables the trout to identify the origin, position, size and speed of the source of the vibrations.

The lateral line helps the trout manoeuvre, detect the slightest change in temperature, and distinguish vibrations that alert the trout to the presence of careless anglers, natural predators, and potential prey.

A *blind* trout can rely on its lateral line to hunt prey, feed and navigate its way around the water. Blind trout turn black in colour, although not all black-coloured trout are blind.

Smell

Trout have a highly developed sense of smell, enabling them to identify minuscule traces of natural scent and track prey for long distances in murky water and at night.

A wary trout will not toy long with an artificial fly impregnated with the telltale smell of human manufacture, storage and handling.

WE MUST BE QUICK TO TIGHTEN OUR LINE AND DRIVE THE HOOK INTO THE MOUTH OF A TROUT INVESTIGATING AN ARTIFICIAL FLY TIED TO OUR FISHING LINE.

Taste

The trout's mouth has sensitive taste buds. Trout are familiar with the normal feel and flavour of their favourite natural foods.

The *unfamiliar* taste and texture of an angler's artificial fly may lead to the artificial's immediate rejection.

The presence of a metal hook will soon be detected and the artificial fly ejected.

WHEN A TROUT INTERCEPTS AND SEIZES OUR ARTIFICIAL FLY, WE HAVE *AT BEST* SECONDS TO ACT BEFORE THE TROUT REALIZES ITS MISTAKE, EJECTS THE FLY AND ESCAPES.

21
The Trout's Food

The trout is an extremely active predator, and relies on a high-protein, largely carnivorous (flesh-eating) diet to supply the extraordinary level of energy it expends each day.

A trout's daily food intake may include aquatic flies, insects, larvae, daphnia (water-fleas), shrimps, snails, small fish and frogs; plus any edible morsel that might fall into or be washed into the water, including: earthworms, caterpillars, beetles, slugs, spiders, ants, wasps, bees, craneflies, grasshoppers, berries and small rodents (rats and mice).

The fly-fisher aims to deceive feeding trout into accepting a skilfully presented artificial fly as a *real* insect.

To capture a *wary* trout's interest, the artificial fly should imitate the appearance and motion of a real insect.

To hook the trout, our artificial fly may have to compete successfully with *real* insects already on or in the water.

To be expert fly-fishers, we must first become competent entomologists: learn which insects trout are likely to be feeding on in specific months, and recognize those insects when they are visible on or in the water.

We can then offer feeding trout an artificial fly that closely resembles the insects on which they are dining.

IT PAYS TO HAVE THE RIGHT FLY IN THE RIGHT PLACE AT THE RIGHT TIME.

In Britain, there are four orders of aquatic insects of particular importance to the fly-fisher. Trout eat these aquatic insects avidly at every stage of the insects' development from nymph or larva to adult winged fly: Ephemeroptera ("mayflies"), Trichoptera (sedge-flies), Plecoptera (stoneflies), and Diptera (gnats, midges, etc.).

MAYFLIES
Order: **Ephemeroptera**
The different species of fly belonging to the order *Ephemeroptera* are commonly called "mayflies".

113

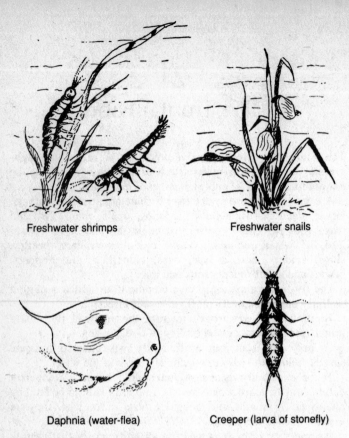

Freshwater shrimps

Freshwater snails

Daphnia (water-flea)

Creeper (larva of stonefly)

Fig. 56 Some aquatic creatures trout eat.

The mayfly has existed for at least 325 million years. There are over 1,500 different species of mayfly worldwide. The mayfly is found in all continents except Antarctica.

There are about 40 different species of mayfly in Britain.

The largest mayfly in Britain is *Ephemera danica*. The adult mayfly is about 19mm (3/4 inch) long, with 16mm (5/8 inch) wingspan and two or three 25mm (1 inch) long tails.

All mayflies of the order *Ephemeroptera* have two large, upright, transparent or opaque wings, and are often referred to by anglers UPWINGED FLIES.

The life-cycle of the mayfly from fertilized egg to adult consists of four stages:

114

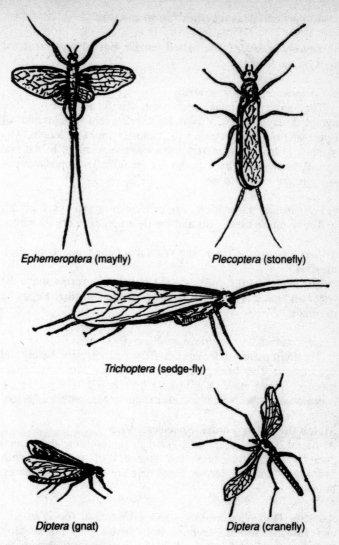

Ephemeroptera (mayfly)

Plecoptera (stonefly)

Trichoptera (sedge-fly)

Diptera (gnat)

Diptera (cranefly)

Fig. 57 Aquatic insects.

a) Fertilized egg
b) Nymph
c) Dun (also called sub-imago or sub-adult)
d) Spinner (adult mayfly).

Anglers call dead mayflies *"spent spinners"*.

a) *Beginning stage:* The mated female mayfly lays fertilized eggs on the water.

b) *Underwater stage:* NYMPH
The mayfly nymphs hatch from the fertilized eggs. The nymphal stage normally lasts from 1–2 years. The nymph of *Ephemera danica* grows up to 25mm (1 inch) in length. The nymphs graze on algae and underwater vegetation. In the late spring, summer and autumn months the fully developed nymphs swim to the water surface.

c) *First surface stage:* DUN (also called sub-imago or sub-adult).
The nymph's case splits and the fly emerges to dry its wings.

d) *Second surface stage:* SPINNER (also called imago or adult mayfly).
The adult mayflies, wings dried, collect in swarms above the water and mate. The mated females lay their fertilized eggs on the water.

Finally: SPENT SPINNER (dead adult mayfly)
The adult male and female mayflies die soon after mating and egg laying. The life-cycle from emerging *"dun"* to *"spent spinner"* (dead mayfly) is usually over in a few days; during warm weather the cycle is sometimes completed within 24 hours.

Match the hatch – order: *Ephemeroptera*
Artificial nymphs, duns and spinners representing the natural "mayfly" nymphs, duns and spinners of the indigenous UPWINGED "mayfly" species listed here are of particular interest to us.

Autumn Dun *(Ecdyonurus dispar)*: Common; found in still, and flowing waters; favours stony rivers and lakes. Most abundant July-September, when the duns emerge during the DAY.

Blue Winged Olive Dun *(Ephemerella ignita)*: Common; found mainly in flowing waters and some still-waters. Most abundant May-October, when the duns emerge during the AFTERNOON/EVENING.

1 Mature nymph.   2 Swims to surface.   3 Emergence.
4 Dun (sub-imago) sheds nymphal skin.   5 Flight.

Fig. 58 The mayfly hatch.

117

Broadwings (*Caenis & Brachycercus* – six species), also known as Angler's Curse: Common; tiny flies; found in still, and flowing waters. Most abundant June–August, when the duns emerge during the DAY/EVENING.

Claret Dun (*Leptophlebia vespertina*): Common; found in still-waters, and occasionally slow-flowing waters. Most abundant May–June, when the duns emerge during the DAY.

Dusky Yellowstreak Dun (*Heptagenia lateralis*): Widespread, not common; found in stony still-waters and stony flowing waters. Most abundant May–September, when the duns emerge during the DAY/EVENING.

Iron Blue Dun (*Baetis niger & Baetis muticus*): Common; found in flowing waters. Most abundant May–October, when the duns emerge during the DAY.

Lake Olive Dun (*Cloeon simile*): Common; found in still, and flowing waters. Most abundant April–June, and again August–October, when the duns emerge during the DAY.

Large Brook Dun (*Ecdyonurus torrentis*): Common; found in stony flowing waters. Most abundant April–July, when the duns emerge during the DAY/EVENING.

Large Dark Olive Dun (*Baetis rhodani*): Common; found in flowing waters. Most abundant February–May; also September–November. The duns emerge during the DAY.

Large Summer Dun (*Siphlonurus lacustris*; also *Siphlonurus armatus* and *Siphlonurus alternatus*): Localized; found mainly in north-west England, Wales, Scotland, western Ireland, in still, and flowing waters. Most abundant June–August, when the duns emerge during the DAY.

March Brown Dun (*Rithrogena germanica*): Widespread, except southern England, though not common; found in stony flowing waters. Most abundant March-May, when the duns emerge during the AFTERNOON.

Mayfly Dun (*Ephemera danica & Ephemera vulgata*): The mayfly dun *Ephemera danica* is common; found in still, and flowing waters. Most abundant May-June, when the duns emerge during the DAY. The mayfly dun *Ephemera vulgata* is localized; found in still, and slow-flowing waters in the Midlands and southern England. Most abundant May–June, when the duns emerge during the DAY.

Medium Olive Dun *(Baetis vernus & Baetis tenax)*: Widespread, though not common, in England and Scotland; found in flowing waters. Most abundant May–October, when the duns emerge during the DAY/EVENING.

Olive Upright Dun *(Rithrogena semicolorata)*: Common; found in stony flowing waters. Most abundant May–August, when the duns emerge during the AFTERNOON/EVENING.

Pale Watery Dun *(Baetis fuscatus)*: Common in Wales, north-west and southern England; found in flowing waters. Most abundant May–October, when the duns emerge during the DAY.

Pond Olive Dun *(Cloeon dipterum)*: Common; found in still, and flowing waters. Most abundant June–September, when the duns emerge during the DAY.

Sepia Dun *(Leptophlebia marginata)*: Widespread, not common; found in still-waters. Most abundant April–May, when the duns emerge during the AFTERNOON.

Small Dark Olive Dun *(Baetis scambus)*: Widespread, not common, found in flowing waters. Most abundant June–October, when the duns emerge during the AFTERNOON/EVENING.

Small Spurwing Dun *(Centroptilum luteolum)*: Common; found in still, and flowing waters. Most abundant May–September, when the duns emerge during the DAY.

Yellow May Dun *(Heptagenia sulphurea)*: Common; found in flowing waters and some still-waters. Most abundant May–August, when the duns emerge during the DAY/EVENING.

SEDGE-FLIES (also know as CADDIS-FLIES)
Order: **Trichoptera**
There are approximately 7,000 species of sedge-fly (called

caddisfly in North America); about 190 species are known in Britain, most of which are either too small to be of value to the fly-fisher, or too localized in distribution to be of general interest.

Adult sedge-flies resemble moths, have four hairy wings that fold sloping roof-like back along the body when at rest, and no tails.

Adult sedge-flies live near water and most species are active at night.

The largest sedge-fly in Britain is the Great Red Sedge *(Phryganea grandis)*. The body of an adult Great Red Sedge is about 25mm (1 inch) long, and wingspan 51mm (2 inches).

The antennae of sedge-flies are very long; up to three times the length of the body.

The life-cycle of the sedge-fly from fertilized egg to adult consists of four stages:

a) Fertilized egg
b) Larva (commonly called a *caddis, caddis worm* or *caddis grub*)
c) Pupa
d) Adult.

a) *Beginning stage:* The mated female sedge-fly lays fertilized eggs on the water or on exposed aquatic plants.

b) *First underwater stage:* LARVA (commonly called a *caddis, caddis worm*, or *caddis grub*).

The sedge-fly larvae hatch from the fertilized eggs. The larvae of most species build a protective open-ended cylindrical case from pieces of plants, sticks, stones, gravel and any other suitable materials found. The protective case is bound together with silk produced from glands on the larva's lower lip.

The case-bearing larva's head and upper body protrude, and it moves by pulling the case along with its abdomen.

The larva can conceal itself within the case at moments of danger.

The larvae of some species of sedge-fly do not build protective cases; they remain free-living and crawl amongst stones on the waterbed, or construct sheltered lairs – complete with tubes or nets of silk to trap food.

The sedge-fly larvae feed on algae, underwater vegetation and aquatic larvae of other insects.

After about one year, the larva is ready to begin its pupal

120

stage; secures its protective cylindrical case to something solid and seals itself inside;

Larvae that have not built protective cases construct a cocoon of silk in which to pupate.

c) *Second underwater stage:* PUPA

The pupa takes 2–3 weeks to develop fully (pupate), and when ready, bites out of the protective case or cocoon and swims or crawls to the water surface.

d) *Surface stage:* ADULT

At the water surface, the pupa inflates and splits its pupal skin, and emerges as a winged adult sedge-fly.

Adult sedge-flies mate and die within a few weeks.

The entire life-cycle of the sedge-fly is normally completed in just over one year.

Match the hatch – order: *Trichoptera*

Artificial representations of the sedge-fly larva (commonly called *caddis, caddis worm,* or *caddis grub*), sedge-fly pupa and adult sedge-fly of the indigenous sedge-fly species listed here are of particular interest to us.

Black Sedge *(Silo nigricornis):* Common; found on flowing waters. Most abundant June–August, when the new adults emerge during the AFTERNOON/EVENING.

Brown Sedge *(Anabolia nervosa):* Common; found on still, and flowing waters. Most abundant June, and again August–September, when the new adults emerge during the EVENING.

Brown Silverhorns *(Athripsodes cinereus):* Widespread; found on still, and slow-flowing waters. Most abundant June–August, when the new adults emerge during the AFTERNOON/EVENING.

Caperer *(Halesus radiatus):* Widespread; found on flowing waters. Most abundant August–October, when the new adults emerge during the AFTERNOON/EVENING.

Cinnamon Sedge *(Limnephilus lunatus):* Common; found on still, and flowing waters. Most abundant June–October, when the new adults emerge during the DAY/EVENING.

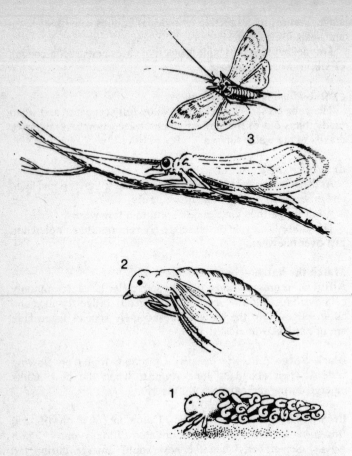

1 Sedge larva.   2 Sedge pupa.   3 Adult sedge-fly.

Fig. 59 Life-cycle of the sedge-fly.

Grannom *(Brachycentrus subnubilus)*: Widespread; found on flowing waters. Most abundant April–June, when the new adults emerge during the DAY/EVENING.

Great Red Sedge *(Phrygania grandis)*: Common; found on still, and flowing waters. Most abundant May–June, when the new adults emerge during the AFTERNOON/EVENING.

Grey Flag *(Hydropsyche instabilis)*: Common; found on fast-flowing waters. Most abundant June–July, when the new adults emerge during the DAY/EVENING. The Grey Flag is a DAY-FLYING species.

Grey Sedge *(Odontocerum albicorne)*: see **Silver Sedge**.

Grouse-Wing *(Mystacides longicornis)*: Common; found on still-waters. Most abundant June–August, when the new adults emerge during the AFTERNOON/EVENING.

Marbled Sedge *(Hydropsyche contubernalis)*: Widespread; found on flowing waters. Most abundant June–July, when the new adults emerge during the AFTERNOON/EVENING.

Medium Sedge *(Goera pilosa)*: Common; found on still, and flowing waters. Most abundant May–July, when the new adults emerge during the DAY/EVENING. The Medium Sedge is a DAY-FLYING species.

Mottled Sedge *(Glyphotalius pellucidus)*: Widespread; found on still-waters. Most abundant May–September, when the new adults emerge during the AFTERNOON/EVENING.

Sand Fly *(Rhyacophila dorsalis)*: Common; found on flowing waters. Most abundant April–September, when the new adults emerge during the AFTERNOON/EVENING.

Silver Sedge *(Odontocerum albicorne)*, also known as **Grey Sedge**: Widespread; found on fast-flowing waters. Most abundant June–September, when the new adults emerge during the DAY/EVENING.

Small Red Sedge *(Tinodes waeneri)*: Common; found on still, and slow-flowing waters. Most abundant May–September, when the new adults emerge during the AFTERNOON/EVENING.

Welshman's Button *(Seriscostoma personatum)*: Widespread; found on flowing waters and some still-waters. Most abundant June–July, when the new adults emerge during the DAY/EVENING. Welshman's Button is a DAY-FLYING species.

STONEFLIES
Order: **Plecoptera**

There are approximately 1,550 species of stonefly; about 34 species are found in Britain, most of them too rare or localized to be of interest to the fly-fisher.

Adult stoneflies range in size from the Needle Fly *(Leuctra fusca)*, which is about 6mm (¼ inch) long, to the Large Stonefly *(Perla bipunctata)*, which grows to just over 25mm (1 inch) in length, with a wingspan of 51mm (2 inches).

Adult stoneflies have four wings that lie flat over the body when at rest, and two tails.

The adult stonefly is a weak and poor flier, spending much of its short life hiding on or near the ground.

Some short-winged species of stonefly are incapable of flight.

The adults of most species of stonefly are found near clean, well-oxygenated fast-flowing stony rivers and streams; some species are found near slow-flowing waters or the rocky shores of large still-waters.

The life-cycle of the stonefly from fertilized egg to adult consists of three stages:

a) Fertilized egg
b) Nymph (nymph of larger species commonly called *creeper*)
c) Adult.

a) *Beginning stage:* The mated female stonefly lays fertilized eggs on the water.

b) *Underwater stage:* NYMPH (nymph of larger species commonly called creeper).

The stonefly nymphs hatch from the fertilized eggs. The nymphs crawl among the stones of the waterbed and feed on algae and underwater vegetation. Nymphs *(creepers)* of the larger species are voracious predators, seizing and eating small aquatic creatures including worms, sedge-fly pupae *(caddis)*, mayfly nymphs, other stonefly nymphs and small fish-fry.

The nymphal stage can last from 1–4 years, depending on the species. During this time some nymphs shed their skin (moult) over 30 times, before the mature nymph finally crawls out of the water onto land.

c) *Surface stage:* ADULT
Once out of the water and on land, the nymph completes its

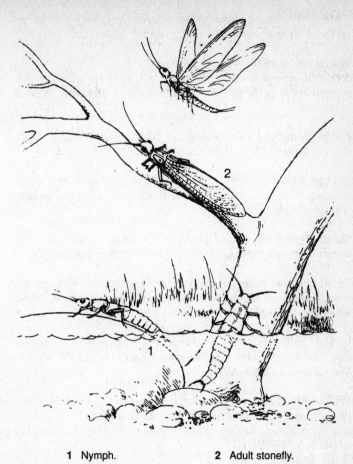

1 Nymph.   **2** Adult stonefly.

Fig. 60 Life-cycle of the stonefly.

final moult – splitting the nymphal skin to emerge as a winged adult stonefly.

Having lived underwater as a nymph for between 1–4 years, the adult winged stonefly mates and dies within 5 weeks.

NOTE: Because stonefly nymphs *crawl* (don't swim) from the water to land to begin their final moult, artificial representations of the natural stonefly nymph are difficult, though not impossible, to present to feeding trout.

Many fly-fishers prefer to concentrate on offering trout an artificial representation of an "egg laying" adult female stonefly.

Match the stonefly – order: *Plecoptera*
Artificial representations of the adult female stoneflies of the indigenous stonefly species listed here are of particular interest to us.

Large Stonefly *(Perla bipunctata)*: Widespread; found on stony flowing waters. Most abundant May–June.

Needle Fly *(Leuctra fusca)*: Widespread; found on stony flowing waters and stony still-waters. Most abundant August–October.

Small Brown *(Nemoura cinerea)*: Common, found on still-waters and slow-flowing waters. Most abundant March–July.

Small Yellow Sally *(Chloroperla torrentium)*: Widespread; found on stony still-waters and stony flowing waters. Most abundant April–July.

Yellow Sally *(Isoperla grammatica)*: Widespread; found on stony flowing waters, and shores of rocky large still-waters. Most abundant May–August.

Willow Fly *(Leuctra geniculata)*: Widespread; found on stony flowing waters. Most abundant August–October.

GNATS, MIDGES, ETC.
Order: **Diptera**
Some natural flies of special interest to the fly-fisher belong to the order Diptera.

The Diptera order of insects contains more than 85,000 species commonly called flies; over 500 species of Diptera are found in Britain – many have aquatic larvae.

The life-cycle of the different species of fly (order Diptera), which have aquatic larvae, consists of four stages:

a) Fertilized egg
c) Larva
c) Pupa
d) Adult.

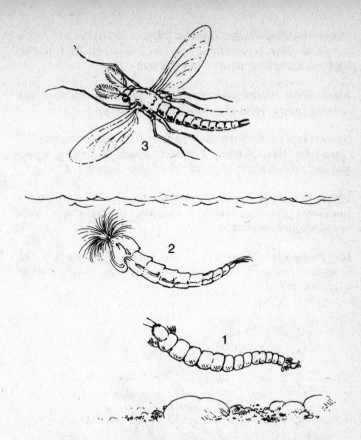

1 Midge larva.   **2** Midge pupa.   **3** Adult midge.

Fig. 61 Life-cycle of the midge.

a) *Fertilized egg*
Mated female lays fertilized eggs on the water.

b) *Larva*
Larvae hatch from the fertilized eggs and live underwater.

c) *Pupa*
Larvae develop and become pupae.

d) *Adult*
Adult flies emerge at the water surface from split pupal skin.

Match the flies – order: *Diptera*

Artificial flies representing the natural adult flies (order: Diptera) listed here are of particular interest to us.

Black Gnat *(Bibio johannis)*: Common; found on still, and flowing waters. Most abundant May–September.

Black Fly (Genus: *Simulium,* many species), commonly called "Smut" or "Black Curse": Common; found on flowing waters and large still-waters. Most abundant May–September.

Cranefly (Genus: *Tipula*, many species), also know as **Daddy Longlegs**: Common; found on still, and flowing waters. Most abundant June–September.

Hawthorn Fly *(Bibio marci)*; also know as **St. Mark's Fly**: Common; found on still, and flowing waters. Most abundant May–September.

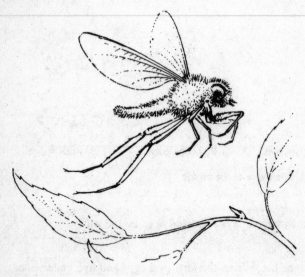

Fig. 62 Hawthorn fly.

Heather Fly *(Bibio pomonae)*: Common in Scotland, the north of England, and Wales (also occurs elsewhere – often near heather); found on still, and flowing waters. Most abundant August–September.

Midge (family: *Chironomidae,* numerous species). The non-biting midge species, commonly called *"Buzzers"* are of particular interest to the fly-fisher. Most species are predominantly black, brown or green (some red), in colour; other species are olive, golden-olive, orange-silver in colour. Non-biting midge species are common, and found on still, and flowing waters. Most abundant March–September. The aquatic larvae of non-biting midges are commonly called *"bloodworms"*.

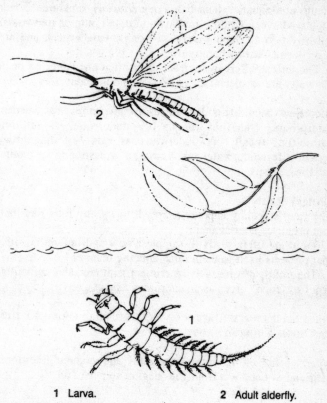

1 Larva.   2 Adult alderfly.

Fig. 63 Life-cycle of the alderfly.

OTHER AQUATICS

The natural flies of the orders Ephemeroptera, Trichoptera, Plecoptera, Diptera, and their nymphs, larvae, and pupae are of principal importance to the fly-fisher.

Other aquatic creatures of special interest to us, include:

Alderfly larvae, aquatic beetles, cranefly larvae, damselfly nymphs, dragonfly nymphs, small fish (minnows, sticklebacks, etc.), small fish-fry (any species of fish), leeches, freshwater lice, freshwater shrimps, freshwater snails, tadpoles, water-mites.

TERRESTRIALS

Many non-aquatic, land-based *(terrestrial)* creatures hover slightly above, alight on, are blown into, fall into, or are washed into (by rain or flood water), still or flowing waters, and are eagerly snatched by hungry trout.

The terrestrial creatures trout most often encounter on or in the water are of special interest to us, and include:

Alderflies (begin life underwater as *nymphs*), ants, bees, beetles, caterpillars, craneflies (begin life underwater as *larvae*), damselflies (begin life underwater as *nymphs*), dragonflies (begin life underwater as *nymphs*), grasshoppers, moths, sawflies, wasps.

Hungry trout

The trout's healthy appetite *tempts* it to try any food-like item that promises nourishment.

Trout are often ready to sample a new and unfamiliar titbit that presents itself to them in an enticing manner.

The trout's readiness to experiment with new and unfamiliar types of "food" gives us an enormous advantage.

THE SKILFULL PRESENTATION OF ANY ARTIFICIAL FOOD-LIKE ITEM CAN HOOK A HUNGRY TROUT.

Note: A list of the more successful and popular traditional artificial dry and wet trout-flies begins on page 168.

22

Tackle, Lines
Knots and Accessories

Notes to help you select and assemble the right tackle, line rigs and tackle accessories, for maximum fly-fishing success.

Tackle dealers
Visit your local fishing tackle dealer, view the fly-fishing tackle and accessories on display. Ask the tackle dealer's expert advice on tackle choice, and buy quality items the dealer recommends which you have inspected, like the look and feel of, and are certain will suit your purpose.

Be wise and happy with your choice of fly-fishing tackle and you will be expertly equipped and supremely confident when you begin fly-fishing for trout.

Rods
A fly-fishing rod of about 2.6m (8½ ft) – 2.9m (9½ ft) in length is ideal for streams, rivers and most fly-fishing on still-waters.

To achieve long distance casts of around 32m (35 yds), sometimes necessary to reach feeding trout on the still-waters of *large* lakes, lochs and reservoirs, a fly-fishing rod of about 2.9m (9½ ft) – 3m (10 ft) in length may prove a practical choice.

Reel
A fly-fishing reel should be light in weight and of strong construction.

A fly-fishing reel of about 89mm (3½ inches) – 102mm (4 inches) in diameter is ideal for streams, rivers and fly-fishing on still waters.

Fly-fishing reel spool line capacities vary: for fly-fishing on streams and small rivers, a full reel spool capacity of *at least* 73m (80 yds) backing line and attached fly-line (see page 134) is usually adequate; for fly-fishing on large rivers, and still-waters, a full reel spool capacity of *at least* 96m (105 yds) backing line and attached fly-line (see page 134) is desirable.

A fly-fishing reel with a large line capacity can be used for fly-fishing on rivers, streams and still-waters.

AFTM

Fly-fishing rods and fly-fishing lines carry an AFTM *(Association of Fishing Tackle Manufacturers)* number. The rod's AFTM number indicates the range of fly-line weights the rod has been designed to cast.

The heavier a fly-line, the higher the line's AFTM number.

For optimum line-casting performance, match the recommended AFTM number of the rod and fly-line. For example: a fly-fishing rod with an AFTM line rating of 5–7 (AFTM 5–7) is designed to cast fly-lines of weights numbered AFTM 5, 6 or 7.

A fly-line too light or too heavy for the rod will not cast properly.

AFTM fly-line numbers 1–4 are ideal for fly-fishing on brooks, becks and burns for small trout.

AFTM fly-line numbers 4–6 are ideal for fly-fishing on streams.

AFTM fly-lines numbers 6 and 7 are suitable for fly-fishing on rivers and most still-waters.

AFTM fly-line numbers 7–9 are suitable for fly-fishing on *large* lakes, lochs and reservoirs, where strong winds blow, and long distance casts of round 32m (35 yds) may sometimes be necessary to reach trout feeding far from the bank or shore.

AFTM fly-line numbers 10–12 are mostly used by fly-fishers pursuing sizeable salmon.

Fly-line tapers

A fly-fishing line is tapered to assist its flight through the air when cast, and enable the fly-fisher to present the artificial fly in the most delicate and natural manner possible to feeding trout.

Double taper (DT)

The double taper fly-line is tapered at both ends of its length and can be reversed on your reel spool when one regularly-fished tapered end is reduced through normal cutting, breakage and trimming.

The double taper fly-line is an excellent and economical choice

Fig. 64 Double taper fly-line.

of line where delicate presentation of your artificial fly is desired at close to medium distance on streams, rivers and still-waters.

Weight forward (WF)

The weight forward fly-line tapers at one end only, and is

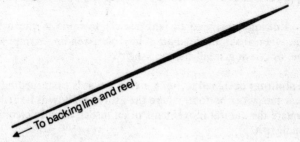

To backing line and reel

Fig. 65 Weight forward fly-line.

specially designed to achieve long distance casts on rivers and still-waters.

Shooting head, also called Shooting taper (ST)

The shooting head or shooting taper fly-line has a tapered head

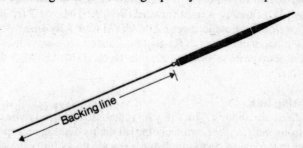

Backing line

Fig. 66 Shooting head or shooting taper fly-line.

133

which enables proficient casters to achieve very long distance casts on the still-waters of *large* lakes, lochs and reservoirs.

Floating and sinking fly-lines

In addition to being tapered, fly-lines are manufactured to float on the water surface, or sink through the water at particular speeds.

Floating: designed for use when trout are feeding at the water surface on adult flies emerging, or newly emerged, from their nymphal or pupal skins, egg-laying female flies, or insects alighting on or blown onto the water surface, and struggling to get out of the water; also when trout are feeding just below the water surface on nymphs or pupae; recently drowned flies/insects, etc.

Slow sinking: designed to sink slowly towards a mid-water depth, when trout are feeding avidly on ascending nymphs or pupae, or chasing small fish or fish-fry.

Fast sinking: designed to sink quickly towards trout feeding on or near the water bottom, where the artificial fly will be fished to imitate the natural movements of an insect, aquatic creature, or small fish.

The right rod, reel and lines for beginners

I suggest (it's *your* choice!) the following rod, reel and fly-line combinations to begin fly-fishing on rivers, streams and still-waters:

Fly-fishing rod, AFTM line rating in the range AFTM 5–7, of about 2.6m (8$\frac{1}{2}$ ft) – 2.9m (9$\frac{1}{2}$ ft) in length; fly-fishing reel of about 89mm (3$\frac{1}{2}$ inches) – 102mm (4 inches) in diameter (see page 131); floating weight forward (WF) AFTM 6 or 7 fly-line, and/or floating double taper (DT) AFTM 6 or 7 fly-line.

Beginners intending to fly-fish for trout on *streams* will enjoy better sport with a floating double taper (DT) AFTM 5 or 6 fly-line.

Backing line

Fly-lines are about 27.4m (30 yds) in length, and need to be tied to strong *backing line*, which helps fill the fly-fishing reel spool, gives extra line to cast long distances, and allows for occasional line-stripping sprints by especially large trout.

The reel spool should be filled with backing line and attached fly-line to within about 6mm (¼ inch) of the reel spool's full line capacity (see page 131).

Backing line to reel

Secure the backing line to your reel, using the **reel knot** (see fig 67). Ensure the line is tight and evenly wound – loose line can tangle and lead to reel jams.

Fly-line to backing line

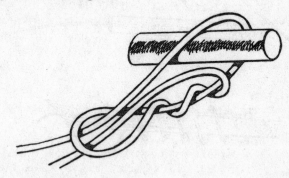

Fig. 67 Reel knot.

Tie your fly-line to the backing line using either the **needle knot** (see fig 68), or the **Albright knot** (see fig 69).

Leaders, also called casts

The tapered leader line (also called a *"cast"*) assists to present your artificial fly in the most delicate and "natural" way possible to feeding trout.

A leader line is the tapered link between fly-line and artificial fly.

Your tapered leader line should normally be about 2.7m (9 ft) – 3.3m (11 ft) in length.

Knotless leaders

Commercially manufactured, ready-made *knotless* continuous taper leader lines are marketed and available from your local fishing tackle dealer.

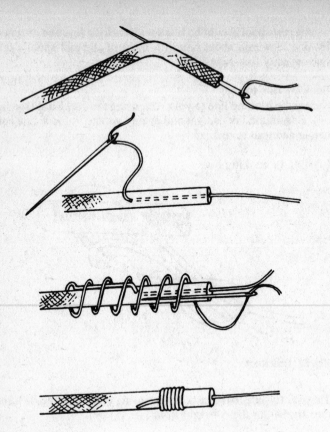

Fig. 68 Needle knot.

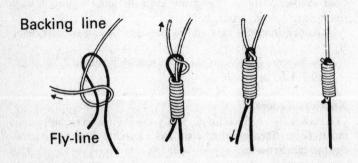

Backing line

Fly-line

Fig. 69 Albright knot.

Follow the manufacturer's instructions and cut the *knotless* continuous taper leader line to achieve the final breaking-strain line strength you require; then tie on an *additional* line of the final breaking-strain you require, about 610mm (2 ft) in length, using the **double grinner knot** (see fig 70), or the **water knot** (see fig 71) or the **blood knot** (see fig 72). By tying on the additional line, you avoid having to cut back along the knotless continuous taper leader line whenever you tie on a different artificial fly.

Make your own leaders

You may choose to make your own tapered leader line by knotting lines of different breaking-strain strengths together to give you a tapered leader line of about 2.7m (9 ft) – 3.3m (11 ft) in length.

Tying a leader

Note: To tie your own tapered leader line, use the **double grinner knot** (see fig 70), or the **water knot** (see fig 71), or the **blood knot** (see fig 72).

A simple example: To make your own tapered leader line of 3m (10 ft) in length, tie 610mm (2 ft) of 9kg (20 lb) breaking-strain line to 610mm (2 ft) of 6.7kg (15 lb) breaking-strain line, tie on 610mm (2 ft) of 4.5kg (10 lb) breaking-strain line, finally tie on 1.2m (4 ft) of 2.7kg (6 lb) breaking strain line (the *leader point* or *tippet*).

To make a tapered leader line of 2.7m (9 ft) in length, reduce the measurement of each of the four sections by 76mm (3 inches).

To make a tapered leader line of 3.3m (11 ft) in length, increase the measurement of each of the four sections by 76mm (3 inches).

You can step down the leader line knotted sections to a leader point or tippet breaking-strain strength of your choice.

Some fly-fishers tie their leader lines with up to 6 or 7 separate sections of line, each section steadily reducing in breaking-strain strength towards the final 6th or 7th leader point or tippet section.

Leader to fly-line

The thick, high breaking-strain-strength end of your tapered leader line is tied to the fly-line using the **needle knot** (see fig 68), or the **nail knot** (see fig 73).

Fig. 70 Double grinner knot.

Fig. 71 Water knot.

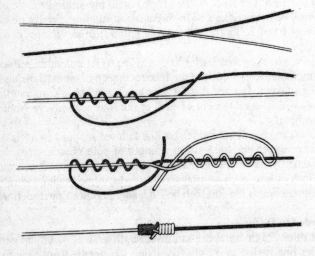

Fig. 72 Blood knot.

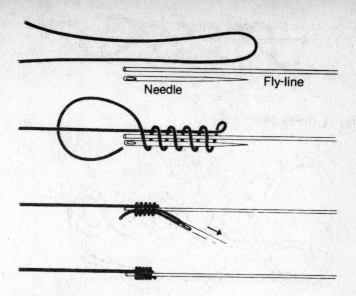

Fig. 73 Nail knot.

Leader point or tippet

The fine, low breaking-strain-strength end section of your tapered leader line is called the **leader point** or **tippet.**

Before fly-fishing, your artificial fly is tied to the leader point or tippet, using the **grinner knot** (see fig 74), or **tucked half blood knot** (see fig 75).

TO SUM UP: THE BACKING LINE IS TIED TO THE REEL SPOOL, THE FLY-LINE IS TIED TO THE BACKING LINE, THE LEADER LINE IS TIED TO THE FLY-LINE., THE ARTIFICIAL FLY IS TIED TO THE LEADER LINE'S POINT OR TIPPET.

TIP

Should you wish to make swift and easy changes of complete leader lines, tie a line of about 9kg (20 lb) breaking-strain, and about 457mm (18 inches) in length, to your fly-line using the **needle knot** (see fig 68) or the **nail knot** (see fig 73). Tie a loop at the end of the line, using the **loop knot** (see fig 76).

Tie a loop at the thick, high breaking-strain "butt" end of your leader line, using the **loop knot** (see fig 76); simply connect the two looped lines as shown in fig 77.

Leader lines can be disconnected and replaced in minutes!

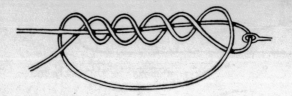

Fig. 74 Grinner knot.

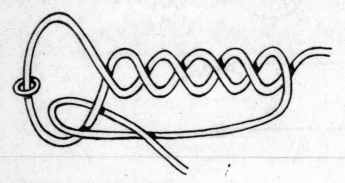

Fig. 75 Tucked half blood knot.

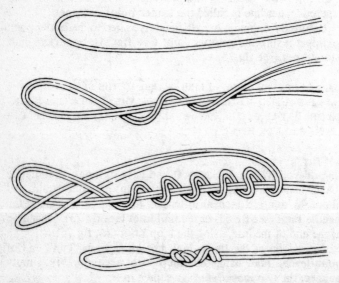

Fig. 76 Loop knot.

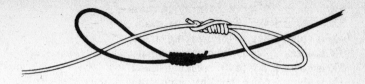

Fig. 77 To join looped lines.

TIP
To tighten knots fully, lubricate them with saliva or by dipping them in water before pulling tight. Saliva or water moistens the knot, easing the turns of line together firmly under pressure. Trim the knot loose ends *close* to the knot.

Leader point or tippet strengths
To balance the overall line strength and reduce the risk of a large trout breaking your leader line, match the leader point or tippet breaking-strain strength to the AFTM number of your fly-line.

AFTM fly-line numbers 1–4 should be tied to leader line with a leader point or tippet breaking-strain strength of about 0.91kg (2 lb) – 1.81kg (4 lb).

AFTM fly-line numbers 5 or 6 should be tied to a leader line with a leader point or tippet breaking-strain strength of about 1.81kg (4 lb) – 2.7kg (6 lb).

AFTM fly-line numbers 7 or 8 should be tied to a leader line with a leader point or tippet breaking-strain strength of about 2.7kg (6 lb) – 3.6kg (8 lb).

AFTM fly-line number 9 should be tied to a leader line with a leader point or tippet breaking-strain strength of about 3.2kg (7 lb) – 4 kg (9 lb).

The "X" Scale
Sometimes leader line point or tippet breaking-strain strengths are referred to by an "X" scale.

6X is about 0.91kg (2 lb) breaking strain.
5X is about 1.4kg (3 lb) breaking strain.
4X is about 1.8kg (4 lb) breaking strain.
3X is about 2.3kg (5 lb) breaking strain.
2X is about 2.7kg (6 lb) breaking strain.
1X is about 3.61kg (8 lb) breaking strain.
0X is about 4kg (9 lb) breaking strain.

Artificial flies

Buy artificial flies expertly tied *("dressed")*, on best quality *sharp* hooks.

Artificial dry flies are designed to be fished floating on the water surface.

Artificial wet flies, including artificial nymphs, pupae and larvae (also "lures"), are designed to be fished sunk just beneath or well below the water surface.

Weighted artificial nymphs, pupae, larvae and lures, are designed to descend quickly in deep or fast-flowing water.

Ready-made artificial flies are tied or *"dressed"* to various designs or *patterns*. The same artificial fly may be commercially available tied as a dry fly, using a dry-fly pattern, and tied as a wet fly, using a wet-fly pattern.

Lures: some lures resemble small fish or small fish-fry; many lures represent no known aquatic life form.

Lures are fished "wet", and may be presented at all water levels from just beneath to deep below the water surface; skilful *lively* retrieval of the lure attracts, excites and entices trout to snatch the lure.

Lures can be effective, fished wet, at any time of year.

Lures resembling small fish-fry can be especially effective June–October, fished wet on still or flowing waters.

Successful and popular lures, fished mostly on still-waters, **include:** Ace of Spades, Appetiser *(fry)*, Baby Doll, Black Chenille, Dog Nobbler, Jersey Herd *(fry)*, Missionary *(fry)*, Muddler Minnow *(fry)*, Perch Fry *(fry)*, Sweeney Todd, Viva, Whisky Fly.

TIP

Consistently successful "all-round" artificial trout flies to carry ready for use on flowing or still-waters, **include:** Coachman (dry and wet patterns), Gold Ribbed Hare's Ear "GRHE" (dry and wet patterns), Greenwell's Glory (dry and wet patterns), Grey Duster (dry pattern), Palmer (dry and wet patterns), Pheasant Tail (dry and wet patterns), Wickham's Fancy (dry and wet patterns).

Chapter 27, Traditional Artificial Flies lists some of the more successful and popular traditional dry and wet trout-flies.

Line and fly accessories
Important and useful line and artificial fly accessories, available from your local fishing tackle dealer, **include:**

"Floatants" : fly-line grease to make your leader line float; also dry-fly oil, paste or spray to help artificial dry flies float on the water surface.

"Sinkants" : commercial preparations to remove grease from your leader line and make the leader line sink.

Cast carriers: spare leader lines can be tied and wound onto circular cast carriers, then stored and carried with you on fly-fishing trips.

TIP
Spare reel spool: often useful; when filled with ready-tied backing line, fly-line and leader line, makes possible speedy waterside changes of complete fly-fishing line in one swift action.

Fly boxes: essential for safe storage and transporting of your artificial flies. Always dry used artificial flies *before* returning them to their box.

Hook sharpener: to keep the hook point of your artificial flies trout-hooking sharp.

Tackle accessories
Important and useful fly-fishing tackle accessories, available from your local fishing tackle dealer, **include:**

Landing-net: adjustable (telescopic) long-handled large (wide-mouthed) landing-net; essential to land hooked big trout, that threaten to break your leader line.

Artery forceps: to remove the hook from a trout's mouth with speed, and without harm to the trout, should you intend returning the trout to its water.

Scissors: a small pair of *sharp* scissors to snip line and trim loose ends of knots at the waterside.

Priest: weighty blunt instrument to kill trout instantly and humanely (see page 166); called a "priest" because it administers the trout's last rites – an old angling joke!

Marrow spoon: to scoop out the stomach contents of a freshly caught and killed trout, to see what the trout has been feeding on.

Rod bag or rod tube: to store, protect and transport your fly-fishing rod.

Reel case: to store, protect and transport your fly-fishing reel.

Tackle bag: to store, protect and transport your fly-fishing tackle and accessories.

Bass bag: specially designed to carry home your bumper fresh catch of big trout.

Clothing: (Refer also to Chapter 11 Personal Safety.) Check you have adequate warm and waterproof clothing. A special fly-fisher's many-pocketed *waistcoat* or *"vest"* supplies handy places to lodge nick-nacks ready for easy access when required.

A *peaked cap* or *floppy hat* and *polarized sunglasses* provide protection for your eyes and head (see Chapter 11); the peaked cap or floppy hat also shades your eyes and together with the polarizing sunglasses, reduces glare from the water, enabling you to see trout ordinarily hidden from view.

Insect repellent: never be without it!

23
Casting

Casting a fly-line is not difficult. Correctly cast, your rod and line do the work – powering your artificial fly to the precise point you want the artificial fly to reach.

TO BEGIN FLY-FISHING THE RIGHT WAY, TAKE EXPERT CASTING ADVICE AND TUITION FROM A QUALIFIED CASTING INSTRUCTOR.

The best way to learn the right way to cast a fly-line: take invaluable instruction from a qualified casting instructor. A few hours' personal tuition is all you should need to become reasonably proficient in correct and accurate casting of your fly-line.

Angling clubs offering fly-fishing can arrange casting lessons for members; managers of trout fisheries often organize casting tuition; fishing tackle dealers can usually recommend local qualified casting instructors who give tuition; some local councils offer courses in fly-line casting, and qualified casting instructors advertise their services in local newspapers, angling newspapers and angling magazines.

The right hold
The right hold for a fly-fishing rod – comfortable and firm, see fig 78.

The overhead cast
The overhead cast is the basic fly-fishing cast to master.

Look round to check all is clear – no trees, shrubs, bushes **or people.** Stand comfortably. Strip and loop a metre or more of fly-line from your reel, see fig 79.

Using your forearm and with a final flick of the wrist, bring your rod vertically upright so the length of line at the rod tip straightens out behind – parallel to the ground, bending the rod tip. This is called the **back cast**, see fig 80 (i). Then bring the rod forwards, in the **forward cast**, see fig 80 (ii). If the line cracks like a whip, you have brought the line forwards too soon

– before the line was fully extended behind you. Release the looped fly-line held in your free hand. When the position shown in fig 80 (iii) is reached, the downwards movement of your rod is halted and the artificial fly alights gently on the water.

TIMING AND RHYTHM COME WITH PRACTICE.

Shooting the line
To cast a long distance – "shoot your line".

Hold several metres of fly-line looped in your free hand. Make the overhead cast, and just as the pull of the line exerts pressure on the rod tip, release the looped fly-line held in your free hand.

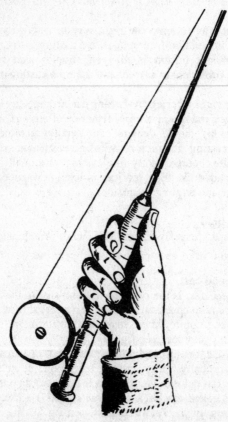

Fig. 78 The right hold for a fly rod.

Fig. 79 Preparing to cast.

When you have become fully proficient in the overhead cast and shooting the line, there are other useful casting techniques to learn, including "double haul", which enables you to cast your fly-line very long distances.

Meanwhile, **practice** helps make perfect!

Advice

Though it may seem obvious advice, do not become *obsessed* with casting your fly-line simply for the sake of casting.

If you can crawl close to a trout feeding near the bank or shore, or stealthily approach a likely trout-holding location, and skilfully present your artificial fly without casting your fly-line, do so!

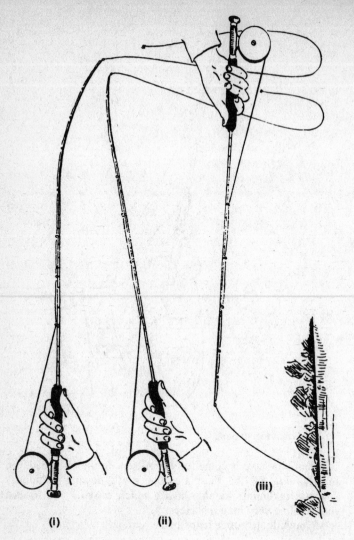

Fig. 80 The cast in progress.

And remember these words of wisdom:

YOU CATCH MORE TROUT WHEN YOUR ARTIFICIAL FLY IS ON OR IN
THE WATER THAN WHEN THE FLY IS IN THE AIR.

24
Fly-Fishing Methods

DRY-FLY FISHING

Dry-fly fishing is the skilful art of presenting an artificial fly on the water surface in imitation of a natural insect.

A *dry* fly is an artificial fly which has been designed to be "fished dry", floating on the water surface.

Fishing the dry fly is a most effective and thrilling way to catch trout rising to snatch natural flies at the water surface.

Fishing the rise

The aim of *"fishing the rise"* is to locate a surface-feeding ("rising") trout and skilfully present the trout with an artificial dry fly which imitates the appearance and motion of the real flies upon which the trout is feeding.

IF YOU DO NOT HAVE THE RIGHT ARTIFICIAL DRY FLY TO MATCH THE NATURAL FLIES ON THE WATER, OFFER A DRY FLY OF SIMILAR SIZE AND COLOUR (MATCHING THE SIZE IS MORE IMPORTANT THAN MATCHING THE COLOUR).

Fishing the water

When you cannot see trout rising to feed at the water surface, try *"fishing the water"*: cast your fly-line to present the artificial dry fly on areas of water where you expect trout to be lying (see Chapter 25, Locating Trout).

A TROUT MAY BE LYING JUST BENEATH THE WATER SURFACE.

A hungry or inquisitive trout may journey from the water bottom to intercept an artificial dry fly presented enticingly on the water surface.

Fishing the water can produce excellent sport.

Tackle notes (see also Chapter 22).

Fly-fishing tackle suitable for dry-fly fishing on rivers, streams and still-waters.

Suitable rods (see page 131), fly-fishing rod; about 2.6m (8½ ft) – 2.9m (9½ ft) in length, AFTM line rating in the range AFTM 5–7. For *large* still-waters, where long distance casts of round 32m (35 yds) may sometimes be necessary, a fly-fishing rod of about 2.9m (9½ ft) – 3m (10 ft) in length, AFTM rating 7–9, may prove a practical choice.

Suitable reels (see page 131), fly-fishing reel; 89mm (3½ inches) – 102mm (4 inches) in diameter.

Suitable fly-lines (see page 132), include: floating double taper (DT), AFTM 5–7; floating weight forward (WF), AFTM 5–7. For *large* still waters: floating double taper (DT), AFTM 7–9; floating weight forward (WF), AFTM 7–9.

Suitable leader point or tippet breaking-strain strengths (see page 141): 0.91kg (2 lb) – 4kg (9 lb).

Suitable artificial flies: Dry flies (see list beginning on page 168); hook sizes: (large) 8/10/12/14/16 (small).

Line and fly accessories: "Floatants" (see page 143), fly-line grease to make your leader line float, and dry-fly oil, paste or spray to help your artificial dry-fly float on the water surface.

Rivers and streams – dry-fly methods
Upstream casting
Approach a rising trout from downstream *(down current)*. Trout living in rivers and streams face upstream *(up current)* – into the water current, and are unaware of a *stealthy* angler's cautious approach. Cast your fly-line upstream *(up current)*, to place the artificial dry fly about 152mm (6 inches) – 457mm (18 inches), and not more than 610mm (2 ft), in front of the surface-feeding trout; let the water current carry your artificial dry fly towards the trout.

Downstream casting
Casting your fly-line downstream *(down current)*, towards a surface-feeding trout – which will be facing towards you – is sometimes the only practical way to present an artificial dry fly to a trout rising in an area of water not easily accessible for an orthodox upstream *(up current)* cast.

A downstream *(down current)* cast can be made to inaccessible areas of water likely to hold trout when *"fishing the water"*, to attract the attention of any unseen trout lying beneath the water surface, or at the water bottom.

Cross-country casting

To present your artificial dry fly to a surface-feeding trout lying near the bank from which you are fishing, or to an area of water close to the bank likely to hold a trout, move quietly to a position directly opposite the rising trout or promising area of water; stand well back from the water – beyond the trout's view; cast your fly-line above and across the bank to place your artificial dry fly just upstream *(up current)* from your target area, and let the water current carry your artificial dry fly to the point you want it to reach.

Still-water – dry-fly methods

Approach the water with stealth and look for signs of trout rising to feed at the water surface. Cast directly to a surface-feeding trout. Aim to place your artificial dry fly about 152mm (6 inches) – 457mm (18 inches), and not more than 610mm (2 ft), in front of the surface-feeding trout; if the trout is slowly feeding its way *across* the water surface, cast your fly-line ahead of the trout, in the direction the trout appears to be heading. Give the line an occasional slight jerk to "twitch" the artificial dry fly into attractive lifelike motion.

When there are no visible signs of trout rising to feed at the water surface, cast your fly-line to a favourable-looking location (see Chapter 25, Locating Trout).

Give the artificial dry fly time to settle, then retrieve the line slowly, with occasional slight jerks to impart trout-attracting, lifelike movement to the artificial dry fly. Allow a few seconds for the artificial dry fly to settle in each new position before retrieving more line. Continue retrieval until you have recovered all the line, then cast again.

Continue casting and retrieving your fly-line until you have thoroughly covered and explored the promising area of water before you, then move along to the next propitious place and begin again.

WET-FLY FISHING

A *wet* fly is an artificial fly which is designed to be "fished wet", sunk below the water surface.

Fishing the wet fly is a challenging and rewarding way to

catch big trout feeding just beneath or well below the water surface, on recently drowned natural flies, nymphs, pupae, larvae, fish-fry, small fish, and other aquatic creatures.

Successful wet-fly fishing demands high levels of skill and patience; the biggest trout are invariably caught using wet-fly techniques.

The aim of wet-fly fishing is methodically to cover areas of water likely to hold large trout. Cast your fly-line to explore every location where a feeding trout can be seen or *ought* to be lying (see Chapter 25, Locating Trout).

Persist with your casting and line retrieval until you hook the trout, or are satisfied there is no feeding trout present. Then move along to another promising patch of water and again begin casting and retrieving your fly-line.

Tackle notes (see also Chapter 22).
Fly-fishing tackle suitable for wet-fly fishing on rivers, streams and still-waters.

Suitable rods (see page 131), fly-fishing rod; about 2.6m (8$\frac{1}{2}$ ft) – 2.9m (9$\frac{1}{2}$ ft) in length; AFTM line rating in the range AFTM 5–7. For *large* still-waters, where long distance casts of around 32m (35 yds) may sometimes be necessary, a fly-fishing rod of about 2.9m (9$\frac{1}{2}$ ft) – 3m (10 ft) in length; AFTM line rating 7–9 may prove a practical choice.

Suitable reels (see page 131), fly-fishing reel; 89mm (3$\frac{1}{2}$ inches) – 102mm (4 inches) in diameter.

Suitable fly-lines (see page 132), floating fly-lines suitable for dry-fly fishing (see page 150) can be used; remove grease from the *leader line* with a "sinkant" (see page 143) to make the leader line sink below the water surface.

You can control the depth to which your leader line sinks by using a "floatant" (see page 143) to grease the length of leader line you wish to float on the water surface, and applying a "sinkant" (see page 143) to remove grease from the length of leader line you want to sink below the water surface. This enables you to present your wet fly at depths ranging from just beneath the water surface, to a depth equivalent to the entire length of your leader line.

Suitable wet-fly only fly-lines (see page 134) include: slow sink double taper (DT), AFTM 5–7; slow sink weight forward

(WF), AFTM 5–7; fast sink double taper (DT), AFTM 5–7; fast sink weight forward (WF), AFTM 5–7.

For *large* still-waters: slow sink double taper (DT), AFTM 7–9; slow sink weight forward (WF), AFTM 7–9; fast sink double taper (DT), AFTM 7–9; fast sink weight forward (WF), AFTM 7–9; fast sink shooting head or shooting taper (ST), AFTM 7–9.

Suitable leader point or tippet breaking-strain strengths (see page 141): 0.91kg (2 lb) – 4kg (9 lb).

Suitable artificial flies: Wet flies (see list beginning on page 168); also artificial nymphs, pupae, larvae, and lures (see page 142). Suitable wet-fly hook sizes: (large) 8/10/12/14/16 (small).

Line accessories: "Sinkants" (see page 143), to remove grease from your leader line and make the leader line sink; also "floatants" (see page 143), when wet-fly fishing with a floating fly-line (see *"Suitable fly-lines"*, opposite).

Rivers and streams –wet fly methods
Upstream wet-fly fishing
Approach a visible trout or likely trout-holding location from downstream *(down current)*; cast your fly-line upstream *(up current)*, ahead of the point you wish the sunken wet fly to reach, casting sufficient fly-line to allow the extra line needed for the wet fly to sink to its target position. Collect slack line in your hand as the current carries the fly-line back towards you; keep your rod tip raised high and tighten the line to hook your trout the moment you feel a trout-taking tremor transmitted through the fly-line from your wet fly.

Downstream wet-fly fishing
Cast your fly-line downstream *(down current)*, so the artificial wet fly is carried downstream and away from you by the current. The taut fly-line will arc across the current and swing back towards the bankside from which you are fly-fishing; retrieve the line with a series of short jerks to impart attractive, lifelike movement to the wet fly. When you have recovered all the line, cast again. Work your way steadily and methodically downstream *(down current)*.

Downstream wet-fly fishing is sometimes the best way to reach otherwise unresponsive trout lurking at the water's bottom, and is a useful technique when night fishing for trout, particularly sea trout – a wide area of water can be searched with a series of "blind" casts.

Still-water – wet-fly methods
Approach the water quietly and look for signs of trout feeding just beneath or below the water surface (see Chapter 25, Locating Trout, especially "rise forms"). Cast your fly-line to reach the position where you can see trout are feeding just beneath or below the water surface. Retrieve the line slowly, with occasional jerks to give your wet fly lifelike movement. Allow the wet fly to settle for a few moments in each new position before continuing line retrieval. Continue casting and retrieving your fly-line until satisfied the trout have ceased feeding or moved to another spot.

When there are no visible signs of trout feeding just beneath or below the water surface, choose a location likely to hold or attract feeding trout (see Chapter 25, Locating Trout), and cast your fly-line to that location.

For maximum chances of success, allow time for your wet fly to reach a slightly different depth with each cast before retrieving your line, and vary the speed of line retrieval.

Continue casting and retrieving your fly-line until you have thoroughly explored the water with your wet fly before moving elsewhere.

A TROUT MAY FOLLOW YOUR ARTIFICIAL WET FLY UNTIL THE MOMENT YOU BEGIN LIFTING IT FROM THE WATER, BEFORE MOVING TO SNATCH THE "ESCAPING" ARTIFICIAL WET FLY.

25

Locating Trout

Where to locate trout in rivers or streams
Notes to help you locate places in rivers or streams where trout may be lying.

- Beneath overhanging trees or shrubs.
- Near submerged tree roots.
- Near water plants and weed-beds.
- In streamy runs of fast water between weed-beds.
- In steady glides of water between rocks or boulders.
- Inside bends on streams or riverbanks, where food is deposited by the current.
- Where inflowing trickles, rivulets or streams of water drain or flow into the main body of water.
- Where swirling and circling eddies of water draw and trap food from the main current.
- Where a rapid flow of water meets calm or shallow water.
- Alongside and behind boulders that break the current and give trout a sheltered spot from which to seize passing prey.
- In shallow bankside runs, sheltered from strong currents, where insects breed and fish fry cavort.
- In deep, oxygen-rich pools of water below weirs or waterfalls, and the streamy runs of water near weirs or waterfalls.
- In deep scoured bankside undercuts, where shallow fast water has eaten down into the bank and waterbed, slowing into a deep, lazy, sleeve-shaped run.
- In deep pools of slow moving water.
- In deep holes or hollows in the stream or river bed.
- In deep stretches of smooth-flowing water – trout often lie close to the bank.
- Where two flowing waters, rivers or streams meet and merge in a confusion of currents.
- Beneath bridges, where trout feel secure; especially old stone bridges, whose small cracks and crevices are home to teeming insects that regularly "plop" into the water.

Fig. 81 Haunts of big trout.

● In rivers or streams with rising water levels (due to rain, or the incoming *flood tide* in tidal waters) – trout feed with enthusiasm, as they also do when the water approaches its "normal" level, after flood or drought.

● Close to the bank in rivers or streams in flood – trout move close to the bank to escape strong currents and feed on insects washed into the water.

● Where large chunks of bankside have newly collapsed into the water – trout are attracted to the area by wriggling insects washed from the mud.

● In pools and stretches of water hidden from view by trees, shrubs and dense undergrowth. These areas of water are seldom fished and often hide big trout.

● Any place where you have caught a big trout before – a captured big trout's vacant favourite spot is soon occupied by another large trout!

TIP

Trout queue according to size for food in the best feeding spots. The biggest trout always takes top place. Find ace feeding spots and catch the biggest trout first, then the smaller ones.

TIP

Big trout usually lie in deep water ("*pools*"), during the day, and move into shallow water at night to feed.

Where to locate trout in still-waters
Notes to help you locate places in still-waters where trout may be feeding.

● Near water plants and weed-beds.
● Beneath overhanging trees or shrubs.
● Near submerged tree roots.
● Near sunken rocks or boulders.
● In comparatively "shallow" areas of water where aquatic insects breed.
● In deep water bordering shallow areas where aquatic insects hatch and fish fry shoal.
● In deep water near the mouth of inflowing rivers or streams.
● In bays and by promontories (where trout shelter and wait to seize insects blown into the water from the land; insects alighting on the water, etc.).

Fig. 82 Favourite trout lies in rivers.

1. Deep shady pools.   2. Near sunken rocks.   3. Deep pool.
4. Rocky stream.

● In deep, overshadowed (shaded) areas of water.
● In streamy and fast water sweeping past rocky headlands on large still-water lakes or lochs.
● In channels around small islands, especially any deep holes or gullies and patches of water beneath island tree-branches or bushy shrubs.
● In heavy reed/weed areas, hollows, deep holes and channels near the shore – all examples of locations occupied by big trout waiting to ambush passing prey.
● Where wind-caused currents and cross-currents carry particles of food to queueing trout; cast into the current.
● Where rippling wind-driven water meets calm stretches of water protected by bank or shore contours and/or vegetation – food is trapped and whirled to waiting trout. Cast to that point and continue casting methodically along the line of rippling water.
● In deep water near newly collapsed chunks of bankside.

Other pointers
● Scout for patches of bank or shore scoured or worn bare by angler's boots. Popular places may have much to recommend them, though not always.

1. Deep overshadowed water.　　2. Off rocky headlands.　　3. Near inflowing streams.

Fig. 83 Where trout feed in lakes or lochs.

● Search for stretches of water hidden from view by trees, bushes and dense growth. These areas of water are seldom fished and often hide big trout.

● Strong gusty winds or squalls drive trout deep in the water, or into sheltered bays. Look for quiet, wind-protected spots, which may offer good sport.

● On sunny summer days, trout feed in stretches of water shaded from strong sunlight. In the evening, the western side of the water will be favoured by trout because it is the first to fall into shadow.

● On windy days fly-fish with the wind blowing from behind you. Trout gather near shallows to feast on insects blown from land into the water. When the wind has ceased, try the opposite bank or shore for bonus catches.

● During cold or changeable weather, expect trout to feed mostly beneath the water surface in deep water, away from the shore. Freezing winter weather may force big trout well down from the water surface.

● During warm weather, trout feed mostly in the upper water level; at the water's surface, and water's edge shallows.

● Check if a detailed map of the water you intend fly-fishing is marketed by the water company/owner, and buy one. The information marked shows obvious "hotspots", and the map is convenient for recording your own secret finds.

● Although trout in still-waters rove widely in search of food, individual brown trout *(Salmo trutta)*, and shoals of rainbow trout *(Salmo gairdneri)*, still have favourite feeding spots, and sometimes become slaves to habit. Careful observation can suggest suitable timing for a shrewdly calculated catch.

● Still-water big trout generally like to have their main meals at dawn, dusk and into the night. At these times they feel safe and are therefore most vulnerable.

Nature's signposts
Let nature signpost the best locations for you to fly-fish for feeding trout.

Look and listen for these signs:

● Rush of small fish (minnows, sticklebacks, etc.) and/or fish fry scattering for cover in shallow water.

● Sudden splashes, ripples, waves or spreading rings on the water surface.

● Watch for kingfishers and herons. They know where small fish are. Big trout won't be far away.

● Birds (swifts, swallows, martins, etc.) snatching insects over the water show you where flies are hatching. Trout will be there too.

● Clouds or swarms of winged-insects above the water.

TIP
Binoculars or a telescope help you spy insect activity and trout-betraying water surface disturbance on large still or flowing waters.

Fig. 84 The swallow – one of nature's signposts.

Take lessons from the way a heron catches fish; remain as inconspicuous and quiet as possible when fly-fishing at or near the water's edge (or afloat in a boat); reduce movement to a necessary minimum; when a trout takes your artificial fly, act immediately with speed and decisiveness to hook and land the trout.

BE PATIENT AND PERSISTENT TO SUCCEED.

Rise forms
To locate feeding trout, watch and listen carefully; there are sometimes clear signals in the water – *"rise forms"* – that tell us where trout are feeding and give clues about what natural food the trout are seeking.

The most important rise forms to look for are:

Surface-breaking *"slashing"* rise
The trout, at speed, breaks the water surface with an audible splash, and may actually twist or leap through the air just above the water surface. The trout is probably snatching at large, fast-moving flies on the water surface – newly emerged or egg-laying sedge-flies; possibly the large mayfly *(Ephemera danica)*; or pursuing a large insect alighting on, flying just above, or blown onto the water surface and struggling to get out of the water: cranefly, dragonfly, hawthorn fly, moth, beetle, grasshopper, etc.

Standard surface *"nosing"* rise
Watch for the trout's nose or head breaking the water surface, followed by outwardly spreading concentric rings of water. The trout is feeding at the water surface on surface hatching insects; adult flies emerging, or newly emerged, from their nymphal or pupal skins. The "nosing" rise is a trout's usual rise for taking duns of a "mayfly" species (order: *Ephemeroptera)*.

The surface *"kiss-sip"* rise
The trout's open mouth appears to kiss and sip at the water surface; there is the barest telltale ripple of water. Sometimes you can hear the soft "smacking-kiss" sound. The trout is lying just below the water surface and probably feeding on nymphs or pupae floating slightly below the water surface; recently drowned flies/insects; flies emerging from their nymphal or

pupal skins; small adult flies newly emerged from their nymphal or pupal skins; and/or small flies/insects alighting on the water surface.

The surface *"head-and-tail"* rise
The trout – head, back, then tail – rolls gracefully out of the water as it descends on an item of food. The trout is probably feeding at, and slightly below, the water surface on surface-bound nymphs or pupae, recently drowned flies, emerging, and newly emerged adult flies unable to take flight.

The underwater *"sub-surface"* boil
The water surface swirls or whirls and appears to hump, bulge or "boil" as the feeding trout, maybe 457mm (18 inches) – 1.52m (5 ft), beneath the surface, twists, turns and rolls to take ascending nymphs, pupae, etc.

Near surface *"bow waving"* rise
Trout chasing fish-fry near the water surface, or herding shoals of fry into shallow areas of water where they can trap and eat them in large numbers, produce fast-moving V-shaped "bow-waves". On still-waters, several trout may be herding the fry, usually into shallow water near the bankside or shore. You may see the water surface erupt, as terrified fry scatter for safety.

The bow-wave rise is most commonly seen July–October, when feeding trout pay special attention to shoals of well-developed fish-fry.

Weather to locate trout
Trout have to eat to live, and a hungry or inquisitive trout can be tempted to take a skilfully presented artificial fly whatever the weather conditions.

Here is a short list of observations about the way the weather may affect trout living in still or flowing waters.

● A spell of settled weather, when the water is at "normal" level, suits trout best; they feed steadily and good sport is practically guaranteed.
● A sharp rise in water temperature makes trout especially active; they feed voraciously. If the water temperature exceeds 70°F (21°C), brown trout *(Salmo trutta)* become torpid and reduce feeding.

Brown trout *(Salmo trutta)* are most active when the water

163

temperature is 45°F (7.2°C) – 60°F (15.5°C).

Rainbow trout *(Salmo gairdneri)* are most active when the water temperature is 60°F (15.5°C) – 75°F (24°C).

A sharp drop in water temperature makes trout less active. When the water temperature drops below 40°F (4.4°C), trout reduce feeding.

● Big trout in all waters keep well under the surface in very hot or very cold weather. To catch them, fly-fish shaded areas of deep water.

● On hot summer days trout often feed fast and furiously early morning (dawn) and late evening (sunset). Big trout may start feeding near sunset and continue into the night.

● Wind and rain after a scorching near-drought period can revive and excite trout into a bout of frenzied near-surface and surface feeding.

● On bright, cloudless days, trout feed mainly in deep water.

● On dull, cloudy days, trout will hunt food in shallow water.

● On a dull overcast day, a brief burst of sunshine sometimes brings on a "hatch" of flies, which starts trout rising to feed at the water surface.

● Trout are excited by rain (which raises the oxygen content of the water), and often feed at or near the water surface shortly before, during and after rainfall.

● Heavy rain washes airborne and terrestrial insects/creatures into the water. Trout gobble them live at the water surface, and drowned just beneath the surface.

● A sudden shower of heavy rain or hail sometimes brings on a "hatch" of flies, which starts trout rising to feed at the water surface.

When *very* heavy rain or hail teems into the water, trout may well wait below the surface, until the rain or hail eases.

● When a wind blows from the west or south, trout are often active near the water surface. Good catches are likely when there is a steady south-westerly breeze on a dull day. When a wind blows from the east or north, trout often stay well down in the water.

● Big trout feed steadily on moonless, mild nights, which can yield fine catches.

26

Playing a Trout

Having enticed a trout to take your skilfully presented artificial fly (nymph, pupa, larva or lure), the next step is to set your hook firm in the trout's mouth and "play" the trout into your landing-net.

To detect a take and hook the trout
Keep line taut as possible between artificial fly and rod tip; do not permit loose line to wander unchecked across or through the water. Once the trout has tasted your artificial fly, it will soon be spat out. You have not a moment to waste. Look for a trout snatching or nonchalantly taking in its mouth, an artificial fly fished on or slightly below the water surface; *at all times*, feel the taut line for tugs or tremors; watch line on the water for sudden movement – curling, running, straightening, etc. – or an unexpected stop in motion. In all cases *immediately* tighten the line (hold the line near your reel firmly with one hand, and smartly raise the rod tip with your rod-holding hand), and hook your trout.

Aim to get the hooked trout out of the water and into your landing-net quick as possible.

EVERY SECOND A HOOKED TROUT STAYS IN THE WATER GIVES IT A CHANCE TO ESCAPE.

A powerful trout, fighting for its life, will use every trout-cunning trick it knows to dislodge the hook or break your line. A hooked trout may rocket straight towards line-tangling underwater cover; weed-beds, tree roots, submerged tree trunk, rocks or boulders, etc.

Always work out where a hooked trout is likely to race *before* fly-fishing, and steer the hooked trout from the safety of line-snapping underwater snags.

A hooked trout may leap from the water in an attempt to dislodge the hook, thrash your line with its body and tail, then dive deep into the water to stretch and strain the line further, and test your knots.

I've seen trout shed the hook and leap from a landing-net to water bottom safety.

To play a hooked trout
Keep your rod upright and line taut – a taut line seldom tangles on underwater snags; apply as much pressure on the racing trout as you dare – timid playing loses trout. A particularly powerful and pugnacious trout may be made to yield by applying side-strain (hold your rod parallel to the water surface; side-strain pulls the hooked trout's head from the side and puts the trout off balance). Pump the trout towards you, by reeling-in line while lowering the rod tip, then raise the rod tip and keep the recovered line on your reel. Never give out line unless judged absolutely necessary to avoid breakage.

Defeat a leaping trout's attempt to strain and snap the line by momentarily lowering your rod tip to reduce line tension.

On the flowing waters of rivers or streams, keep downstream (*down current*) of the hooked trout, then the trout can't use the strength of the water's current in its fight against you, and by turning the trout and pulling it downstream (*down current*), you force the trout's gills shut and it has difficulty breathing. The trout's capacity to fight is reduced.

To land a hooked trout
Steer the hooked trout through the water towards the wide *mouth* of your long-handled landing-net (the mouth of the net should be submerged just below the water surface). When the trout is above the submerged mouth of the landing-net, raise the net and land your trout.

Wet your hands before touching the trout to remove the hook from its mouth. Dry fingers may damage the trout's tiny protective scales, leading to infection if the trout, not wanted for eating, is gently released back into its watery home.

To return a trout caught from the flowing waters of rivers or streams, carefully lower the unhooked trout back into the water, facing upstream (*up current*) into the water current, and gently hold the trout steady until it feels strong enough to swim away.

Should you wish to take the captured trout home to make a meal of it, kill the trout quickly and humanely by striking it heavily across the base of its head with a weighty blunt instrument (a "priest", see page 144, is an ideal weapon).

I have seen trout squirm free and leap from the hands of fly-fishers preparing to kill them, back into the water, or thrash their way over the bank or shore or out of a boat and back into the water.

A TROUT NEVER SURRENDERS, IT NEVER GIVES IN.

TIP
Kill trout you want to keep and eat while the trout is in the landing-net, *before* removing the hook from its mouth.

27

Traditional Artificial Flies

The more successful and popular **traditional** dry and wet trout-flies **include:**

Alder: *Dry and wet patterns.* Represents the natural Alderfly *(Sialis lutaria* and *Sialis fuliginosa);* especially effective April–July, fished dry or wet on still or flowing waters.

Alexandra: *Wet pattern.* A general representation of a small fish-fry; especially effective June–October, fished wet on still or flowing waters.

Ant: (Black/Brown/Red): *Dry pattern.* Represents a winged ant (order: *Formicidae);* especially effective July–September, fished dry on still or flowing waters when mating winged-ants swarm.

Bibio: *Wet pattern.* A general representation of a natural fly of the family *Bibionidae* (order: *Diptera*) which includes the Black Gnat *(Bibio johannis),* Hawthorn Fly *(Bibio marci),* and Heather Fly *(Bibio pomonae).* Especially effective May–September, fished wet on still or flowing waters.

Black-And-Peacock-Spider: *Wet pattern.* A general representation of a natural fly/insect (can be used to represent a freshwater snail or beetle); can be effective March–October, fished wet on still or flowing waters.

Black Gnat: *Dry pattern.* Represents the natural fly *(Bibio johannis,* of the order *Diptera*)*;* especially effective May–September, fished dry on still or flowing waters.

Blae and Black: *Wet pattern.* Represents a pupa of the Black Midge *(Chironomus anthracinus,* of the order *Diptera*)*;* especially effective March-September, fished wet on still-waters.

Blue Upright: *Dry pattern.* A general representation of a natural fly/insect. Can be used to represent a Large Dark Olive Dun *(Baetis rhodani)*, or Iron Blue Dun *(Baetis niger* and *Baetis muticus)* mayfly, or a Willow Fly *(Leuctra geniculata)* stonefly; can be effective March-October, fished dry on still or flowing waters.

Blue Winged Olive: *Dry pattern.* Represents the natural mayfly *(Ephemerella ignita)*; especially effective May–October, fished dry on flowing waters, or still-waters where this mayfly is present.

Brown Silverhorns: *Dry pattern.* Represents the natural sedge-fly *(Athripsodes cinereus);* especially effective June–August, fished dry on still or slow-flowing waters.

Butcher: *Wet pattern.* A general representation of a small fish-fry; especially effective June–October, fished wet (can be successful fished dry!), on still or flowing waters.

Caenis: *Dry pattern.* Represents the natural mayflies called Broadwings *(Caenis & Brachycercus* – six species); especially effective June–August, fished dry on still or flowing waters.

Caperer: *Dry pattern.* Represents the natural sedge-fly *(Halesus radiatus);* especially effective August–October, fished dry on flowing waters.

Caterpillar: *Dry pattern.* A general representation of a caterpillar (larva of butterfly or moth); especially effective May–August, fished dry, near overhanging trees or bushes on still or flowing waters.

Cinnamon Sedge: *Dry pattern.* Represents the natural sedge-fly *(Limnephilus lunatus);* especially effective June–October, fished dry on still or flowing waters. The **Cinnamon and Gold** is often used to represent a pupa of the Cinnamon Sedge, and is especially effective June–October, fished wet on still-waters.

Coachman: *Dry and wet patterns.* A general representation of a natural fly/insect (can be used to represent a sedge-fly pupa when fished wet, or a moth when fished dry). A good all-purpose artificial fly; effective March–October, fished wet or dry on still or flowing waters.

Coch-Y-Bonddu: *Dry and wet patterns*. Represents the natural beetle *(Phyllopertha horticola,* of the order *Coleoptera)*; can be used to represent any species of beetle. Effective March–October, fished wet or dry on still or flowing waters.

Corixa: *Wet pattern*. A general representation of an aquatic beetle of the family *Corixae* (about 30 species, commonly called *lesser water boatmen*). Especially effective June–September, fished wet on still-waters (can be fished wet on slow-flowing waters).

Cranefly: (also known as **Daddy Longlegs**): *Dry pattern*. Represents the natural cranefly (genus: *Tipula,* many species); especially effective June–September, fished dry on still or flowing waters.

Daddy Longlegs, see **Cranefly,** above.

Damselfly Nymph: *Wet pattern*. A general representation of the natural nymphs of the Damselflies (order: *Odonata;* sub-order: *zygoptera,* 17 species). Especially effective June–August, fished wet, just below the surface, on still-waters (can be fished wet on flowing waters).

Dunkeld: *Wet pattern*. A general representation of a small fish-fry; especially effective June–October, particularly on large still-waters, fished wet.

Ginger Quill: *Dry pattern*. A general representation of the Pale Watery Dun *(Baetis fuscatus)* and Medium Olive Dun *(Baetis vernus & Baetis tenax)* mayflies. Can be used as a general representation of light-coloured Olive Dun mayflies; effective May–October, fished dry on flowing waters.

Gold Ribbed Hare's Ear: *Dry and wet patterns*. Commonly called **"GRHE"**; a general representation of the mayflies: Medium Olive Dun *(Baetis vernus & Baetis tenax),* Large Dark Olive Dun *(Baetis rhodani),* and Small Dark Olive Dun *(Baetis scambus)*. The GRHE can also be fished as a general representation of other mayfly duns, or a mayfly nymph. Effective March–October, fished dry or wet on still or flowing waters.

Grannom: *Dry pattern.* Represents the natural sedge-fly *(Brachycentrus subnubilus)*; especially effective April–June, fished dry on flowing waters.

Greenwell's Glory: *Dry and wet patterns.* A general representation of all the Olive Dun mayflies; can be used to represent the Iron Blue Dun *(Baetis niger & Baetis muticus);* can also be fished to represent a mayfly nymph. Effective March–October, fished dry or wet on still or flowing waters.

Grey Duster: *Dry pattern.* A general representation of a natural fly/insect; can be effective March–October, fished dry on still or flowing waters.

Grey Sedge, see **Silver Sedge.**

Grouse and Claret: *Wet pattern.* Represents the Sepia Dun *(Leptophlebia marginata)* mayfly; can also be used to represent the Claret Dun *(Leptophlebia vespertina)* mayfly, and the nymphs of both species. Especially effective April–June, fished wet (can be fished dry), on still or flowing waters.

Hawthorn Fly: *Dry pattern.* Represents the natural fly *(Bibio marci)*; also known as **St. Mark's Fly.** Especially effective May–September, fished dry on still or flowing waters.

Heather Fly: *Dry pattern.* Represents the natural fly *(Bibio pomonae);* especially effective August–September, fished dry on still or flowing waters where this fly is present.

Hofland's Fancy: *Dry pattern.* A general representation of a natural fly/insect. Can be used as a general representation of a natural sedge-fly (order: *Trichoptera*). Can be effective April–October, fished dry on still or flowing waters.

Iron Blue Dun: *Dry pattern.* Represents the natural mayfly *(Baetis niger & Baetis muticus);* especially effective May–October, fished dry on still or flowing waters

Kite's Imperial: *Dry pattern.* A general representation of a natural fly; can be used to represent the natural Claret Dun *(Leptophlebia vespertina)*, Large Dark Olive Dun *(Baetis rhodani)*, Medium Olive Dun *(Baetis vernus & Baetis tenax),*

Olive Upright Dun *(Rithrogena semicolorata)*, and Small Dark Olive Dun *(Baetis scambus)* mayflies. Effective March–October, fished dry on flowing waters (can be fished dry on still-waters, as a general representation of a natural fly).

Lake Olive Dun: *Dry pattern*. Represents the natural mayfly *(Cloeon simile)*; especially effective April–June, and again August–October, fished dry on still or flowing waters.

Lunn's Particular: *Dry pattern*. Represents the Medium Olive Dun *(Baetis vernus & Baetis tenax)* mayfly spinner, also the Large Dark Olive Dun *(Baetis rhodani)* mayfly spinner. Effective March–October, fished dry on still or flowing waters.

Mallard and Claret: *Wet pattern*. A general representation of a nymph-like creature; can be used to represent a sedge-fly pupa, or a mayfly nymph. Effective March–September, fished wet on still or flowing waters.

March Brown: *Dry and wet patterns*. Represents the natural mayfly *(Rithrogena germanica);* especially effective March–May, fished dry or wet on flowing waters.

Mayfly (also known as **Greendrake**): *Dry pattern*. Represents the natural mayflies *Ephemera danica* and *Ephemera vulgata;* especially effective May–June, fished dry on still or flowing waters.

Midge (Black/Brown/Green/Red; also Golden/Olive/Orange-Silver); *Wet pattern*. A general representation of a non-biting midge (order: *Diptera,* family *chironomidae,* numerous species; commonly called **"Buzzers"** by anglers). The **black midge** can be especially effective March–April, and again July–October; the **brown midge** June–September; the **green midge** March–October; the **red midge** June–September; the **golden midge** June–August; the **olive midge** May–June, and again August–September; the **orange-silver midge** (commonly called *"grey boy"* by anglers), April–July. Midges are usually fished wet (can be fished dry) on still-waters. Midges can be fished wet (or dry), on flowing waters where they are present. The **Hatching Midge Pupa** can be effective March–October, fished wet (deep to just below the surface), on still-waters, or flowing waters where hatches are occurring.

Moth (White/Brown): *Dry pattern*. A general representation of an insect (moth) of the order *Lepidoptera;* especially effective June–September, fished dry, at dusk or after dark, on still or flowing waters.

Olive Dun: *Dry pattern*. Represents the natural Medium Olive Dun mayflies *(Baetis vernus & Baetis tenax);* especially effective May–October, fished dry on flowing waters.

Pale Watery Dun: *Dry pattern*. Represents the natural mayfly *(Baetis fuscatus);* especially effective May–October, fished dry on flowing waters.

Palmer: (Black/Brown/Grey/Red): *Dry and wet patterns*. A general representation of a natural fly/insect or beetle; can be effective March–October, fished dry or wet on still or flowing waters. Can also be used, fished wet, to represent a freshwater shrimp, nymph or pupa, or almost any small aquatic life form.

Peter Ross: *Wet pattern*. A general representation of a small fish-fry; especially effective June–October, fished wet on still or flowing waters.

Pheasant Tail: *Dry and wet patterns*. A general representation of a natural fly/insect; can be particularly effective, fished dry, to represent a mayfly spinner of the Blue Winged Olive Dun *(Ephemerella ignita)*, Iron Blue Dun *(Baetis niger & Baetis muticus)*, Pale Watery Dun *(Baetis fuscatus)*, or Medium Olive Dun *(Baetis vernus & Baetis tenax)*. Can be effective March–October, fished dry or wet on still or flowing waters. Can also be used, March–May, fished wet, to represent a nymph of the March Brown Dun *(Rithrogena germanica)* mayfly, on flowing waters where this mayfly is present.

Pheasant Tail Nymph: *Wet pattern*. A general representation of a nymph/small fish-fry/aquatic creature; can be effective March – October, fished wet on still or flowing waters.

Red Spinner: *Dry and wet patterns*. A general representation of the female spinners of the Medium Olive Dun *(Baetis vernus & Baetis tenax)*, and Small Dark Olive Dun *(Baetus scambus)* mayflies. Especially effective May–October, fished dry or wet on flowing waters. The **Large Red Spinner** represents the female spinner of the Large Dark Olive Dun *(Baetis rhodani)* mayfly; especially effective February–May, fished dry or wet on flowing waters.

Rough Olive: *Dry pattern.* Represents a Large Dark Olive Dun *(Baetis rhodani)* mayfly; especially effective February–May; also September–November, fished dry on flowing waters.

Sand Fly: *Wet pattern.* Represents the natural sedge-fly *(Rhyacophila dorsalis);* especially effective April–September, fished wet on flowing waters.

Sedge: (Dark/Medium/Light): *Dry pattern.* A general representation of an adult sedge-fly of the order *Trichoptera;* can be effective April–October, fished dry on still or flowing waters.

Sherry Spinner: *Dry pattern.* Represents the female spinner of the Blue Winged Olive Dun *(Ephemerella ignita)* mayfly; especially effective May–October, fished dry on flowing waters, or still-waters where this mayfly is present.

Shrimp: *Wet pattern.* Represents the natural freshwater shrimp (genus: *Gammarus,* several species); can be effective March–October, fished wet on still or flowing waters.

Silver Sedge (also known as **Grey Sedge**): *Dry pattern.* Represents the natural sedge-fly *(Odontocerum albicorne);* especially effective June–October, fished dry on fast-flowing waters.

Smut: *Wet pattern.* Represents the natural Blackfly (order: *Diptera,* genus: *simulium,* many species); especially effective May–September, fished wet on flowing waters, or large still-waters.

Snail: *Wet pattern.* A general representation of a natural freshwater snail (phylum *Mollusca,* class: *gastropoda,* many species); especially effective July–September (when some species of freshwater snail migrate to the water surface on still-waters), fished wet – just below the surface on still-waters.

St. Mark's Fly, see **Hawthorn Fly.**

Tadpole: *Wet pattern.* represents a natural tadpole (larva of frogs or toads; also newts); especially effective March–June (when tadpoles mass in shallow water), fished wet on still waters.

Teal, Blue and Silver (also Teal & Red/Black/Green, etc.): *Wet pattern.* A general representation of a small fish-fry; can be effective June–October, fished wet on still or flowing waters.

Tup's Indispensable: *Dry and wet patterns.* A general representation of the female spinners of the Pale Watery Dun *(Baetis fuscatus)*, Small Spurwing Dun *(Centroptilum luteolum)*, Large Dark Olive Dun *(Baetis rhodani)*, and Medium Olive Dun *(Baetis vernus & Baetis tenax)* mayflies. Can be effective May–October, fished dry or wet on still or flowing waters.

Water Cricket: *Wet pattern.* Represents the natural insect *(Velia caprai,* of the order *Hemiptera);* especially effective March–June, fished wet (can be fished dry), on still-waters.

Welsh Partridge: *Wet pattern.* A general representation of a natural fly/insect; can also be fished wet to represent a nymph-like creature. Can be effective March–October, fished wet on still or flowing waters.

Welshman's Button: *Dry pattern.* Represents the natural sedge-fly *(Seriscostoma personatum);* especially effective June–July, fished dry on still or flowing waters.

Wickham's Fancy: *Dry and wet patterns.* A general representation of a natural fly/insect; can be effective March–October, fished dry or wet on still or flowing waters.

Willow Fly: *Dry pattern.* Represents the natural stonefly *(Leuctra geniculata);* especially effective August–November, fished dry on stony flowing waters.

Woodcock and Hare's Ear: *Wet pattern.* A general representation of a nymph-like creature; can be effective March–September, fished wet on still or flowing waters.

Yellow May Dun: *Dry pattern.* Represents the natural mayfly *(Heptagenia sulphurea);* especially effective May–August, fished dry on flowing waters, or still-waters where this mayfly is present.

Yellow Sally: *Dry and wet patterns.* Represents the natural stonefly *(Isoperla grammatica),* also the natural stonefly Small Yellow Sally *(Chloroperla torrentium);* especially effective April–August, fished dry or wet on stony flowing waters or stony still-waters.

Zulu: (Black/Blue/Gold/Silver): *Wet pattern.* A general representation of a natural fly/insect. The Black Zulu can also be fished to represent an aquatic or terrestrial beetle. Can be effective March–October, fished wet on still or flowing waters.

Part 3

Sea Fishing

28

Sea Fishing

Oceans and seas cover 71% of the world's surface. Vast areas of the sea have yet to be explored; its mysterious depths hide many unfamiliar species of fish.

When sea fishing we're never quite sure what we might catch!

Each of us lives within easy travelling distance of the sea; no costly rod licence or permit is required to begin fishing, and there's no close season. You may choose to fish from beach, rock outcrop, river estuary, pier, harbour wall or boat.

Sea fishing is a healthy, popular and fast-growing sport that offers thrilling pursuit of big fish, most of which provide a satisfying and nutritionally excellent meal later.

You can fill the freezer with fish fillets and cutlets, and regularly enjoy economical fish dishes that more than repay the price of tackle, bait and travel.

Should you wisely decide to join a sea fishing club, you'll benefit from the friendly, happy and helpful atmosphere; expert instruction and advice, plus valuable discounts on equipment and organised shore and boat fishing expeditions.

Reel screamers
Some giant fish will strip line from your reel and make it scream with strain. Conger eels, halibut and skate grow scaringly huge; sometimes large sharks come close inshore.

When you hook a sea fish, you're never certain what's on the other end of the line. In 1938 fishermen in the Indian Ocean caught a 2m (6 ft) coelacanth *(Latimeria chalumnae)* of the family *Latimeriidae* – thought to have been extinct for at least 60 million years. The coelacanth family was widespread in our oceans 350 million years ago – about 200 million years before dinosaurs roamed the earth!

Since the first coelacanth was captured and recognised, several more have been caught off the Comoro Islands in the

Mozambique Channel, where the islanders, unaware of the fish's supposed extinction, had long regarded it as a tasty food dish.

And what of legendary sea monsters like the Norwegian "Kraken", and the Biblical "Leviathan". Do they exist? Now, they would be real, reel screamers!

29

Sure Way to Catch Fish

The sure way of catching fish is to *know* which *species of fish* frequent the area of coast you anticipate fishing, and then scheme *the right way* to catch them.

There's no substitute for *local knowledge*. Visit local specialist tackle shops; talk with staff – buy a few items of necessary tackle and/or bait in exchange for their valuable and expert advice. Read the latest local "hotspots" sea angling news in angling newspapers and magazines. Chat to "locals" angling near spots you intend fishing; find out the fish species currently feeding along the coast; their favourite foods and baits. Then refer to the relevant chapters here and *plan* your fishing expedition.

Care and attention to detail bring success.

TIPS
1. Concentrate on one small stretch of coast; learn its secrets, then move on. Keep written records of your discoveries – after a few seasons your records will be worth their weight in gold!
2. In popular holiday months, a courteous phone call to the local tourist information centre often brings up-to-the-minute intelligence on sea fishing prospects.

TIDES
A tide is the action of rise and fall in sea level, influenced by the gravitational "pulling" power of the moon and to a lesser degree, the sun.

Along most areas of coastline, the tide rises and falls *twice* each day. So we should expect 2 high tides and 2 low tides in a period of 24 hours.

About every *two weeks* throughout the year, at new and full moon, sun and moon are in line with the earth, and exert enormous pulling power on the sea, causing high *spring tides*. The strongest seabed-churning storms usually occur during spring tides.

The highest spring tides rise at spring (21st March) and autumn (21st September) equinoxes. During all spring tides, the sea not only rises to a very high level, but also falls to a specially low level.

In the weeks between spring tides, smaller tides (rising and falling to a lesser extent) prevail; these smaller tides are called *neap tides*.

Around many coastal areas, the rising (flood) tide takes about 6 hours to reach its high tide level, and 6 hours to fall (ebb) to its low tide level. The period when the tide has reached and briefly settled at its high point is commonly called "slack water". The term "slack water" is occasionally also used to mean the briefly settled state of the sea at low tide. In essence, "slack water" simply means still, unmoving water.

Tides, listed from high to low level:

HIGH WATER SPRING (HWS).

HIGH WATER NEAP (HWN).

LOW WATER NEAP (LWN).

LOW WATER SPRING (LWS).

The precise times of tides vary from place to place around the coast, and become a little later every day. Times of tides (tidal constants) are published for all areas in national angling newspapers and sea angling magazines.

TIPS

1. Low water spring (LWS) tide is an ideal opportunity to explore the seabed and chart in your records the promising patches to fish (see Chapters 34–38) at high tide.

2. Gathering natural baits (see Chapter 32 page 234) is best carried out at low water spring (LWS) tide or low water neap (LWN) tide.

3. High water spring (HWS) tide carries snooping fish close inshore, grubbing food previously hidden from them.

4. Admiralty charts, available for reference in some public reference libraries, or purchase to order from specialist tackle shops and bookshops, show water depths, seabed types (sand, reef, rocks etc.) and contours, including the position of known wrecks!

WHERE, WHEN, WHY?

Fish shoals generally follow regular routes to feeding and breeding grounds at customary and predictable times of year;

but routes and timing are subject to change, and may be altered owing to such factors as: cliff erosion and deviation of currents; exhaustion or disappearance of food sources; fluctuation of weather conditions and/or water temperature; presence of trawlers, pollution, noise etc. We must constantly update our records.

Fish choose to stay awhile in an area because: there's plenty of food; it's got convenient hang-outs to lurk in ambush, or hide from attack, like rocks and reefs, weeds, wrecks and/or sunken debris, breakwaters, pier or jetty supports, cracked stone harbour walls etc.

Fig. 85 The Black-Backed Gull.

1. Fish will be found near areas of seabed offering food and security.
2. Never rely on fish behaving *exactly* as they're supposed to behave according to books. The fish haven't read the books! If fish *have* read *this* book, they didn't pay for it!

WATCH THE BIRDIE
Some birds are accomplished fishers. Watch for them and know where fish can be caught! Herons are partial to estuary flounders and freshwater eels; cormorants and gannets greedily devour mackerel, sandeels, flounders and wrasse; gulls and terns snatch whole small shoal fish and the floating remains of fish shredded by hunting packs of bass or mackerel. Big predatory fish are seldom far from shoals of small fish.

TIP
Spot a bird to find the fish!

GROUNDBAITING
Whether fishing from harbour wall, pier or jetty, rock outcrop, estuary or boat – groundbaiting helps hook fish!

You'll need some freshly caught fish (mackerel, herrings, sprats and pilchards are best); shellfish (optional) like limpets, mussels, cockles etc.; also bran and/or angler's fish meal, and angler's pilchard oil.

A tough, medium or "small" sized fine-meshed net bag (weighted with a few stones if necessary) is filled with delicious titbits – chopped and diced fish; crushed shellfish, bran and/or fish meal – topped with piquant pilchard oil. The net bag is bunched tight at the top; tied shut with string; knotted to the end of a length of strong cord, and lowered into the water to rest about 1.21m (4 ft) from your baited hook.

The groundbait bag *attracts feeding fish* to your hookbait. Jiggle the bag now and again to release minute juicy morsels into the current. Fish track the glorious scent for many metres!

Fishes' favourite groundbait dinner consists of about 85% chopped fish (or 70% chopped fish and 15% crushed shellfish) plus about 15% bran and/or angler's fish meal, laced with a liberal lashing of appetizing pilchard oil.

Prepare at least 680g (1½ lb) for use in your fine-meshed net bag. Estuary, harbour and rock anglers sometimes find (small approximately golf-ball sized) balls of groundbait mixture, scattered 3 to 5 at a time onto the water above the hookbait at 15 to 25 minute intervals, more convenient and successful than the net bag. When using the scattered groundbait technique, add a few chopped samples of your hookbait for bonus results!

DETECTING BITES

Keep your rod tip high and the line tight. Hold the line near your reel gently between thumb and forefinger. When a fish bites the baited hook, you'll feel slight vibrations or tremors run up the line. With experience, you'll be able to identify the species of fish biting from the distinctive "feel" as it mouths the bait. Different species of fish investigate and seize food in their own unique way. Your rod tip will tremble, waver and may swing down sharply. If the rod bends double you've hooked a biggie!

Floats indicate a bite by wobbling, dipping, diving, disappearing, or speeding across the surface in suspicious fashion and/or against the current.

Immediately you detect a bite, *tighten your line* and reel-in!

TIP

Check you've packed *all* your tackle before travelling home!

CONSERVATION

Fish shoals fight for survival against natural predators *and* trawlers; and sea anglers.

Please help conserve declining fish stocks by returning small fishes, and fish not wanted for freezing and cooking (see Chapter 40), *alive* to the sea. Thank you.

30

Get Fish-Wise –
Know your Fish

Over 350 different species of sea fish swim in the coastal waters round Britain, Northern Ireland and Eire. Many of the fish popularly sought after, or encountered by sea anglers, are discussed in this chapter, which reveals the essential facts necessary to begin catching the species of fish of your choice.

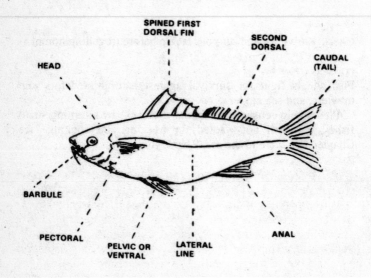

Fig. 86 General features of sea fish.

A clear understanding of fish behaviour helps us discover the best fishing methods. Get "fish-wise"; know the right way to catch big fishes, and enjoy consistent sea angling success!

ANGLER FISH *(Lophius piscatorius).*
Family: Lophiidae
Average weight: Big rod-caught angler fish can weigh 27.21kg
(60 lb) or above. The average angler fish weighs about 9.07kg
(20 lb).

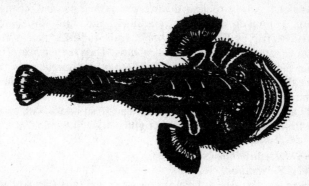

Fig. 87 Angler fish.

Description: Easily identifiable. Huge head and mouth; dark
brown body and large pectoral fins.
WARNING: Beware of the angler fish's powerful jaws. It's earned
the nickname "Sea Devil"!
*Angler fish may be cooked and eaten (see Chapter 40).

Catch angler fish! Hints:
Best locations: All parts of Britain, notably the south coast and
West Country.
Season: Summer visitor. MAY/JUNE/JULY/AUGUST/SEPTEMBER.
Withdraws to ocean depths at onset of wintry weather.
Favourite feeding places: Prefers mud, sand, rocks and wrecks
lying under deep water – about 40 fathoms (73.15m).
Sometimes comes into shallower inshore waters.
Successful baits: Any whole fresh fish, or generous fish strips
(mackerel, herring, pollack, pouting and whiting are
recommended).

Right methods and rigs include:
Shore fishing: Basic leger with a wire trace attaching hook to
swivel on line: cast from beach, or rocks into deep water.
Boat fishing: Boat leger with a wire trace attaching hook to
swivel on line: simple paternoster where bait is to be offered

slightly above snag-ridden stretch of seabed, with a wire trace attaching hook to swivel on line, or rotten bottom with a wire trace attaching hook to swivel on line.

EXPERT TIPS

1. Angler fish love rooting themselves in mud or sand; change colour to match their surroundings, and lure shoals of inquisitive fish by flicking and bobbing the rod-like spine of the dorsal fin above their cavernous mouths. Then they strike! The angler fish seldom pursues a moving bait and rarely rises far above the seabed to swallow food – so fish your bait on, or close to, the seabed.

2. Be alert. The angler fish removes bait from hooks with ease. Feel for faint knocks or tugs and tighten your line quickly.

BASS *(Dicentrachus labrax).*
Family: Serrandiae.
Average weight: Big rod-caught bass can weigh 6.35kg (14 lb) or above. The average bass weighs about 2.26kg (5 lb).

Fig. 88 Bass.

Description: Silvery sides; blue-grey back; cream – white belly. Two separate fins; the first with 9 spines; the second with 13. Large mouth – sharp teeth: WARNING: Watch for the dorsal spines; keep hands clear.
***Bass are good to eat (see Chapter 40).

Catch bass! Hints:
Best locations: Mainly south and south-west coasts of Britain, and southern Eire.
Season: All year. Best results in MAY/JUNE/JULY/AUGUST/ SEPTEMBER/OCTOBER. Many big bass migrate around November to deeper southern waters; returning about May/June.

Favourite feeding places: Rough, turbulent inshore waters; off rocky shorelines; over reefs and in fast tidal currents ripping along sandy shores. Also river estuaries; harbours and frequently many metres up tidal "freshwater" rivers.

Successful baits: Almost anything! Whole small fresh fish (sprats) or fish strips (mackerel, herring, squid); sandeels; shrimps: hermit crab (claws removed); crabs (peeler or soft back); prawns; shellfish; ragworms and lugworms (especially after dark).

Artificial baits: rubber or plastic sandeels; spoons; plugs and devon minnows; specially-tied flies or salmon or large trout flies (in river estuary or harbour waters, using freshwater fly fishing tackle and techniques).

Right methods and rigs include:

Shore fishing: Running paternoster; 2 hook running leger cast from beach; spinning from steep sloping shore.

Rocks, harbour, pier or jetty: Sliding float; spinning; driftlining.

Boat fishing: Sliding float; boat leger; driftlining; trolling.

EXPERT TIPS

1. In estuaries and harbours, look for bass cruising near the surface.

2. At sea, watch for gulls, gannets or terns feeding on torn fish leavings; victims of large bass shoals.

3. Spot patches of water broken by shoals of terrified small fish herded to the surface by bass; to be attacked and eaten.

4. Don't cast too far! Bass often feed in shallow water close inshore. A long cast may overshoot hungry hunting bass.

5. Big bass feed at all depths; mid-water level is an ideal float setting when fishing from rocks.

6. To catch BIG bass, use a big bait!

BREAM, BLACK *(Spondyliosoma cantharus).*

Family: Sparidae.

Average weight: Big rod-caught black bream can weigh 2.26kg (5 lb) or above. The average black bream weighs about 0.68kg (1½ lb).

Description: Purple-grey back; silver-grey sides. Dark, broad vertical lines on sides. Dark spots on dorsal and anal fins. Ten or eleven sharp spines on dorsal fin. WARNING: Avoid dorsal spines when unhooking black bream.

***Black bream are good to eat (see Chapter 40).

Fig. 89 Black Bream.

Catch black bream! Hints:

Best locations: South coast of England, West Country and Channel Islands, Sussex and Littlehampton in particular, produce notable bream. Fine catches come also from the Isle of Wight, Hampshire and Dorset.

Season: Summer only visitor. MAY/JUNE/JULY/AUGUST/SEPTEMBER. Black bream return to the Mediterranean when the weather (and water) turns cold.

Favourite feeding places: Deep water, about 10 fathoms (18.53m) down, above weed covered rocks; although black bream do rise to feed near the surface when the tide is rushing in, or running out.

Successful baits: Fish strips (mackerel, pilchard and squid effective); ragworm, lugworm, shellfish, shrimps, small sandeels.

Right methods and rigs include:

Shore fishing: Basic leger or running paternoster from beach.
Rocks, pier or jetty: Sliding float or driftlining.
Boat fishing: Sliding float; boat leger; 2 hook paternoster, and driftlining.

EXPERT TIPS

1. Groundbaiting is effective from rocks, piers, jetties or boats.
2. The black bream sucks food into its little and sensitive mouth, so use the smallest (and therefore least detectable) hook suited to the bait fished.

3. Keep your bait on the move. Active baits excite black bream and invite attack. When fishing bait on the seabed, occasionally jerk and jiggle the line with your rod; raise the bait one or two metres and periodically wind bait, in stops and starts, to the surface. Black bream will follow and seize food near the top of the water.

BREAM, RED *(Pagellus bogaraveo).*
Family: Sparidae.
Average weight: Big rod-caught red bream can weigh 2.72kg (6 lb) or above. The average red bream weighs about 0.90kg (2 lb).

Fig. 90 Red Bream.

Description: Crimson back, orange/gold sides, silvery-orange underneath. Mature red bream have a distinctive black patch at the beginning of the lateral line (see fig 86). Twelve sharp spines on dorsal fin. WARNING: Keep clear of the dorsal spines. ***Red bream are good to eat (see Chapter 40).

Catch red bream! Hints:
Best locations: South and south west coasts of Britain; particularly the West Country, also Eire.
Season: Summer visitor. MAY/JUNE/JULY/AUGUST/SEPTEMBER.
Favourite feeding places: Deep water, about 12 fathoms (21.94m), over weed and rocks; can be caught in shallow water, mainly after dark.
Successful baits: Shellfish, sandeels, whole small fish, or fish strips; ragworm, lugworm etc. Eats almost anything that looks and/or smells attractive and nourishing!

Right methods and rigs include:
Shore fishing: Basic leger or running paternoster from beach.
Rocks, pier or jetty: Sliding float or driftlining.
Boat fishing: Sliding float; boat leger; 2 hook paternoster, and driftlining.

EXPERT TIPS
1. A stationary bait fished on or near the seabed achieves best results during daytime.
2. Red bream feed prolifically after dark, often rising to the surface in search of food. Driftlining (see page 282) near the surface can prove a productive form of night fishing.

BRILL *(Scophthamlus rhombus).*
Family: Bothidae.
Average weight: Big rod-caught brill can weigh 4.53kg (10 lb) or above. The average brill weighs about 1.81kg (4 lb).
Description: Closely resembles the turbot (see fig 111), speckled brown body on top; white underneath. Brill are frequently mistaken for turbot. However, the brill is less broad-bodied and more oval in outline than the turbot; brill – unlike turbot – have small scales on their bodies and none of the turbot's "tubercles" (see the turbot's description, page 224).
***Brill are good to eat (see Chapter 40).

Catch brill! Hints:
Best locations: All round British Isles and Eire; good catches of brill are taken off shores of southern Britain.
Season: Throughout the year; best in JUNE/JULY/AUGUST/SEPT-EMBER/OCTOBER/NOVEMBER/DECEMBER/JANUARY/FEBRUARY.
Favourite feeding places: Offshore sand and sand/mud seabed beneath 30 fathoms (54.86m) of water; occasionally ventures closer inshore.
Successful baits: Whole live or freshly killed small fish (sprats, sandeels), or fish strips (mackerel); prawns, ragworms, lugworms.

Right methods and rigs include:
Shore fishing: Basic leger cast into deep water.
Boat fishing: Boat leger.

EXPERT TIP
1. When boat fishing for brill with leger rig, raise and lower

your rod tip and/or reel-in, then unwind about 304mm (1 ft) of line, at regular intervals – to lend attractive and extra-inviting movement to your bait.

COALFISH *(Pollachius virens).*
Family: Gadidae.
Average weight: Big rod-caught coalfish can weigh 8.16kg (18 lb) or above. The average coalfish weighs about 3.17kg (7 lb).

Fig. 91 Coalfish.

Description: Cousin to the cod. Young coalfish are called "billet". Coalfish are black on the back, have blue-green sides and a silver-grey belly. Nearly straight white-dashed lateral line (see fig 86). Lower jaw juts out just beyond upper jaw; there's a small barbule (feeler) on the coalfish's chin.
*Coalfish may be cooked and eaten (see Chapter 40).

Catch coalfish! Hints:
Best locations: Rocky shores. Most common off coast of northern England, Scotland and Northern Ireland. Can be caught in deep water above West Country rocks, reefs and wrecks.
Season: Throughout the year. Best sport in MAY/JUNE/JULY/AUGUST/SEPTEMBER/OCTOBER/NOVEMBER.
Favourite feeding places: Weed-covered rocks; estuaries and harbours. Big coalfish feed in deep water over offshore reefs and wrecks, but return inshore when the weather turns cold. Coalfish feed near the seabed and at mid-water depth.
Successful baits: Any whole small fish, or fish strips (cod, mackerel, herring, squid, whiting); lugworms, ragworms, sandeel, shrimp, prawn.

Artificial baits: rubber or plastic sandeels; spoons; devon

193

minnows; pirks, specially tied or salmon or large trout flies (in river estuary or harbour waters; from boats on a calm sea, using freshwater fly-fishing tackle and techniques).

Right methods and rigs include:
Shore fishing (from rocks, piers, jetties, harbour walls): Sliding float; spinning.
Boat fishing: Driftlining deep water; trolling; pirk "jigging"; feathering; rotten bottom fished over rocks or reefs – raised and lowered by 1 metre (3 ft) every 3–5 minutes (raise and lower rod tip) to attract coalfish.

EXPERT TIPS
1. Look out for gulls and terns circling over the debris of torn floating fish marking the position of a shoal of feeding coalfish.
2. When float fishing without success, a slow "jerky" rewinding of line may tempt tardy coalfish to take your bait.
3. Big coalfish hunt food away from large shoals of smaller coalfish, and prefer whole fish or fish strip baits, especially herring and small cod.
4. Boat fishing in deep water over rocks; first offer your bait about 1 metre (3 ft) above the rocks. If you haven't caught a coalfish after 20 minutes, raise your bait a further 1 metre (3 ft) and so on... until you contact a feeding coalfish shoal.
5. Keep hooked coalfish away from rocks and/or submerged snags and obstructions. Draw coalfish quickly to the surface on a tight line.
6. Coalfish often rise to feed near the surface at dawn and dusk.

COD *(Gadus morhua)*.
Family: Gadidae.
Average weight: Big rod-caught cod can weigh 14.5kg (32 lb) or above. The average cod weighs about 5.44kg (12 lb).
Description: Big head; bulky brown-green or olive-green body. Large mouth, bedded with small sharp teeth; barbule (feeler) below chin.
***Cod are good to eat (see Chapter 40).

Catch cod! Hints:
Best locations: All round British Isles, particularly northern and eastern waters. Some good boat fishing for BIG cod in West Country waters above sunken ship wrecks, and around Isle of Wight in Hampshire.

Fig. 92 Cod.

Season: Autumn and winter visitor to many coastal areas of Britain and Eire; though can be caught off Scottish coast throughout the year. Cod may be caught in northern waters from JUNE to MARCH; cod shoals arrive off the south coast round OCTOBER and melt away about FEBRUARY.

Favourite feeding places: Prefer deep water; scour the seabed for food. Cod shoals rove remorselessly in search of rich feeding grounds; consume everything edible – then move on.

Successful baits: Almost anything! Cod snatch and digest all natural baits: whole fish or fish strips; lugworms, ragworms, sandeels, shellfish, crabs etc.

Right methods and rigs include:

Shore fishing: Basic leger; simple paternoster cast into deep water.

Boat fishing: Boat leger; driftline fished deep; trolling; feathering; jigging.

EXPERT TIPS*

1. Big cod feed enthusiastically when the tide is changing; either ebbing (flowing out) or flooding (rushing in). Cod are most active in their search for food when the sea is rough.

2. Watch for gulls diving at shoals of sprat; cod won't be far away!

3. Don't be afraid to fish a large bait for cod. A 4.5kg (10 lb) cod can swallow a 1kg (2¹/₄ lb) whole fish AND a few sprats as an appetizer before the main meal!

4. Some boat anglers, fishing for big cod, like to attach a wire trace of about 11.33kg (25 lb) breaking strain between hook and swivel on line.

CONGER EEL *(Conger conger).*
Family: Congridae.
Average weight: Big rod-caught conger eels can weigh 27.21kg (60 lb) or above. Commercial fishermen have reported catching conger eels of approximately 100kg (220 lb) in weight. Such monsters have also been sighted by deep-sea divers. The average rod-caught conger eel weighs about 9.07kg (20 lb).

Fig. 93 Conger Eel.

Description: Serpent-like head; wide protruding eyes; slime-covered scaleless body; powerful jaws and razor sharp teeth! WARNING: Dodge those teeth!!
***Conger eels are good to eat (see Chapter 40).

Catch conger eels! Hints!
Best locations: All round British Isles; Northern Ireland and Eire.
Season: All year; inshore conger eels are more responsive to bait offered in warm weather. During very cold winter weather, some conger eels withdraw to deep offshore hideaways, returning about MAY. The *monster* deep water conger eels live in a world of perpetual cold and dark, and strike at bait in all seasons; day or night! The most profitable months to fish for big inshore conger eels are JUNE/JULY/AUGUST/SEPTEMBER/OCTOBER.
Favourite feeding places: Conger eels live in rocky crevices, holes, hollows, caverns and sunken wrecks; by harbour walls, breakwaters and underneath piers and jetties. Conger eels set up home and stay put(!) unless extremely cold conditions drive them temporarily into deeper water, or they outgrow their lair

196

and must move somewhere more spacious. Conger eels seldom stray far from the safety of their hideouts and prey on passing fish.

Successful baits: Whole *live* fish, hooked through the upper jaw behind the lip (mackerel, pouting, whiting) or whole freshly killed fish (squid, herring, bunch of sprats or pilchards); $1/2$ fresh fish (top and bottom halves effective); or occasionally fish strips – large helpings preferred! Also crabs and lobsters.

Right methods and rigs include:

Shore fishing: Basic leger with a wire trace attaching hook to swivel on line.

Boat fishing: Boat leger with a wire trace attaching hook to swivel on main line; running paternoster with a wire trace attaching hook to swivel on line.

EXPERT TIPS

1. Big conger eels lurk in some pretty obvious places close inshore, and in "shallow" water not more than 2 fathoms (3.7m) deep! Because inshore conger eels stay hidden 'til night, their presence is often unsuspected. Look for likely lairs – sunken boat hulls, broken pipes, dumped scrap, old collapsing jetties, cracked or holed harbour walls, narrow underwater clefts in rock outcrops etc.

2. Herring, mackerel, sprat and pilchard make good bait because their high oil content lays a scent trail which conger eels quickly detect and find irresistible.

3. Conger eels respond to groundbaiting. In deep offshore water, weight a large and strong brown paper bag (or 2 strong brown paper bags, one inside the other, for extra strength) with a few heavy stones; top up with conger's favourite goodies – fresh fish blood and guts, mixed with bran soaked in cod liver oil or angler's pilchard oil; bunch the bag tight shut; fasten round with fishing line or wire, and heave into the sea. The bag breaks open upon hitting the seabed and the conger eel community thinks it's Christmas! Conger eels live alone, but belong to small sociable groups; so where there's one big conger eel, other members of the conger's clique won't be far away!

4. The tingling feel in the air on hot, humid evenings shortly before a thunderstorm breaks, electrifies conger eels into a feeding frenzy; they frequently snatch baits in suicidal haste.

5. Conger eels normally play cat and mouse with baits before gulping them down. Don't reel-in line at the first tug; wait until line strips off your reel and the running conger's bending your rod – then recover the line and begin fighting the conger eel to the surface. Immediately you apply pressure, the conger eel knows it's hooked and dives towards obstacles around which to wrap and snap your line. Don't let this happen – maintain pressure and pump the eel upwards through the water by lowering your rod; reeling-in line; raising the rod, then lowering, smartly reeling-in and so on...

6. Manoeuvre the landed conger eel straightaway into an old sack; cut line (or unclip, if using a link swivel attachment). Should you intend keeping the conger for cooking, tie sack top with string; store away from easy reach of the sea. Conger eels may be stunned by a blow from a heavy object to the head, but can only be killed by severing the spine with a sharp knife or striking the head off with an axe. Neither method of execution ought to be risked in a small boat or on slippery rocks – wait until you're safely ashore. And don't be fooled by congers playing "dead". Some survive out of water for *hours!*

DAB *(Limanda limanda).*
Family: Pleuronectidae.
Average weight: Big rod-caught dabs can weigh 0.68kg (1½ lb) or above. The average dab weighs about 340g (12 oz).

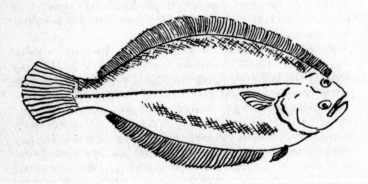

Fig. 94 Dab.

Description: Rounded, thin body. Sandy-brown back (sometimes with dark spots), white underneath.
***Dabs are good to eat (see Chapter 40).

198

Catch dabs! Hints:

Best locations: Found along sandy estuaries and shallow water close inshore. Dabs don't dwell round really rocky coastlines; otherwise common to Britain and Eire. Adult dabs move into deeper offshore waters in spring/summer to spawn, and head out to sea in severe wintry weather.

Season: Small dabs can be caught close inshore throughout the year; big dabs inshore (except during freezing weather): AUGUST/ SEPTEMBER/OCTOBER/NOVEMBER/DECEMBER/JANUARY/FEBRUARY: busy breeding and recovering off-shore for remaining months.

Favourite feeding places: On the bottom of shallow sandy bays; sand/mud estuaries and sometimes many metres up river.

Successful baits: Small pieces of fish; ragworm, lugworm, cockles, hermit crabs, sandeels, peeled shrimps, razorfish.

Right methods and rigs include:

Shore fishing and *boat fishing:* Basic leger; 2 hook paternoster.

EXPERT TIP

1. Dab shoals seek food in the same spots at regular times; so find their local time-table and accurately predict the precise moment to cast out and pull dabs in!

DOGFISH

Several species of dogfish may be caught round the shores of the British Isles. Each of the species listed below is a dogfish:

SMOOTHHOUND *(Mustelus mustelus)*

SMOOTHHOUND, STARRY *(Mustelus asterias)*

BULL HUSS *(Scyliorhinus stellaris)*

DOGFISH, LESSER SPOTTED *(Scyliorhinus canicula)*

SPURDOG *(Squalus acanthias)*

Dogfish are related to the tope and *sharks!*

SMOOTHHOUND *(Mustelus mustelus). Family: Triakidae.*

SMOOTHHOUND, STARRY *(Mustelus asterias). Family: Triakidae.*

Average weight: Big rod-caught smoothhounds and starry smooth-hounds can weigh 9.07kg (20 lb) or above. The average smoothhound and starry smoothhound weigh about 4.53kg (10 lb).

Description: The smoothhound closely resembles the tope, and is often mistaken for a tope (see fig 110). The smoothhound is slightly less streamlined in appearance than the tope; the smoothhound's first dorsal fin is positioned further forward, closer to its head, and the smoothhound's teeth are short close-set, slab-like grinders; the tope has long and sharp, flesh-tearing teeth.

The smoothhound has a grey back; light grey sides and white belly.

The starry smoothhound is of similar shape to the smoothhound, but its grey body is dotted with white spots or "stars".

NOTE: Both smoothhound and starry smoothhound may be caught using similar methods, rigs and baits; in the following notes both species will be referred to simply as "smoothhounds".

***Smoothhounds are good to eat (see Chapter 40).

Catch smoothhounds! Hints:

Best locations: All round Britain; numerous along southern shores, especially the south-east.

Season: Summer; shoals of smoothhounds come close inshore in MAY; their feeding peaks in JUNE/JULY/AUGUST. Smoothhounds move into deeper offshore waters in SEPTEMBER/OCTOBER.

Favourite feeding places: Wide ranging. Smoothhounds patrol the seabed at offshore depths of about 60 fathoms (109.72m); then steer inshore and cruise contentedly in 2 metres (6½ ft) of water. Smoothhounds enjoy hunting across areas of sand or sand/mud seabed.

Successful baits: Strips of fresh fish (mackerel, herring, squid); peeler and soft-backed crabs, ragworms, shellfish, prawns.

Right methods and rigs include:

Shore fishing: Basic leger; running paternoster.
Boat fishing: Boat leger; running paternoster.

EXPERT TIPS

1. Some sea anglers like to attach a wire trace of about 9.07kg (20 lb) breaking strain between hook and swivel on line.

2. Smoothhounds feed voraciously on hot summer's evenings, as light begins to fade. Dawn may bring good catches.

3. Smoothhounds often play with food before eating it, so allow time for a toying smoothhound to finish its game before tightening your line. Begin reeling-in when the line moves out; pulls taut and starts bending your rod tip.

4. When you hook a smoothhound, land it quickly and cast for another. The shoal stays in one place for a short spell only; sometimes as little as 20 minutes, then moves onwards. But during their brief visit, they mop up all appetizing food in sight!

5. Get to know the smoothhound shoal's patrol routes. The shoal sticks to regular routes and feeding times – until there's a sudden change in temperature, or a new patrol route is explored and adopted.

BULL HUSS *(Scyliorhinus stellaris). Family: Scyliorhinidae.*
DOGFISH, LESSER SPOTTED *(Scyliorhinus canicula). Family: Scyliorhinidae.*
SPURDOG *(Squalus acanthias). Family: Squalidae.*
Average weights: Big rod-caught bull huss can weigh 7.25kg (16 lb) or above. The average bull huss weighs about 3.62kg (8 lb).

Big rod-caught lesser spotted dogfish can weigh 1.59 kg (3$^1/_2$ lb) or above. The average lesser spotted dogfish weighs about 1kg (2$^1/_4$ lb).

Big rod-caught spurdogs can weigh 6.80kg (15 lb) or above. The average spurdog weighs about 3.17kg (7 lb).
Descriptions: Both bull huss and lesser spotted dogfish are of shark-like appearance; have a sand-brown or rust-brown body, dotted with dark brown spots, and white belly. The bull huss has one separate frilled flap of skin beneath each nostril. The lesser spotted dogfish has a continuous, unfrilled nasal flap between nostrils.

The spurdog is also of shark-like shape; blue-grey or brown-grey body; smattering of light-grey/white spots on sides.

WARNING: Bull huss and lesser spotted dogfish have sand-paper rough skin – handle with care! Don't let these "dogs" wrap their body round unprotected arms. A thick leather glove or gauntlet provides welcome protection. Also BEWARE of large bull huss' teeth!

Spurdogs have a sharp spine or "spur" at the front of each of their two small dorsal fins. These two spurs can inflict painful wounds!
***Bull huss, lesser spotted dogfish and spurdogs are good to eat (see Chapter 40). These fish are sometimes marketed as "huss" and "rock salmon".
NOTES:
Bull huss are "loners"; they lie in offshore water over rough, rocky ground. Bull huss are commonly caught during the summer round Britain, but may be found all around the British Isles, and in any season. Bull huss feed on or near the seabed; their favourite food includes: crabs, sandeels, ragworms, lugworms, whole small fish (sprats) or fish strips (mackerel, whiting, pilchard, squid).

Bull huss habitually swim away with bait before biting and getting hooked. Tighten your line firmly *twice* or *thrice* when you judge you might have a bull huss on the other end of the line.

Lesser spotted dogfish swim in shoals off all coastal areas of Britain; found all year round – close inshore from JUNE to OCTOBER. Lesser spotted dogfish prefer feeding over soft (non-rocky) ground; taking baits fished near the surface, or on the seabed. Successful baits include: strips of fresh fish (mackerel, herring, pilchard) and whole fresh small fish.

Spurdogs hunt in packs along shores all around Britain; feed close inshore in summertime, and at varying depths. Spurdogs pursue shoals of small fish relentlessly. Spurdogs respond to almost any bait, especially strips of fresh fish and whole small fish.

Right methods and rigs include:
Bull huss, lesser spotted dogfish and spurdogs can be caught using similar methods and rigs to those recommended for smoothhounds (see page 200).

FLOUNDER *(Platichthys flesus).*
Family: Pleuronectidae.
Average weight: Big flounders can weigh 1.58kg (3½ lb) or above. The average flounder weighs about 0.45kg (1 lb).

Fig. 95 Flounder.

Description: Dark green-brown back; pearl-white underside. Rows of small knobs or "tubercles" can be found where the lateral line meets the gill-cover. Flounders may be dark blotched top and bottom.

202

***Flounders are good to eat (see Chapter 40).

Catch flounders! Hints:
Best locations: All round British and Irish coasts.
Season: Throughout the year, though mature flounders move into deep offshore water to spawn mid-winter, and may be absent from shallow inshore waters for 3–4 months, usually JANUARY/FEBRUARY/MARCH or JANUARY/FEBRUARY/MARCH/APRIL. Naturally, flounders depart and return according to water temperature rather than calendar, and there can be variation in the months flounders spawn.
Favourite feeding places: On or near the bottom of sand and/or mud covered estuaries and harbours. Flounders are frequently found several kilometres up tidal rivers, often well into fresh water. Flounders also feed beneath piers and jetties.
Successful baits: Ragworm, lugworm, shellfish, fish strips (herring, mackerel, pilchard, sprat); shrimps, sandeels, hermit crab tail, peeler crab, soft-backed crabs.

Artificial baits: flounder spoons (baited with a titbit of one of the above listed baits).

Right methods and rigs include:
Shore fishing: Basic leger; 2 hook paternoster; 3 hook paternoster; spinning; light float or sliding float set to present bait slightly above bottom in estuary and harbour waters.
Boat fishing: Boat leger; 2 hook running leger; 2 hook paternoster; trolling.

EXPERT TIPS
1. Flounders follow the flood tide onto beaches and into estuaries to investigate disturbed sand and mud for lugworms, ragworms and any food on offer. Fish for flounders on a racing and rising tide for great results.
2. Flounders feed in extremely shallow water; sometimes sufficient only to cover their backs. Long distance casts into deep water are seldom necessary.
3. Pack all of a bait firmly onto the hook; flounders filch loosely fixed baits and flapping bits of bait clean away from the hook in a trice.
4. Reel in line regularly and re-cast to arouse interest of flounders, and check your bait is intact!
5. Flounders travel in mixed-size small shoals; moving with the current. One shoal follows another at intervals of up to about

137m (150 yds). To track a particular shoal you've located, follow the current, making allowance for the flounder shoal's modest pace. If you lose a shoal, don't despair – there's another shoal behind!

6. Flounders continue to feed hungrily in the coldest wintry weather; so don't be deterred by frost on your ear lobes. The flounders are feeding!

GARFISH *(Belone belone)*.
Family: Belonidae.
Average weight: Big rod-caught garfish can weigh 0.90kg (2 lb) or above. The average garfish weighs about 454g (1 lb).

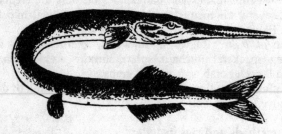

Fig. 96 Garfish.

Description: Cross between an eel and a long-beaked bird! Blue-green body; silvery sides. The garfish's sword-like beak/mouth is equipped with rows of small sharp teeth, which might give a nasty nip – be careful! Related to the flying fish, garfish love leaping from the sea to turn aerial somersaults over the waves.

*Garfish may be cooked and eaten (see Chapter 40). Don't be put off by the appearance of its cooked green bones!

Catch garfish! Hints:
Best locations: Swims happily in most waters along Britain's coastline; caught mainly off southern shores of England and the West Country.

Season: Summer visitor. Arrives off British coast about MAY/JUNE, stays through JULY and AUGUST; disappears around SEPTEMBER/OCTOBER.

Favourite feeding places: Surface and mid-water level of any patch of sea holding small fish. Dives down towards seabed in rough and stormy weather. Cruises over wide area of sea seeking food. Frequently found close inshore.

Successful baits: Small whole fish (sprats, sandeels, whitebait) or fish strips (mackerel, herring); lugworm, ragworm, prawns.
 Artificial baits: spoons, devon minnows.

Right methods and rigs include:
Shore fishing: (rocks, pier, jetty, harbour wall): Light float; sliding float; spinning also spinning from steep sloping beach.
Boat fishing: Light float; sliding float; spinning; driftlining near surface; trolling.

EXPERT TIPS
1. Garfish are often found in the company of mackerel shoals.
2. Garfish respond to groundbaiting.
3. Rapidly retrieved artificial spinning lures can be super-successful. The brighter your lure the better!
4. Tighten line on a garfish swimming away with your bait by sweeping your rod *sideways* (not straight up). A sideways action drives your hook securely into the side of the garfish's mouth. An upwards motion of the rod pulls your bait from its hard beak!

GURNARD, YELLOW *(Trigla lucerna).* Also known as "Tubfish".
Family: Triglidae.
Average weight: Big rod-caught yellow gurnard can weigh 3.62kg (8 lb) or above. The average yellow gurnard weighs about 1kg (2¼ lb).

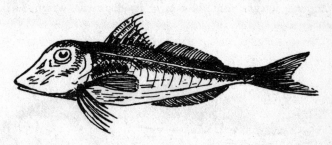

Fig. 97 Gurnard.

Description: Distinctive shape; glorious colour: deep red-orange/yellow; pectoral fins edged by bright blue bands.
Warning: The gurnard's spine ribbed fins can cut skin.
 NOTE: Of similar shape is the GREY GURNARD *(Eutrigla*

205

gurnardus), average weight about 227g ($^1/_2$ lb); purple-grey back. And the RED GURNARD *(Aspitrigla cuculus)*, average weight about 454g (1 lb); brilliant red body.

Yellow, grey and red gurnard may each be caught in similar locations, using identical methods, rigs and baits. The grey gurnard is the more common of the three; the yellow gurnard is generally the heaviest, and makes the most filling meal!

***Gurnard are good to eat (See Chapter 40).

Catch gurnard! Hints:
Best locations: Found round coasts of Britain, Northern Ireland and Eire.
Season: Gurnard come close inshore during the summer months, JUNE/JULY/AUGUST/SEPTEMBER and return to deeper offshore waters from OCTOBER to APRIL/MAY.
Favourite feeding places: On or near the bottom of soft sand or sand/mud areas of seabed between rocks and reefs; inshore and offshore.
Successful baits: Fish strips (herring, mackerel); sandeel, shrimps, crabs (soft-backed).

Right methods and rigs include:
Shore fishing: Basic leger; running paternoster.
Boat fishing: Boat leger; simple paternoster.

HADDOCK *(Melanogrammus aeglefinus)*.
Family: Gadidae.
Average weight: Big rod-caught haddock can weigh 3.62kg

Fig. 98 Haddock.

(8 lb) or above. The average haddock weighs about 1kg (2¼ lb).
Description: Grey-brown/bronze back, shading into white belly.
Black lateral line; black mark above each pectoral fin; small
barbule (feeler) on chin. Related to the cod.

Haddock are good to eat. However, the species has become
scarce around British shores due to past commercial over-
fishing, and where possible captured haddock should be
returned ALIVE to the sea.

Catch haddock! Hints:

Best locations: The haddock is now steadily re-establishing its
numbers, and is most plentiful around the coasts of Scotland,
north-eastern England, Northern Ireland, and deep water off the
West Country.

Season: All year round, especially JUNE/JULY/AUGUST/SEPTEMBER/
OCTOBER/NOVEMBER/DECEMBER. Come close inshore during
winter months.

Favourite feeding places: Haddock feed on or near the bottom
of deep water off steep-sloping beaches or rocky outcrops.
Haddock shoals sift sandy and soft sand/mud seabed areas for
food.

Successful baits: Ragworm, lugworm; shellfish (mussels and
cockles are haddock favourites); whole small fish (sprat,
pilchard) or fish strips (mackerel, herring, squid); shrimps, crabs
(soft-backed), starfish.

Right methods and rigs include:

Shore fishing: 2 boom paternoster; 2 hook paternoster; simple
paternoster – *cast into deep water.*
Boat fishing: Boat leger; 2 boom paternoster; 2 hook
paternoster.

EXPERT TIPS

1. When boat fishing safely away from rocks and reefs, be
prepared to move your boat in the same direction and at the
same speed as feeding shoals of haddock you hook into;
haddock shoals are constantly on the move, combing the seabed
for food.

2. In water 20 fathoms (37m) or more deep; adjust paternoster
rigs to present one baited hook about 1m (3 ft) above the seabed,
and a second (if any) baited hook about 1.82m (6 ft) above the
seabed.

HALIBUT *(Hippoglossus hippoglossus).*
Family: Pleuronectidae.
Average weight: Big rod-caught halibut can weigh 40.82kg (90 lb) or above. Commercial deep sea trawlers have netted single halibut over 113.39kg (250 lb) in weight. Halibut are believed to reach weights in excess of 317kg (700 lb)! Fancy hooking one? The average rod-caught halibut weighs about 13.60kg (30 lb).

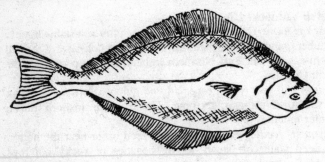

Fig. 99 Halibut.

Description: Dark olive-brown on top; white underside. Lateral line curves over pectoral fins. Strong jaws and sharp teeth! WARNING: Treat the halibut's mouth with the caution its teeth command.
***Halibut are good to eat (see Chapter 40).

Catch halibut! Hints:
Best locations: The deep, cold seas round northern Scotland; Orkneys, Shetland, and occasionally Northern Ireland.
Season: All year round. Best sport likely JULY/AUGUST/SEPTEMBER/OCTOBER/NOVEMBER.
Favourite feeding places: Deep offshore waters. Halibut feed at depths ranging from 30 fathoms (54.86m) and above to 600 fathoms (1,097m) and below! Take plenty of line!
Successful baits: Whole live fish (coalfish, pollack, mackerel, haddock, whiting, squid); freshly killed whole fish, or fish strips.

Right methods and rigs include:
Boat fishing: Rotten bottom over rocky ground, with a wire trace attaching hook to swivel on main reel line; or boat leger with a wire trace attaching hook to swivel on main reel line;

driftlining with a wire trace attaching hook to swivel on main reel line, fished deep – a few metres above the seabed.

EXPERT TIPS

1. Live bait is best (fish hooked through its upper jaw behind the lip). Put enticing movement into freshly killed whole fish or fish strips, by raising and lowering your rod and/or reel-in a metre or two of line, then slowly release the same length of line. Repeat this action at regular intervals.

2. If you're chasing MONSTER halibut, employ standard giant common skate or shark fishing tackle. You'll need a strong shoulder harness and rod-butt holder; at LEAST 365.76m (400 yds) of 36.28kg (80 lb) breaking strain line; wire trace of around 40.82kg (90 lb) breaking strain and nerves of steel!

JOHN DORY *(Zeus faber)*.

Family: Zeidae.

Average weight: Big rod-caught john dory can weigh 4kg (9 lb) or above. The average john dory weighs about 0.90kg (2 lb).

Description: Brown-olive body: yellow-gold stripes and whisps. Black spots on each side – St. Peter's thumb prints, or so legend says. John dory is known as "St. Peter's fish".

WARNING: Don't touch the sharp-spiked dorsal fin. Note where St. Peter (a professional fisherman) placed his thumbs, and do likewise, or you'll be sorry!

***John dory are good to eat (see Chapter 40).

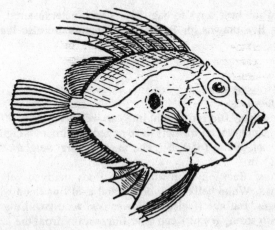

Fig. 100 John Dory.

209

Catch john dory! Hints:

Best locations: Inshore and deep offshore water – as far down as 110 fathoms (201m). Caught mainly off West Country coastline; western Northern Ireland and Eire. Also found round shores of southern England.

Season: Throughout the year. Big john dory move from inshore to deep offshore water in cold and/or rough weather.

Favourite feeding places: Wherever shoals of small fish gather, there will be john dory. Near rocks and reefs; round wrecks, wherever fish make easy prey, there drifts john dory!

Successful baits: Small whole fish (herring, sprat, pilchard); fish strips (squid, herring, mackerel); prawns, shrimps, sandeels.

Right methods and rigs include:

Shore fishing: Simple paternoster cast into deep water; running paternoster cast into deep water.

Boat fishing: 2 hook paternoster; simple paternoster; driftlining at mid-water or deep water depth.

EXPERT TIPS

1. To catch fish for meals, john dory, who can't swim fast, drifts in harmless fashion towards unsuspecting victims; opens his mouth, and SUCKS them in! An anchored or slow moving bait is therefore most likely to succeed in arousing john dory's interest.

2. John dory feed largely on fish, preferably live; certainly fresh.

3. One of the best ways to bag dory is with paternostered live sandeels; live prawns, or freshly killed sprats are also highly effective.

LING *(Molva molva).*

Family: Gadidae.

Average weight: Big rod-caught ling can weigh 18.14kg (40 lb) or above. Commercial trawlers have netted specimens weighing in excess of 294kg (650 lb)! The average ling weighs about 6.80kg (15 lb).

Description: Back olive-brown/yellow. Body marbled yellow/gold/brown. White belly. Tail, dorsal and anal fins lined white along edges. Barbule (feeler) on lower jaw. WARNING: Ling are armed with strong teeth! Keep your finger away from the jaws.
***Ling are good to eat (see Chapter 40).

Fig. 101 Ling.

Catch ling! Hints!

Best locations: Found all round Britain. Noteworthy catches are made off the coast of Scotland, northern England, the West Country and Eire.

Season: All year round; good catches made JUNE/JULY/AUGUST/SEPTEMBER.

Favourite feeding places: Deep offshore water. Big ling mostly feed near the seabed; depths of 50 fathoms (91.44m) and below yield large catches, especially over wrecks and rocks. Ling may pursue shoals of fish to mid-water level and sometimes swim close to the surface – chasing behind and well below trawlers, ready to snatch fish falling from nets.

Successful baits: Whole fresh fish (herring, mackerel, squid, pouting) or fish strips.

Artificial baits: sizeable pirks, with baited hook.

Right methods and rigs include:

Shore fishing: Basic leger with a wire trace attaching hook to swivel on line; cast into deep water.

Boat fishing: Boat leger with a wire trace attaching hook to swivel on line; running paternoster with a wire trace attaching hook to swivel on line; driftlining with a wire trace attaching hook to swivel on line – fish the driftline deep; jigging with a wire trace attaching pirk to line.

EXPERT TIPS

1. Use big baits to catch large ling. A whole live pouting or freshly killed mackerel is merely a snack to a monster ling!

2. Stop hooked ling lunging down into rocks, caves or subterranean tunnels, or you'll lose the ling in a seabed tangle. Halt the ling's dive for freedom; fight it to the surface without surrendering line!

211

MACKEREL *(Scomber scombrus).*
Family: Scombridae.
Average weight: Big rod-caught mackerel can weigh 1.58kg (3¹/₂ lb) or above. The average mackerel weighs about 0.56kg (1¹/₄ lb).
Description: Streamlined; glistening; metal-blue/green body; wavy black bands along the back.
***Mackerel are good to eat (see Chapter 40).

Fig. 102 Mackerel.

Catch mackerel! Hints:
Best locations: All round coasts of British Isles in summer.
Season: Begin arriving along the coast in MAY/JUNE; stay through JULY/AUGUST; depart about SEPTEMBER/OCTOBER. The largest catches are frequently made in AUGUST.
Favourite feeding places: On or near the surface over any type of seabed. Always on the move; chasing shoals of small fish across the ocean.
Successful baits: Live sandeels; fish strips (mackerel, herring, pilchard, sprat).

Right methods and rigs include:
Shore fishing: (pier, jetty, harbour wall, rocks): Sliding float; spinning, also spinning from a steep sloping shore.
Boat fishing: Sliding float; driftlining; trolling; feathering; fly-fishing, using freshwater fly-fishing tackle, techniques, and specially tied flies, or large artificial trout flies.

EXPERT TIPS
1. Groundbait is effective.
2. Gulls wheel and dive above surface-feeding mackerel shoals; watch for their position.
3. Mackerel will pursue shoals of small fish into estuaries (see Chapter 34) and occasionally well up river!

MULLET, THICK-LIPPED *(Chelon labrosus).*

Family: Mugilidae.

Average weight: Big rod-caught thick-lipped mullet can weigh 3.62kg (8 lb) or above. The average thick-lipped mullet weighs about 1kg (2¼ lb).

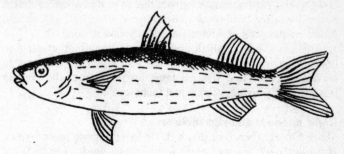

Fig. 103 Thick-Lipped Mullet.

Description: Grey-blue back; silvery sides and belly. Dark grey-brown stripes along each side.

NOTE: Of similar shape, though less numerous and smaller average size are:

THIN-LIPPED MULLET *(Liza ramada);* as the name suggests, thinner lips than its cousin; average weight about 0.68kg (1½lb).

GOLDEN GREY MULLET *(Liza aurata);* comparatively rare in British waters. The golden grey mullet has easily seen gold patches on its gill covers. Average weight about 340g (12 oz).

Collectively these three species are called GREY MULLET and may be caught using similar methods, rigs and baits.

Mullet are not generally considered good to eat.

Catch mullet! Hints:

Best location: All round British isles, Northern Ireland and Eire. Abundant in the south of England, West Country and southern Eire.

Season: Feed mainly through the summer and autumn months; MAY/JUNE/JULY/AUGUST/SEPTEMBER/OCTOBER. Mullet also feed in warm winter and spring weather; throughout the year in some "warm" harbour and estuary waters of southern England.

Favourite feeding places: At the water bottom; mid-water and frequently near or at the surface. Harbours, estuaries; many metres (even kilometres!) up tidal rivers; round rock outcrops, pier and jetty supports, bays, coves and creeks. The mullet is

213

quite content to swim and feed in surprisingly shallow water – barely covering its back!

Successful baits: Small ragworm; little strips of fresh fish (mackerel, herring, pilchard); small crabs (soft-backed), shrimps, prawns (peeled).

In rivers: earthworms, maggots, bread paste, sweetcorn; also boiled macaroni (add some grated cheese when boiling); cheese paste; small cubes of peeled banana (dipped in honey!).

Artificial baits: small flounder spoons (with bait attached to hook); special angler's mullet spoon (with bait attached to hook); specially tied flies or large artificial trout flies (using freshwater fly-fishing tackle and technique).

Right methods and rigs include:
Shore fishing: (beach or pier): Basic leger; simple paternoster.
Harbour wall, rocks, pier, jetty, river bank: Light float; spinning; fly-fishing (freshwater style).
Dinghy fishing (harbour, estuary, close inshore): Basic leger; simple paternoster; spinning.

EXPERT TIPS

1. Freshwater fishing tackle and small freshwater fishing hooks and baits (see above) may be used to catch mullet feeding "up river".

2. The best time to catch mullet is dawn/daybreak, when the tide is rising.

3. Mullet shoals invariably follow the flood tide into rivers and withdraw on the ebb tide.

4. Be quiet, crouch low and keep out of sight; mullet are shy and sudden movement or unexpected sound send the shoal scooting for cover.

5. Mullet forage through weed for food; check heavily-weeded pier and jetty supports, hulls of moored boats and harbour walls for frequented "food larders".

6. Groundbaiting is effective.

7. Surface-feeding mullet in rivers can be caught by fishing your line greased 1 metre (3 ft) from the hook towards reel with freshwater fly-fishing line grease; bait the hook with a small square of fresh bread crust and cast your bread upon the water. No float or weights necessary.

8. Mullet suck food into their mouth, so tighten your line the second a bite is seen, felt or indicated by a bobbing float, or the bait may be sucked off your hook!

9. Mullet have exceptionally soft lips. Don't tighten your line too smartly or the hook tears out. Always use a long-handled landing-net or drop net to lift mullet from the water.

10. Shy mullet shoals are scared away by the sound of a hooked mullet splashing in the water; direct captured mullet away from the main shoal with your rod; get it out of the water as quickly and quietly as possible.

MULLET CAN BE TRICKY FISH TO CATCH!

PLAICE *(Pleuronectes platessa).*
Family: Pleuronectidae.
Average weight: Big rod-caught plaice can weigh 2.26kg (5 lb) or above. The average plaice weighs about 1kg (2¼ lb).

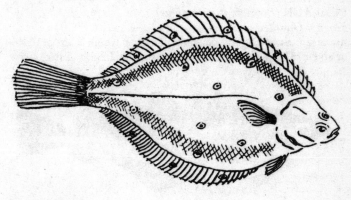

Fig. 104 Plaice.

Description: Brown back, dotted with large bright orange spots; white underside. Smaller head; slimmer body and smaller tail fin than the flounder, which it closely resembles.
***Plaice are good to eat (see Chapter 40).

Catch plaice! Hints:
Best locations: Widespread around British Isles.
Season: Best catches are made in APRIL/MAY/JUNE/JULY/AUGUST/ SEPTEMBER/OCTOBER. Plaice stay fairly close inshore until about January, when they move into deeper offshore water to spawn; returning close to shore around April/May.
Favourite feeding places: On the bottom of sand, shell-grit/ gravel, sand/mud seabed, beneath about 6 fathoms (10.97m) of water.

Successful baits: Ragworm, lugworm, shellfish (mussels, cockles), shrimps, hermit crabs.

Right methods and rigs include:
Shore fishing: Basic leger; 2 hook running leger.
Boat fishing: Boat leger; 2 hook running leger.

EXPERT TIPS
1. Plaice feed around the clock, in nearly all weather and water conditions.
2. Plaice travel in shoals; where you hook one — expect more!
3. Patches of seabed sand surrounded by rocky, rough ground draw plaice shoals.

POLLACK *(Pollachius pollachius).*
Family: Gadidae.
Average weight: Big rod-caught pollack can weigh 7.25kg (16 lb) or above. The average pollack weighs about 2.26kg (5 lb).

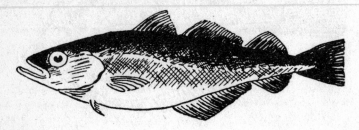

Fig. 105 Pollack.

Description: Dark, olive-green back; gold/silver sides; silver-white belly. Lower jaw protrudes.
*Pollack may be cooked and eaten (see Chapter 40).

Catch pollack! Hints:
Best locations: Notable specimens are caught in deep water off the West Country, and southern Eire; though pollack can be caught from many rocky areas round the British Isles.
Season: All year round; best inshore sport, MAY/JUNE/JULY/AUGUST/SEPTEMBER. Pollack withdraw into deeper offshore waters from mid-October to April.
Favourite feeding places: Close to the base of weed-covered rocks and reefs, and wrecks.

Successful baits: Whole fresh small fish (sprats, pilchards, sandeels) or fish strips (mackerel, herring); ragworms, prawns, peeler crabs, shrimps.

Artificial baits: rubber or plastic sandeels; spoons; devon minnows; pirks.

Right methods and rigs include:
Shore fishing: (from rocks, piers, jetties, harbour walls): Sliding float; rotten bottom cast onto rocky seabed; spinning; driftlining.
Boat fishing: Driftlining; trolling; pirk "jigging"; feathering; rotten bottom fished over rough or rocky seabed.

EXPERT TIPS
1. Live small fish, hooked through the upper jaw behind the lip, make successful bait.
2. Dawn and dusk often bring the best sport; when pollack rise to feed near the surface.
3. During daytime pollack usually stay deep; close to the seabed and tight against rocks.
4. Stop hooked pollack diving amongst rocks and snapping your line! Keep line taut and reel-in fast.
5. Pollack swim in shoals; once you've located a shoal, expect a fine catch of fish!
6. The biggest pollack are caught above rocks, and especially wrecks in deep offshore water.

POUTING *(Trisopterus luscus)*.
Family: Gadidae.
Average weight: Big rod-caught pouting can weigh 1kg (2¼ lb) or above. The average pouting weighs about 0.56kg (1¼ lb).

Fig. 106 Pouting.

Description: Red-brown/copper coloured, deep body; 4–5 dark bands on sides. Black spot at base of pectoral fins. Small barbule (feeler) underneath chin.

Pouting are not generally considered good to eat.

Catch pouting! Hints:

Best locations: Common round most areas of British Isles, particularly southern Britain and Eire.

Season: All year. Close inshore shallow water during JUNE/JULY/AUGUST/SEPTEMBER. Withdraws to the greater warmth of deeper water OCTOBERish to MAY.

Favourite feeding places: Near, or close to, the seabed. Sometimes rising to feed near the mid-water level. Pouting prefer feeding over sand-grit; rough and rocky ground; wrecks; weed-covered boulders; pier supports etc.

Successful baits: Fish strips (mackerel, herring, squid); ragworms, lugworms, mussels, cockles, small crabs, shrimps, prawns, sandeels, razorfish.

Right methods and rigs include:

Shore fishing: Basic leger; 2 hook paternoster.

Piers, jetties, harbour walls: Sliding float; simple paternoster; 2 hook paternoster; 3 hook paternoster; 2 boom paternoster.

Boat fishing: Driftlining deep; 3 hook paternoster; 2 boom paternoster.

EXPERT TIPS

1. Groundbaiting is effective from piers, jetties, harbour walls or boats.

2. When fishing with float or paternoster rig, or driftlining from a boat, present your baited hook(s) between about 355mm (14 inches) and 1m (3 ft) from the seabed.

3. Keep small pouting off your hook by attaching a large bit of bait.

RAY, STING *(Dasyatis pastinaca).*

Family: Dasyatidae.

Average weight: Big rod-caught sting rays can weigh 18.14kg (40 lb) or above. The average sting ray weighs about 6.80kg (15 lb).

Description: Brown-grey back; white-grey underneath. The ray with a sting in its tail! The long tail is endowed with a serrated arrow-like spine – its sting! WARNING: Dodge that tail. When you

Fig. 107 Sting Ray.

see you've caught a sting ray, consider cutting your line and letting it return to the sea. The sting may pierce boots and clothing and slash a wound into which venom is injected. Temporary paralysis could follow; certainly profuse bleeding. Should you be stung, hurry to the nearest hospital, or doctor.

If you are determined to take a closer look at the ray, tread on the tail *away from the sting*. Be doubly cautious – some sting rays carry *two stings!!* Why not cut it loose?

Sting rays are not generally thought good to eat.

Location: The sting ray is active in summer and autumn, mainly along the shores of southern Britain. The sting ray is hooked offshore by boat anglers, and comes close inshore, where it's caught from beach and pier. Sting ray's favourite bait seems to be ragworm or lugworm, although it eats whole small fish or fish strips lying on or near the seabed.

Please remember the warning given regarding the sting ray's sting(s).

I suggest the sting ray ought not be a species you set out to capture.

RAY, THORNBACK *(Raja clavata)*.
Family: Rajidae.
Average weight: Big rod-caught thornback rays can weigh 9.07kg (20 lb) or above. The average thornback ray weighs about 4.53kg (10 lb).

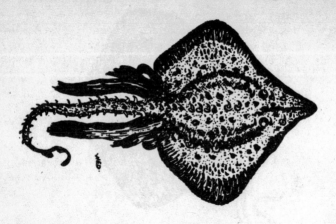

Fig. 108 Thornback Ray.

Description: Brown/grey back with thorn-like spines. White underneath. WARNING: The spines are sharp, and so are the teeth! Handle with care.

NOTE: The *small-eyed ray (Raja microocellata)* resembles the thornback ray in shape; without thorn-like spines. The small-eyed ray has a sand-brown back, decorated (painted) with pale, curling lines and pretty markings. The average small-eyed ray weighs about 2.26kg (5 lb); is common around the shores of southern and south-eastern Britain, and Eire. The small-eyed ray may be caught employing similar methods recommended for the thornback ray.

*Thornback rays (wings only) and small-eyed ray (wings only) may be cooked and eaten (see Chapter 40).

Catch thornback rays! Hints:

Best locations: All round Britain, Northern Ireland and Eire.

Season: All year. Close inshore from MARCH/APRIL; gives excellent sport in MAY/JUNE/JULY/AUGUST/SEPTEMBER. Can be caught in deeper offshore water OCTOBER to FEBRUARY/MARCH.

Favourite feeding places: Shallow or deep water, over sand, sand/mud or clean gravel seabed; doesn't like rocks or rough ground.

Successful baits: Whole small fish (sprats) or fish strips (herring, mackerel, pilchard); sandeels; peeler, soft back and hermit crabs; shellfish, ragworms.

Right methods and rigs include:
Shore: Basic leger with a wire trace of about 9.07kg (20 lb) breaking strain attaching hook to swivel on line.
Boat: Boat leger with a wire trace of about 9.07kg (20 lb) breaking strain attaching hook to swivel on line.

EXPERT TIPS
1. Thornback rays toy with their bait before consuming it. Wait until your line pulls away strongly; then tighten and reel-in.
2. Thornback rays journey across the seabed in small, sociable groups. After one is caught and removed, the remaining thornback rays hover in the area for a fair time until moving on. During the thornbacks' "confused" waiting period, it is possible to catch the entire group, one by one!

SKATE, COMMON *(Raja batis).*
Family: Rajidae.
Average weight: Big rod-caught common skate can weigh 68kg (150 lb) or above. Common skate are known to exceed 181.43kg (400 lb) in weight! The average common skate weighs about 20.41kg (45 lb).
Description: Grey-brown back, "patchworked" with light-coloured blotches; blue-grey underneath.
*Common skate (wings only) may be cooked and eaten (see Chapter 40).

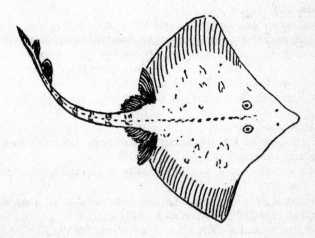

Fig. 109 Common Skate.

Catch common skate! Hints:

Best locations: All round Britain; Scotland, Northern Ireland and Eire provide the best fishing for *big* common skate.

Season: Throughout the year.

Favourite feeding places: Likes deep or shallow water over sand, sand/mud and mixed "rough" sand/rock seabed. Common skate frequently feed close inshore.

Successful baits: Wide range, especially whole fresh fish, ½ whole fish or fish strips (mackerel, herring, coalfish, pouting, pollack, whiting, squid); sandeels; crabs; shellfish; ragworms.

Right methods and rigs include:

Shore fishing: Basic leger with a wire trace attaching hook to swivel on line.

Boat fishing: Boat leger with a wire trace attaching hook to swivel on line.

EXPERT TIPS

1. Common skate mouth and "play" with bait before biting; wait for a definite and strong pull on your line, then tighten and reel-in.

2. Common skate "cling" to the seabed with great power; once drawn clear, steadily pump them to the surface. Don't permit forceful downward glides back towards the bottom!

SOLE *(Solea solea).*

Family: Soleidae.

Average weight: Big rod-caught soles can weigh 1.36kg (3 lb) or above. The average sole weighs about 0.56kg (1¼ lb).

Description: Long, oval bodied "flatfish" (see sketch of the plaice, fig 104 on page 215). Brown/grey-green on top, with dark blotches; white underneath.

***Soles are good to eat (see Chapter 40).

Catch soles! Hints:

Best locations: Caught mainly off southern and south-eastern Britain, and southern Eire.

Season: All year; best catches usually made JUNE/JULY/AUGUST/SEPTEMBER.

Favourite feeding places: On the bottom of sand, sand/mud seabed, especially between rocks and reefs.

Successful baits: Ragworm, lugworm; small fish strips (mackerel, herring, sandeel).

Right methods and rigs include:
Shore fishing: Basic leger; 2 hook running leger.
Boat fishing: Boat leger; two hook running leger.

EXPERT TIPS
1. Soles feed mostly after dark.
2. Present your hookbait near the shore on a night-time rising tide for good catches.

TOPE *(Galeorhinus galeus).*
Family: Carcharhinidae.
Average weight: Big rod-caught tope can weigh 20.86kg (46 lb) or above. The average tope weighs about 11.33kg (25 lb).

Fig. 110 Tope.

Description: Shark! The tope is a member of the shark family. Grey/brown back, rough skin; white belly. Distinctive "notched" tail. WARNING: Beware of tope's shark-sharp teeth!
*Tope may be cooked and eaten (see Chapter 40).

Catch tope! Hints:
Best locations: Widely distributed round British Isles, Northern Ireland and Eire.
Season: Feeds close inshore summer and autumn. The best months to catch tope are generally JUNE/JULY/AUGUST/SEPTEMBER. However, big tope can be caught in deep offshore water throughout the year.
Favourite feeding places: On or near the bottom of sandy seabed, particularly near rocky ground.
Successful baits: Whole live or freshly killed fish (mackerel, dabs, herring, pouting, whiting, sprats, squid); fish strips; sandeels.

Right methods and rigs include:

Shore fishing: Basic leger with a wire trace attaching hook to swivel on line; running paternoster with a wire trace attaching hook to swivel on line.

Boat fishing: Boat leger with a wire trace attaching hook to swivel on line; running paternoster with a wire trace attaching hook to swivel on line.

EXPERT TIPS

1. Keep a tight hold on your rod; hooked tope tow unattended rods into the sea in a flash!

2. Tope feed enthusiastically on a rising tide, day or night.

3. Tope hunt alone *and* in packs. Quick unhooking; re-baiting and casting often rewards with handsome catches!

TURBOT *(Scophthalmus maximus).*

Family: Scophthalmidae.

Average weight: Big rod-caught turbot can weigh 9 kg (20 lb) or above. The average turbot weighs about 3.17kg (7 lb).

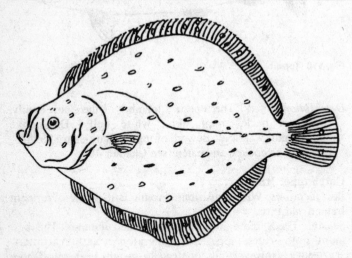

Fig. 111 Turbot.

Description: Broad, speckled brown, diamond-shaped and scale-less body; covered with small and rounded bony lumps or "tubercles". White underneath.

***Turbot are good to eat (see Chapter 40).

Catch turbot! Hints:

Best locations: Found widely around the British Isles; caught mainly along the coast of southern and south western England; also southern Eire.

Season: Summer months give good sport, JUNE/JULY/AUGUST/SEPTEMBER. Move into deep offshore water from October to May.

Favourite feeding places: The turbot's ideal feeding station seems to be a sand or sand/mud seabed; approximately 1.2km (³/₄ mile) offshore beneath about 14 fathoms (25.6m) of water. Sometimes seeks comfortable sandbanks in shallow water closer inshore, or descends to a convenient ambush spot in much deeper water – 40 fathoms (73.15m) or thereabouts.

Successful baits: Small whole fish (sprats, sandeels, pouting) or strips of fresh fish (mackerel, herring).

Right methods and rigs include:

Shore fishing: Basic leger; running paternoster.
Boat fishing: Boat leger; trolling.

EXPERT TIPS

1. Turbot like live baits best. A small fish, hooked through its upper jaw, behind the lip, is guaranteed to tempt turbot.

2. When fishing freshly-killed whole fish or fish strips; put motion into the bait by raising and lowering your rod tip at regular intervals.

3. Be gentle with hooked turbot. Hooks may rip through the soft-skinned mouth and the turbot escape! Reel-in hooked turbot with minimum applied pressure; raise the fish from the sea with a large landing net.

4. Turbot gather in small groups in good feeding places; so after you've caught number one turbot, fish a few metres further on for number two!

WEEVER, GREATER *(Trachinus draco)*.

KNOW THIS FISH: Drab yellow/brown body; sloping dark lines on sides; average weight about 227g (¹/₂ lb). Potentially LETHAL POISON is injected by spines in the first dorsal fin and gill covers. The greater weever is an inshore AND deepwater fish – BOAT ANGLERS BEWARE! If you hook a greater weever, carefully cut your line and let the weever drop back into the sea.

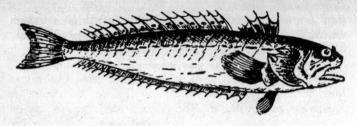

Fig. 112 Greater Weever.

The tiny LESSER WEEVER *(Trachinus vipera)* – only about
152mm (6 inches) long – is MORE VENOMOUS than its big
cousin, the greater weever. Lesser weevers are inshore fish; they
like to lie half buried in the seabed beneath shallow waters.

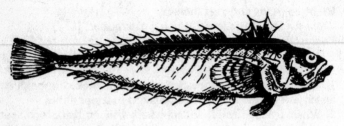

Fig. 113 Lesser Weever.

WEEVERS (greater and lesser) can kill!

Sadly, people have been killed by weever venom. Happily,
death is very rare and most victims of weever stings fully
recover after hospital treatment. NEVER TOUCH A WEEVER
and never kill a weever and leave its body where someone might
come in contact with it; the spines remain poisonous for several
days after the weever's death!

If a weever stings you, don't panic. Get to the nearest hospital
or doctor as quick as possible. *Stay calm;* shock may cause more
harm to your nervous system than the weever's venom.

You'll survive!

WHITING *(Merlangius merlangus).*
Family: Gadidae.
Average weight: Big rod-caught whiting can weigh 1.36kg (3 lb)
or above. The average whiting weighs about 0.45kg (1 lb).

Description: Large and pointed head; slim body; gold-green back and silver-white sides. Small, sharp teeth. WARNING: Nips from whiting teeth can infect your fingers – handle with care! ***Whiting are good to eat (see Chapter 40).

Fig. 114 Whiting.

Catch whiting! Hints:
Best locations: Round most parts of British Isles.
Season: Arrive inshore early autumn, SEPTEMBER/OCTOBER; stay close to shore through winter months: NOVEMBER/DECEMBER/JANUARY/FEBRUARY. Move to deeper offshore water about MARCH/APRIL.
Favourite feeding places: On or near bottom of sand, sand/mud or shell-grit seabed; will feed over rough, rocky ground and at mid-water level.
Successful baits: Ragworm, lugworm, shellfish, shrimps, prawns, sandeels, strips of fresh fish (herring, mackerel, sprat, pilchard, whiting), hermit crab.
   Artificial baits: small pirks (see fig 124) baited or unbaited and jigged.

Right methods and rigs include:
Shore fishing: 2 hook paternoster; 3 hook paternoster.
Boat fishing: 2 hook paternoster; 2 boom paternoster; 3 hook paternoster; 2 hook running leger; driftlining deep.

EXPERT TIPS
1. Groundbaiting is effective.
2. Whiting feed hungrily soon after dusk on frosty nights when the sea's calm and continue feeding into the night.
3. Have your bait supply ready to slip straight on the hook immediately a caught whiting is unhooked. Once whiting begin

biting, speedy and methodical unhooking, re-baiting, casting out and reeling-in, can catch a fair weight of tasty food for your freezer!

WRASSE, BALLAN *(Labrus bergylta).*
WRASSE, CUCKOO *(Labrus mixtus).*
Family: Labridae.
Average weight: Big rod-caught ballan wrasse can weigh 2.72kg (6 lb) or above. The average ballan wrasse weighs about 1kg (2¼ lb).

Big rod-caught cuckoo wrasse can weigh 0.56kg (1¼ lb) or above. The average cuckoo wrasse weighs about 227g (½ lb).

Fig. 115 Cuckoo Wrasse.

Description: Male cuckoo wrasse: brilliant blue black; orange-gold sides. Female cuckoo wrasse: vivid pink-red body; black spots on back.

Ballan wrasse: green or red/rust-brown body; sometimes infused with blue. Pale orange/white underneath. Colour pattern variable. Breeding ballan wrasse build nests to lay their eggs in!

Wrasse are not generally considered good to eat.

Catch wrasse! Hints:
Best locations: The BALLAN WRASSE is found round most of the British coast. The CUCKOO WRASSE is caught mainly along the shores of southern Britain.
Season: Wrasse are especially active close inshore during MAY/ JUNE/JULY/AUGUST/SEPTEMBER/OCTOBER.
Favourite feeding places: Near the base of inshore rocks; slightly offshore rocks; weed-covered reefs; old holed and cracked harbour walls; sandy patches of seabed between rocks and/or reefs. Where there are rocks you'll likely find wrasse!

Successful baits: Sandeels, small pieces of fresh fish (herring, mackerel, pilchard, squid); ragworms, lugworms; small shellfish (cockles, mussels, limpets); prawns, peeler crabs, soft-backed crabs.

Right methods and rigs include:
Shore fishing: Rotten bottom cast onto sandy area near rocks.
Rocks and harbour walls: Sliding float; rotten bottom.

EXPERT TIPS

1. A rising tide frequently brings large catches of wrasse.

2. Wrasse hustle together very close to the rock face, so position your baited hook as near as you're able to the rocks.

3. Don't let wrasse tangle your line round rocks. Reel-in hooked wrasse fast!

4. You'll need a long-handled landing net or drop net (see page 258) to hoist hooked wrass to a convenient unhooking place.

5. Float fished baits are often most effective presented about 304mm (1 ft) above the point where rock base meets seabed – the bottom. However, if your bait doesn't soon attract bites, adjust the float to raise the bait a bit further from the bottom, 304mm (1 ft) at a time; until you find the popular feeding level of the moment, and begin catching wrasse!

31

Quality Tackle for that Perfect Edge

Even expert skill won't overcome disaster if you hook a powerful fish on cheap, inferior tackle. For superior results buy the best tackle you can afford. Good tackle gives you a winning edge over big and strong, fighting fish. Buy best and always be the winner!

Correctly balanced tackle is essential to achieve ultimate angling performance. The only certain way to buy the right tackle for the type of sea fishing you want to enjoy is to visit your local specialist tackle dealer's shop and ask his professional advice.

Be wise, buy right and have no cause for regret. Quality tackle lends you that perfect edge!

Rods (see also the "suitable rods" section in Chapters 34 to 38). Suitable rods for different types of sea angling are suggested in the "Tackle Notes" section of Chapters 34 to 38.

Beach casting rods (see also page 254): specially designed to cast heavy weights into the surf of breaking waves where fish feed. Beach rods are built to cast a specified range of weights from 85g (3 oz) to 255g (9 oz). Details are supplied with new rods. NEVER EXCEED the maximum weight recommended for your rod, or it might break!

Boat rods (see also page 265): sold according to "line class". A 9.07kg (20 lb) line class boat rod is made to fish most effectively with line of 9.07kg (20 lb) breaking strain.

You may fish with line 2.26kg (5 lb) either side of the stated "line class" *but no more,* or you won't get the best "balanced" action from rod and line.

Reels
Suitable reels for different types of sea angling are suggested in the "Tackle Notes" sections of Chapters 34 to 38.

Fixed spool reels: easy to operate and perfect for the beginner fishing on shore. The reel's spool is "fixed" and unmoving; line simply strips off the spool when cast.

Multiplier reels cast line from a rotating drum; ideal for boat fishing, and reeling-in very heavy fish when shore angling (especially from tall rocks, piers and high harbour walls). A degree of skill is required to beach cast successfully with a multiplier, though once mastered, championship-class casts are possible with multiplier reels.

Ask your specialist tackle dealer to help you match rod and reel. A harmonious balance of weight and design brings amazing results.

Line (see also "Tackle Notes" sections of Chapters 34 to 38). Never buy "cut-price" line. Cheap line can't cope with big catches – it snaps! Fill fixed spool reels neatly to the spool lip with line. Fill multiplier reels with line evenly to the drum rim.

Weights

Also called "sinkers"; come in many shapes and sizes (see "Tackle Notes" sections of Chapters 34 to 38). "Balls", "bombs", "pears" and "torpedoes" are the best shapes for general use.

Weights fitted with grapnel wires grip the seabed in rough conditions, slowing tidal shift of the baited hook. Use the smallest weight necessary to hold your bait at the depth and position you expect fish to be feeding.

Hooks

High quality, non-brittle hooks sharpen to a proper chisel-edge. Check that the points are fish-hooking sharp before angling. Use an angler's sharpening stone to hone hook points to perfection.

Hook sizes

Sea hooks graduate from "small" sizes 6 or 4; 2 or 1 and 1/0 to giant size 10/0 or 12/0.

Match hook size to bait size and fish size. Use generous helpings of bait on large hooks to catch "specimen" size big fish.

Small hook sizes 6 or 4 are adequate for smaller fish: dabs, flounders, garfish, mackerel, wrasse etc.

Small hook sizes 2 or 1 are suitable for "smallish" fish: bass, young cod ("codling"), dabs, flounders, mullet, whiting etc.

Medium hook sizes 1/0 or 2/0 or 3/0 are suitable for larger fish: bass, cod, dogfish, skates, rays, whiting etc.

Big hook sizes 4/0 or 6/0 are suitable for bigger fish: cod, conger eels, dogfish, rays, skates, tope etc.

Monster hook sizes 8/0 and 10/0 or 12/0 are suitable for huge fish: tope, halibut, skates, sharks, Kraken and Leviathan etc.

Beginners usually find hook sizes 2 or 1 or 1/0 satisfactory for general sea fishing. Increase bait size and hook size where BIG fish are expected.

Extras

Invaluable items of tackle stocked by your specialist dealer and freely available for inspection in his shop include:

Tackle boxes and anglers' *haversacks, rucksacks* or *daypaks*.

Tackle boxes are neat and provide a seat but if you have to walk a distance, a rucksack may be better as it sits snug on your back.

Don't forget *boots* and *clothing;* sea anglers' *hook disgorgers* and *artery forceps* for removing hooks from fishes' mouths; *long-nosed pliers* to cut wire and line; *reel lubricant* and *small spanners* for re-fastening bits of rod and reel before they drop off!

Your local tackle shop is an Aladdin's cave of angling treasures. Browse round and be a regular customer. Support your local specialist tackle dealer and he'll be delighted to help you with advice, hints and tips. You can't manage without him!

TACKLE HINT

Salt water corrodes almost anything from leather boots to rod rings and reels. Rinse tackle taken sea fishing with cold tap water before drying, cleaning and storing.

SUPERHOOKERS

12 TOP TACKLE TIPS To Improve Your Fishing Pleasure

1. Hoard plastic bags of all sizes. Take a few on each fishing trip to keep spare clothing and tackle dry. Large, heavy-gauge plastic bin liners are useful for caught fish destined for the freezer. Special heavy-duty, self-sealing plastic bags (available in several sizes) are sold by tackle dealers.

2. Make sure any fishing jacket or waterproofs worn aren't too tight across your shoulders, or under the arms. Tight clothes cramp casting style.

3. Stripes of bright paint or fluorescent strips on tackle box, bag or rucksack, show their position clearly should light conditions fade after you've wandered from them.

4. A roll of waterproof electrical insulating tape is ideal for temporary patching of splits and tears in tackle or clothing; frayed rod whippings, and loose rod or reel fittings.

5. To prevent sand damaging the working parts of reels, rod rings and joints (ferrules) keep reels in reel cases until ready for use; assemble rods before reaching the beach. Brush sand and grit from tackle with a small, soft paintbrush before packing for your homeward journey.

6. An angler's umbrella gives welcome protection from strong winds on exposed beaches. Anchor the umbrella with umbrella guy ropes fitted to the top; tied to tent pegs fixed in the ground and covered with heavy stones.

7. A drop of rod varnish or waterproof Superglue on a well tied knot in fishing line increases the knot's strength.

8. Never put used wet hooks with unused dry hooks. Smear used hooks with angler's pilchard oil to counter the corrosive action of salt water; keep them separate from unused hooks until you've dried and sharpened them.

9. Hooked small ragworm or lugworm baits; soft baits like mussels, and "cocktails" of mixed small and/or soft baits that seem unlikely to stay on the hook after a long, hook-jarring cast, are easily stuck to one another and/or the hook with a tiny dollop of Superglue – which scrapes off hooks with a sharp knife. Don't glue your fingers to the hookbait!

10. An angler's battery-operated headlamp is a boon when fishing after dusk; fastened to your forehead by its comfortable headband, the headlamp leaves your hands free and beams light wherever you look (be safe; have a torch handy for extra instant light).

11. Strips of angler's luminous sticky tape wrapped around your rod at joints and tip show what's happening to the rod when fishing after dark. A fluorescent rod tip is valuable as an after-dusk bite indicator (see page 185).

12. When shore fishing in cold winter weather, or icy after dark hours, pack a camper's plastic "bivvy" or "survival" bag. If you fancy a break, pull the bag up over your legs and chest and enjoy a warming and revitalizing sit down snack.

32

Best Baits for Bites

Any small creature which lives where fish feed can be put on a hook, cast into the water, and catch fish! If in doubt – try it out! Some baits attract fishes better than others.

The best baits for bites vary from one species of fish to another (see Chapter 30) and from one area to another. Pop into the local specialist tackle shop for accurate advice and a supply of fresh, fish-catching bait.

Before collecting bait from the shore, check by-laws (if not displayed on a noticeboard near the shore, visit or phone the public reference library) to be certain bait-gathering and digging is permitted. Take a plastic bucket and lid; one or two sea angler's large plastic bait boxes and a few old newspapers. A full-size garden fork is necessary for digging. Remember to rinse the fork under tap water at home afterwards; oil metal parts to prevent rusting.

SAFETY HINTS
* Tread warily when collecting baits at low tide; be alert for soft "sinking" mud and quicksand!
* Fill in and smooth over holes and hollows dug; *before* someone stumbles into them!
* Watch for weevers lying under shallow water.

TIPS
1. Buy or gather bait the day you go fishing to be sure of fish-attracting freshness.
2. Keep fresh bait covered, in a cool place out of sunshine.
3. Never mix in the same container baits likely to EAT each other. For example, ragworms eat lugworms!
4. Use damaged freshly gathered baits immediately; they won't live long!
5. Stored bait: discard unhealthy looking, injured or dead specimens.
6. Baits can be hooked singly; in bunches; or in "cocktail"

assortments. Ragworm or lugworm and shellfish (mussels, cockles, limpets etc.) is a favourite "cocktail" with many greedy fishes.

7. Big fish prefer big baits; small fish seize small baits. Choose your bait size and hook size according to the species of fish you're hunting.

8. Improve appeal of drab looking baits with a squeeze of angler's pilchard oil.

9. Use a *sharp* filleting knife and securely placed cutting board when slicing fish for bait, and aim to *miss* your fingers!

Fig. 116 Mussels and cockles.
Above: Mussels on rock.
Below: Cockles fresh dug from sand.

Best Baits

CLAMS (shellfish): Live burrowed in sand and sand/mud, about 304mm (1 ft) beneath the surface. Prise open shell with a strong thin-bladed knife, and remove soft clam; thread on hook so the

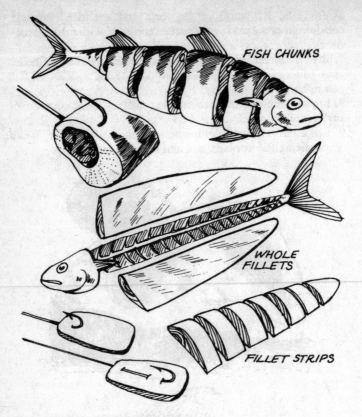

Fig. 117 Fish strip and chunk baits.

clam's tough "foot" is held firm on the hook's bend below the barbed hookpoint.

COCKLES (shellfish): Live burrowed in sand, sand/mud, or mud about 25mm (1 inch) beneath the surface. Prise open the shell with a strong thin-bladed knife and remove cockle; thread hook through cockle so the flesh is held firm on the hook's bend below the barbed hookpoint.

CRABS, COMMON: Shore or "green" crabs are called *peeler* crabs when they are about to "peel" or shed an outgrown shell ready to harden their skin into a new, bigger shell. As soon as a "peeler" crab has peeled the old shell, it's known as a *soft-backed* crab. After several days, the new shell has hardened and the crab is termed a *hard-backed* crab.

Peeler and soft-backed crabs make excellent bait for many species of fish. They can usually be found from May/June onwards, throughout the summer, at low tide in rock pools, shallow bays, estuaries and harbours. Crabs have favourite places to peel; once located, you can return for a regular supply.

Search for "peelers" and "soft backs" under stones, weed, breakwaters, pier or jetty supports etc. Mating female "peelers" may be found clinging for safety to the underside of hard-backed males, who will fight to defend them!

A peeler crab is identifiable by its old, soon-to-be-peeled shell – which looks dull and brittle. It comes away easily if tapped with a knife handle or stone. A soft-backed crab is betrayed by its new-looking, soft-skinned back.

Crabs, not wanted for immediate use, may be kept alive for a few days in a large loosely-covered (not airtight!) plastic bucket containing damp sand and seaweed; stored in a cool, shaded place. Don't mix peelers and soft-backs, and if they become hard-backed, take them to the shore and release them. Hard-backed crabs seldom make successful bait.

Kill crabs by stabbing between the eyes with a sharp knife. Remove claws; insert your hook through the crab's belly from its side. Push the hookpoint out of the crab's back, so the crab rests on the hook's bend below the barbed hookpoint. To be sure your hook isn't torn from the crab by casting, rough water or cunning fish: bunch together and bind the crab's side legs to your hook's long shank with a few turns of strong elastic thread, knotted tightly.

An alternative way of fastening a freshly killed crab to your hook using strong elastic thread is shown in fig 121. Break off the claws; strip away the shell and use the claw flesh as separate bait.

A large crab can be killed and sliced in half lengthways, to provide 2 generous-size baits. A crab may also be broken into pieces, and the shelled flesh threaded onto small hooks to catch fish.

CRABS, HERMIT (shellfish): Live in "borrowed" empty shells – graduating from small periwinkle shells to large whelk shells as the hermit crab grows in size. Small hermit crabs can be found in rock pools at low tide. Large hermit crabs live in deeper offshore water, and are often sold to sea anglers by commercial fishermen. Crack open the shell to remove the crab for hooking. Use either the tail only, or the whole freshly-killed crab, threaded onto the hook through its soft underneath (see fig 121).

Break off legs and claws to bleed scent into the water and make the crab obviously vulnerable and appealing to inquisitive fish.

EARTHWORMS (lobworms): Gather from soil and damp grass. Earthworms are an effective bait for estuary- and river-feeding sea fish (see Chapter 34). Earthworms don't live long in saltwater and aren't suitable for saltwater sea fishing. Thread on hook singly or in small bunches (see fig 120).

FISH: Catch your own fish for bait, or buy freshly-caught fish from a coastal fishmonger, or purchase direct from local commercial fishermen at the quayside.

Fresh herrings, mackerel, sprats and pilchards make the best all-round fish baits, because their natural oil content is high.

TIP

OIL:BLOOD:GUTS = SCENT
SCENT = BIG FISH INVESTIGATING!

Deep-frozen herrings and squid (your own or shop-bought) and sandeels also prove good bait; some species of fish become too soft to stay long on the hook after being deep-frozen.

Squid is a handy all-round bait; every part of a squid may be cut up and used to catch fish. Squid can also be fished whole (see fig 121) to attract *big* fish.

Any fresh fish offered as bait could appeal to predators. Consistently successful fish baits include: coalfish, small cod, garfish, pollack, pouting, whiting.

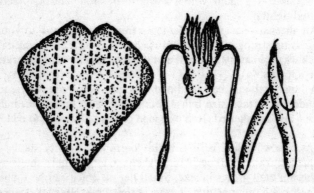

Fig. 118 Using squid as bait.
Left: Body and flap cut into strips.
Middle: Head.
Right: Strips of squid on hook; tied at top with thread to prevent slipping.

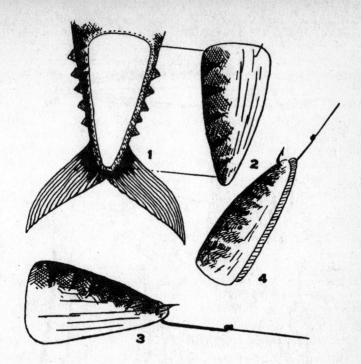

Fig. 119 Making a lask.

Hook live fish through the upper jaw, behind the lip; freshly killed whole or halved fish may be hooked through eye sockets; or your line pulled through the length of a whole freshly killed fish (see fig 121) using an angler's baiting needle. Bind the tail end of the fish bait with thread or elastic, to stop line cutting free from the flesh.

Slice bait fish into chunks, fillets or strips of suitable size to excite the fish you're pursuing. Mackerel "lasks" (see fig 119) cut from fresh mackerel almost always guarantee big bass catches when trolled in summertime.

TIP
Strips of fish, cut in shapes to resemble small fish, especially a tapered sandeel shape, are extraordinarily successful bait!

LIMPETS, COMMON (shellfish): Collected from rocks at low tide, common limpets attract some rock-feeding fish (wrasse, black

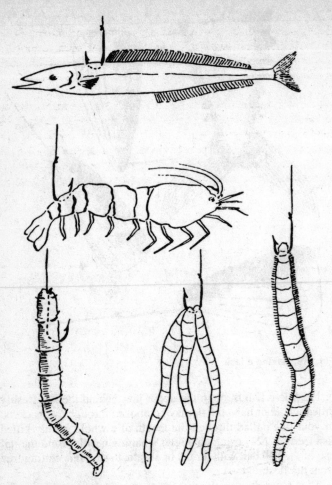

Fig. 120 Natural baits.
Top: Sandeel.
Middle: Prawn.
Below: Lugworm, earthworms, ragworm.

bream etc.), but are mainly added to bait "cocktails" (see page 234) and crushed for groundbait. When used as hookbait, carefully scoop limpet out of shell with a strong thin-bladed knife and thread on hook so the tough "foot" is held firm on the hook's bend below the barbed hookpoint.

LIMPETS, SLIPPER (shellfish): Live clustered together in shallow-water colonies; males on top, females underneath (see fig 122). Heavy seas wash slipper limpets ashore in large numbers. Prise shell clusters apart with a strong thin-bladed knife, carefully scoop out slipper limpet and thread on hook so the tough "foot" is held firm on the hook's bend below the barbed hookpoint.

LUGWORMS: Live burrowed about 0.45m (1½ ft) beneath sand or sand/mud in U-shaped tunnels, topped by coiled "casts" of ejected lugworm excrement. Lugworms average about 152mm (6 inches) in length, and may be dug at low tide. Store lugworms not wanted immediately as bait, spaced roughly 76mm (3 inches) apart from each other on sheets of clean dry newspaper,

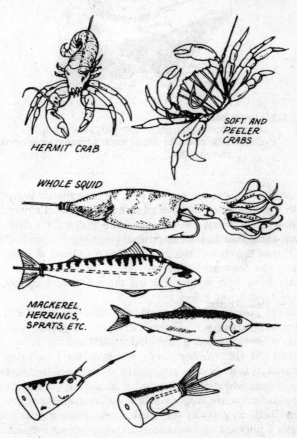

HERMIT CRAB

SOFT AND PEELER CRABS

WHOLE SQUID

MACKEREL, HERRINGS, SPRATS, ETC.

Fig. 121 More natural baits.

241

Fig. 122 Limpet baits.
Above: Common limpet adhering to piece of flint.
Below: Little colony of slipper limpets growing together on a piece of rock.

folded into a large plastic bait box, or large plastic bag pricked with a few air holes, and placed somewhere cool. Lugworms are best used fresh, but can be stored in a fridge for 3 days. They *stink* when dead and decomposing!

Thread onto hook through the lugworm's head, or at the point where the lugworm's thin tail meets the thicker trunk of its body. Some sea anglers tear off the tail before casting – to release fish-luring juices.

MUSSELS (shellfish): Gather at low tide from pier and jetty supports, harbour walls, breakwaters, and exposed rocks. Prise open shell with a strong thin-bladed knife and carefully remove mussel OR take mussels home and keep for 1 to 3 days in a covered plastic bucket containing damp sand and seaweed; stored somewhere cool. Shortly before setting out fishing, drop mussels into warm, slightly salted water; remove mussels from their shells as soon as the shells open. Place a few drops of angler's pilchard oil on mussels to restore scent evaporated by warm water and wrap in plastic bag. Thread mussel on hook so the tough "foot" is held firm on the hook's bend below the barbed hookpoint.

PRAWNS: Can be netted throughout summer months in rock pools at low tide; use a long-handled child's beach net. Prawns are most effective as bait fished alive. Dead or alive, thread on hook through the second or third segment of the tail (see fig 120).

RAGWORMS: Live burrowed in sand, sand/mud and mud. There are many kinds of ragworm; ranging in length from 25mm (1 inch) to "King" ragworm growing as long as 0.91m (3 ft)! Ragworms vary in colour from white or green, to the more familiar brown or bright red. The common ragworm is about 114mm (4½ inches) in length and brown-bronze coloured.

A ragworm's head houses extendable sharp jaws; large ragworms can give your fingers a painful nip!

Ragworms may be dug at low tide from estuaries, beaches, and harbours. Keep ragworms not wanted for immediate use wrapped between layers of clean, dry newspaper – leave a space of approximately 76mm (3 inches) between individual ragworms; fold the newspaper and carefully place in a large plastic bait box, or large plastic bag with a few pricked air holes.

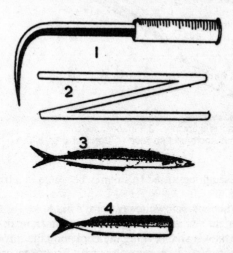

Fig. 123 Sandeels.
1. Rake-hook for getting sandeels out of the sand.
2. Zig-zag method of raking the sand.
3. Sandeel.
4. Sandeel with head and shoulders cut off; an excellent natural bait for spinning.

243

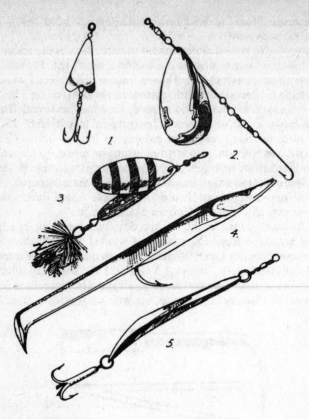

Fig. 124 Artificial baits.
1. Mackerel spinner. *2.* Flounder spoon.
3. Bass and mullet spinner. *4.* Sandeel lure. *5.* Pirk.

Ragworms, though best used fresh, may be stored in a fridge for about 6 days.

Thread onto hook below the ragworm's head (see fig 120), or push the hook into its mouth and slide ragworm along the whole length of the hook's shank; bring the hookpoint out through the ragworm's side. Very long ragworms may be broken in half or into several pieces before placing on one hook, or used to bait several hooks.

RAZORFISH: (shellfish): Live burrowed in sand, sand/mud, or mud; just below the surface, near the low tide line. Prise open the shell with a strong thin-bladed knife and remove the razorfish; thread on hook so the razorfish's tough "foot" is held firm on the hook's bend below the barbed hookpoint.

SANDEELS: Live on sandy seabeds, in estuaries, close inshore and offshore to a depth of about 20 fathoms (36.57m). Sandeels often disappear from shallow inshore waters in autumn, returning about May. Sandeels burrow beneath sand to a depth of about 203mm (8 inches). They can be uncovered by raking wet sand at low tide, in "zig zag" patterns (see fig 123).

Insert hook through body behind the sandeel's head (see fig 120), or through the sandeel's mouth, so the hook's bend and barbed point project from its throat or belly. A sandeel with head cut off; hooked onto an angler's dead bait mount (available from tackle dealers) and clipped to the link swivel on a spinning trace is a deadly attractive natural spinning bait!

PRESERVED BAITS:

Several popular natural baits, specially treated and preserved, are sold by tackle shops as "preserved baits". These baits are second-best to fresh natural baits, but convenient and sometimes reasonably effective. A liberal squeeze of angler's pilchard oil, applied before fishing, restores much of the bait's appetizing appeal. Among successful preserved baits are: lugworm, ragworm, shrimp, sprat, and chopped squid.

ARTIFICIALS

Spinners and *spoons,* many of which can be baited with a tasty morsel of fishes' favourite fresh foods, are designed for spinning (see trace); *pirks* for "jigging" and *sandeel* lures for spinning or trolling.

Artificials rely on movement, vibration, shape and colour to lure and excite fish into seizing them. Many highly successful artificial baits are on sale to today's sea angler.

33

Better Safe Than Dead

The sea is not our friend. The sea is neutral; it could offer us a big fish and drown us –with the same wave! Every year sea anglers drown, sadly the number is increasing. Where relevant, chapters in this book give clear safety hints; take note of them and survive!

And study Chapter 30, "Get Fish-Wise", for details of dangerous fish with skin-tearing teeth, and slashing spines or stings. Given half-a-chance, some fish would eat anglers for breakfast – snap, crackle and pop!

CLOTHING
Dress to stay warm, dry and smiling. Wear a woolly hat; carry a full set of waterproofs and spare pullover.

Put on some bright coloured clothing to give rescuers clear sight of you in the event of accident.

SNACKS
Don't forget to take a packed lunch, flask of hot soup and a couple of chocolate bars for emergencies. Leave the brandy-filled flask at home. Brandy doesn't warm you, quite the reverse – alcohol lowers your body temperature.

GENERAL SAFETY HINTS
* Tell someone where you intend fishing, and when to expect you back.
* Go fishing with a friend.
* Always carry an EMERGENCY SURVIVAL KIT which ought to include: *waterproof torch* + *spare bulb* and *batteries*.

The S.O.S. signal is . . . - - - . . . ; dot (short flash), dot, dot; dash (longer flash), dash, dash; dot, dot, dot. Repeat until answered.

The S.O.S. signal may also be made by reflecting sunlight from a mirror or polished metal.

Take a *whistle* as part of your kit. The international distress signal with a whistle is 6 short blasts in one minute; wait one minute, then repeat.

Map and compass (know how to use them). Sudden thick fog blots out familiar landmarks.

First aid kit: assorted plasters, roll of bandage, safety pins, antiseptic cream and pain killing tablets.

FOUR GOLDEN TIPS

1. Under qualified supervision, learn to swim *at least* 50m (55 yds) fully clothed.

2. Learn basic first aid at evening classes run by the Red Cross, St. John Ambulance Brigade, a similar organisation or qualified instructor.

3. If you find yourself in the water, stay calm and get out *quick!!!* Cold water *kills fast*.

4. Should you see someone in distress and can't immediately help, dial 999 from the nearest telephone. Ask for the police and/or coastguard; describe the exact location of the person requiring assistance.

34

Estuary and Harbour
Success Secrets

River mouth estuaries and harbour walls are easy to fish and careful, cunning anglers bag big catches of sizeable fishes.

Estuaries

An estuary is the meeting point between outflowing fresh water and incoming tidal sea water. The resultant mixture of fresh and salt water is termed "brackish" water.

Brackish estuary water supplies rich feeding for bass, conger eels, mackerel, mullet, flounders and freshwater eels. Bass cheerfully follow the rising tide 2 or 3 kilometres up river. Mullet sometimes venture 4.82km (3 miles) or more inland.

Most estuary-feeding fish move into the river mouth and cruise up river on a rising tide; have a party gobbling small crabs, fish fry, lugworms, prawns, ragworms, sandeels and shrimps and freshwater fishes' usual foodstuffs; then move back down river into the sea on the ebb tide.

Some fish stay in channels or pools. Flounders laze, partly buried, in water-covered sand/mud patches, waiting patiently for the next incoming tide. Small "school" bass and mullet withdraw to the security of deeper estuary water.

Fish remaining in estuary water at low tide respond to a well presented bait.

TIPS

1. As the tide begins to rise, large bass gather on the seaward side of shingle banks, sand/mud flats and sandbars, until the tidal current is high and strong enough to sweep them into the main centre channel of the river. Fishing for bass on the seaward side of an estuary entrance in a rising tide produces pleasing results.

2. Be ready for the run of fish passing up river on the high tide. Stealthily follow shoals along the river bank. Be prepared for the same shoals returning down river as the tide ebbs.

3. Pay special attention to drainage and sewage pipe outlets – always fruitful spots to fish; areas of sand and sand/mud housing lugworm and ragworm; weed-covered rocks, jetties and submerged stone steps beside moorings etc.

4. Groundbait suspended in a fine mesh bag or scattered loose attracts fish.

5. Stay out of sight; be quiet, tread lightly. Kneel low to cast bait and make no sharp, sudden movements against the skyline – or the fish will know you're hunting them.

Harbours

Harbours and cracks and clefts in harbour walls provide fish with a dependable and plentiful supply of natural food; scraps of people's discarded snacks; gutted fish offal thrown overboard by commercial fishermen. They also insulate fish from strong currents and wild weather conditions.

Many harbours are a haven for bass, conger eels, flounders, mackerel, mullet, small pollack, pouting, whiting etc.

TIPS

1. Watch for fishable eddies and deep water runs; gaps between weeds, and beds of sand or sand/mud.

2. Conger eels often live inside holes and cracks in stone harbour walls; outlet pipes and under sunken, rusting parts of wrecks.

3. Groundbait suspended in a fine mesh bag or scattered loose attracts fish.

4. Fish beside steps leading down to the water for easy landing of hooked fish.

Safety hints

* Beware of standing on estuary mud or sandbanks at low tide. You may be swallowed!

* Stay back from the edge of harbour walls and be careful descending slippery stone steps.

Right methods and rigs for estuary and harbour wall fishing include:

Light float; sliding float; basic leger where crabs are unlikely to seize hookbait; simple paternoster; running paternoster; 2 hook paternoster; spinning, driftlining and fly-fishing using freshwater fly-fishing tackle, techniques and artificial flies, to catch surface-feeding bass, mackerel or mullet.

Tackle Notes (see also Chapter 31)

Suitable rods: sea or strong freshwater rods, from 2.74m (9 ft) to 3.65m (12 ft) in length.

Suitable reels: fixed spool or multiplier.

Suitable line strength: from about 3.62kg (8 lb) to 5.44kg (12 lb) breaking strain.

Suitable weights: up to about 56g (2 oz) depending on the distance you wish to cast and strength of current.

* You'll find a long-handled landing net useful; a drop net from high harbour walls.

35

Champion Beach Casting

Shorefishing the tumbling surf from a beautiful beach is a refreshing and lively sport. Beach casting is a branch of sea fishing pursued and enjoyed by many champion sea anglers.

Sometimes fish, notably bass, dabs and flounders, search the seabed for food within 3.65m (12 ft) of the shore. At other times you'll have to cast 91.5m (100 yds) or more to put your baited hook among feeding shoals; though a cast of about 32m (35 yds) normally finds marauding fish.

Beach casting
To learn the secrets of beach casting champions, who cast a weighted line over 228.5m (250 yds) in casting tournaments, watch experts in action. View beach fishing and casting competitions; chat to competitors. Venues are advertised in the local and angling press. Take a course of instruction at Local Education Authority evening classes, a private course, or one at your nearest Sports' Centre. Better still – join a sea angling club!

Basics of beach casting
Stand comfortably with your feet apart; left foot pointing in the direction you wish to cast. Lower the rod behind you and point the tip down low towards the beach; lay 1.21m (4 ft) to 1.82m

Fig. 125 Beach casting style.

(6 ft) of line, including assembled and attached rig (see Chapter 39), on the beach. Grip the lower end of the rod butt with your left hand; with your right hand grip the reel seating (where the reel is fastened to the rod handle). Keep your right thumb on the reel line to prevent line slipping off the fixed spool's "spool" or multiplier's "drum".

Look towards your rod tip; your left shoulder and elbow facing in the direction you're about to cast.

Begin turning your body around; look into the sky above your target area (don't stare into the sun!); bring the rod upwards as you turn.

Firmly and smoothly power the rod forwards; finally whipping the rod out straight in the direction of your target area – release the line from your reel as the weight speeds past the rod tip. Don't move your position until the weight splashes into the sea, then stop your reel.

You'll soon develop a personal style of casting that suits you best. Beach casting is an easy, co-ordinated technique, requiring little physical strength. There should be no strained muscles!

To become a champion beach caster you must have confidence and practise regularly.

Start with modest expectations – 13.5m (15 yds). When you comfortably cast a specific distance, aim for a 9m (10 yds) improvement. It's surprising how quickly a laboured style of casting that barely reaches 23m (25 yds) may be nurtured into a technique effortlessly achieving 110m (120 yds) and beyond!

How to "read" the beach

Pick a place to fish away from car parks; holidaymakers' splashing and screeching "beach" radios. Fish stay further out to sea opposite noisy shores; often swimming along to quiet areas of beach, where they feel safe to venture closer inshore.

Spot likely patches of water from the cliff top. A telescope or a pair of binoculars helps!

Study the sea for dark blotches showing the position of underwater rocks and reefs; brown spreads of seabed sand; dark blue pools of water over deep gullies and channels; light blue expanses of "shallow" water over sand, sand/mud or shingle.

Note the location of large beds of sand between rocks and rough ground, favoured by dabs, flounders, plaice and rays. Sandy and sand/mud beaches may also attract (according to locality and season, see Chapter 30): bass, cod, dogfish (smoothhounds, lesser spotted dogfish, spurdog), mackerel, mullet, sole, tope, turbot and whiting.

Rocky and rough seabed draws (depending on location and season, see Chapter 30): bass, bream, coalfish, cod, conger eels, dogfish (bull huss), mackerel, pollack, pouting, skates, whiting and wrasse.

Jot useful notes and/or markings on Ordnance Survey maps of the area for future references. Keep an exercise book for detailed records of observations.

Having spied the sea from above, next explore the beach itself at low tide. Look for exposed weed-covered rocks, rock pools, hollows and channels hiding small marine creatures and tiny fish; patches of sand or sand/mud.

Check for the natural foods fish will expect to find as they forage through these food-rich dining spots on the incoming tide. Depending upon the type of beach (see Chapter 32), search for clams, cockles, fish fry, limpets, lugworms, mussels, prawns, ragworms, razorfish, sandeels, and shrimps. If, on the rising tide, you present a hookbait at the place fish suspect the "bait" lives naturally, you should catch fish!

Expect excellent catches on the sheltered side of breakwaters; around rocks; whirling currents and eddies; near the point where narrow streams, rivulets or drains flow into the sea; close to dense growths of weed, and power station warm water outflow pipes!

TIPS

1. Don't cast further than necessary. Heavy swells of rolling surf breaking on the shore stir up food particles and small creatures normally buried safe from attack. A cast beyond the 3rd or 4th breaking wave ("breaker") could catch a large bass.

2. For up to 4 or 5 days after a storm, fish feed close inshore.

3. If you're not hooking fish, try further out (or closer in!) until you find where the fish are feeding.

4. Fish seldom feed over barren shingle. Cast to the edge where shingle meets sand or sand/mud.

5. On calm, clear and sunny days fish usually prefer to stay offshore until dusk. But this is not always the case!

6. Dawn and dusk are often fruitful times to fish, especially when either coincides with a rising or high tide.

7. Keep a tight line on hooked fish; pull the rod upright and recover line in time with incoming waves (reel-in as waves come towards the shore), then the tide carries your fish to you. Don't strain too hard on the line, or the hook might rip from the fish's mouth – and lose the fish!

8. Once you've safely "beached" the hooked fish in shallow water, swing it ashore, or "tail" the fish; grab the fish's tail end and carry it ashore *after you're certain it's not a species with poisonous spines or stings or a nasty spur!!!* See Chapter 30; particularly the weevers, sting ray, and spurdog. Be wary of conger eels – they may tail you!

9. A beach caster's rod rest gives YOU a rest, but should not be over employed. Bites are missed when a rod isn't held.

Safety hints

* Don't get cut off by a rapidly rising ride.

* Before fishing isolated beaches, work out escape routes in event of mishap – no climbing cliffs! Clearly mark on your map quick escape routes to safety.

* Tie knots tightly. A heavy weight flying free from line you're casting could kill someone.

* Before casting, see there's nobody close behind.

Right methods and rigs for beach casting include:
Basic leger; simple paternoster; running paternoster; 2 hook paternoster; 2 hook running leger; 2 boom paternoster; spinning in deep water off steep shelving beach.

Tackle Notes (see also Chapter 31)

Suitable rods: beach caster rods from 3.35m (11 ft) to 3.96m (13 ft) in length. A beach caster rod of 3.50m (11½ ft) is ideal.

Suitable reels: fixed spool or multiplier.

Suitable line strength: main reel line from about 6.80kg (15 lb) to 11.33kg (25 lb) breaking strain. A main reel line of 9.07kg (20 lb) breaking strain is a good strength for all-round beach casting.

When beach casting, to absorb the shock on main reel line of casting a heavy weight long distances, a shock *leader line* is tied to the reel using the *leader knot* (see page 270). To be safe the shock leader line should be approximately 7m (23 ft) in length and about *twice* the breaking strain strength of the reel line used. For example, when casting with a main reel line of 9.07kg (20 lb) breaking strain, use the leader knot to tie 7m (23 ft) of 18.14kg (40 lb) breaking strain leader line to the main reel line.

The rig (weight and hook arrangement, see page 271) is tied to the leader line. Always attach the weight either direct to the leader line, or to line of the same breaking strain as the leader line (see rig designs, Chapter 39).

TIP

Tie the leader line to main reel line and wind onto your reel at home, before setting out to beach cast.

Suitable weights: from about 85g (3 oz) to 170g (6 oz) depending on strength of current and the distance you wish to cast. A 142g (5 oz) weight is normally adequate for long distance beach casting in strong currents.

36

Pier into yon Distance

Walking on water takes practice; walking over water on a pier or jetty is easy; a marvellous cheating way to fish deep water – no long casts from the beach to worry about, simply stroll to the end of the pier or jetty and let down your line.

Yes, a pier is the easiest way to present your baited hook to fish swimming out there – in yon distance!

Piers and jetties attract fish. The weed-covered supports are home for many shellfish and shelter shoals of small fish from strong currents and waves. Holiday makers, boat trippers, pier cafes and restaurants – each pitches the odd unwanted sandwich, scraps and leftovers into waves lapping the supports. All scrumptious food for big fish!

Among fish you may expect to catch from piers and/or jetties, depending on locality, season and type of seabed (see Chapter 30) are: bass, bream, coalfish, cod, conger eels, dabs, dogfish, flounders, garfish, mackerel, mullet, plaice, pollack, pouting, skates, whiting, wrasse etc.

Unfortunately, piers and jetties were not erected solely for sea anglers and few extend over prime fishing ground. However, the merits and sporting potential of particular piers and jetties are soon checked by referring to local tackle dealers, sea anglers; angling newspapers or magazines.

NOTE: Most of the following tips and hints apply to piers *and* jetties.

TIPS

1. Study the seabed beneath the pier or jetty at low tide. Look for patches of sand or sand/mud between rocks; dips, holes, hollows and gullies likely to be searched for trapped food particles by fish patrolling the rising tide. Notice their precise position in relation to clearly visible and memorable structures on the pier or jetty. Also look out for iron girders, concrete blocks and other obstacles which, when submerged on the high tide, might snag and snap your line. Check for signs of whirling

currents round supports – fish queue beside these eddies for snatches at spinning food sucked into the vortex. Weed-covered rocks, posts and pier or jetty supporting piles may prove great places to fish.

2. The best times to fish from a pier are generally dawn, dusk and night (if permitted). Many fish are attracted by lights on open-all-night piers. Big fish not fascinated by the lights are drawn to shoals of fish dancing to the underwater disco effect of the lights, and big fish make a meal of the small fish! One and a half hours before high tide is a good time to begin fishing; your sport should peak at high tide. When high tide occurs at dawn or dusk – BONANZA! You'll catch more than your fair share of fish.

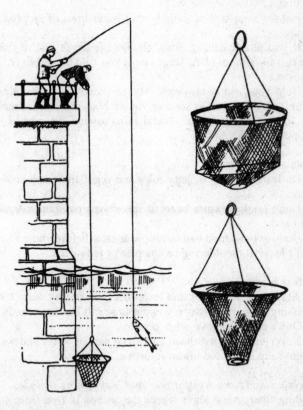

Fig. 126 Drop net in use.

3. Where possible fish on the lower deck of a pier or near a boat landing stage. It's easier to land your fish from a lower level. There you may find a long handled landing net useful (especially on jetties). You'll need a sea angler's drop net to haul hooked heavy fish from the sea to a high pier deck (see fig 126). A helpful friend saves the trouble of lowering the net yourself; manoeuvre your hooked fish over the mouth of the sunken net, then hoist up the cord and net.

4. When the sea's calm, fish in deep water off the pier end. In rough water, fish close to the shore. Heavy swell churns the seabed, dislodging natural food and buried titbits.

5. Groundbait suspended in a fine mesh bag about 1.21m (4 ft) from your hookbait attracts fish.

6. To foil persistent bait-pinching crabs, keep your bait at least 609mm (2 ft) above the seabed.

7. Fishing your bait at roughly mid-water level often produces results.

8. If you're not getting bites, change the depth you're fishing the bait in 609mm (2 ft) stages until you find the depth fish are feeding.

9. Hold your rod at all times – be prepared for a bite. Keep a tight line and reel-in as soon as you've hooked a fish; otherwise the fish wraps your line several turns around the pier or jetty supports and SNAP!

Do's and Don'ts

1. Do learn the pier or jetty rules and regulations and abide by them.

2. Don't hook pleasure boats or speedboats passing underneath your rod.

3. Do give unwanted bait to fellow anglers before you go home; don't leave it mouldering on the pier or jetty deck.

Safety hints:

* Stay clear of the pier and lower decks in stormy seas. A high breaking wave may sweep you out to sea. It has happened!

* Don't push or shove other people.

* Never make an overhead cast from pier or jetty. The weight might snap loose and injure someone.

Right methods and rigs for pier and jetty fishing include:
Sliding float; basic leger where the seabed is free from snags and crabs; simple paternoster; 2 hook paternoster; 3 hook

paternoster; 2 boom paternoster.

From jetties in calm water a light float may be used to catch mullet. When fishing from jetties and the lower decks of piers, spinning frequently brings success; as does driftlining providing the current carries your line away from line-snagging obstacles.

Tackle notes (see also Chapter 31)

Suitable rods: strong rods, from 2.43m (8 ft) to 3.50m (11½ ft) in length.

Suitable reels: fixed spool or multiplier.

Suitable line strength: from about 4.53kg (10 lb) to 6.80kg (15 lb) breaking strain.

Suitable weights: any weight up to about 28g (1 oz) depending on strength of current.

37

Fishing on the Rocks

Fishing from rocks is an exciting and exhilarating experience. You might be on an easily accessible rock outcrop merely a few metres higher than the crashing waves, or 30 metres (100 ft) or more above the sea on top of a sheer rock face.

Rocks are a rich source of fishes' natural food; provide protection from strong tidal currents; security from commercial trawlers, and handy holes and crevices for hiding from predators.

Fig. 127 Huge cliffs and rocks on the coast of North Wales.

The seabed may be mainly sand with some rough ground and small rocks, or rough, rocky ground leading to a solid rock base rising massively above the waves and towering skywards.

Fish eat tiny creatures found in weed growing on rocks; fish also feed on crabs, fish fry, limpets, lugworms, mussels, prawns, razorfish, sandeels, shrimps etc. If you can safely approach the rock base at low tide, check for promising places to fish: clumps of weed and colonies of shellfish; patches of sand or sand/mud between rocks; hollows in the rocks; little caves and caverns; clefts, channels and lanes between rocks – well travelled fish "highways" leading from one feeding "hotspot" to another. Plan to intercept fish at these points with your hookbait. Fish closely hug the rock walls, picking at growths of weed and clinging creatures; playing hide-and-seek with friends and foes.

As the tide rises, so fish ride higher in the water, investigating every nook and cranny for recently deposited morsels of food. And keeping a hungry eye on smaller feeding fish are the BIG predators.

Among the fish that can be caught in season (see Chapter 30) from rocks at various places round the coast are (depending on the nature of the seabed): bass, bream, coalfish, cod, conger eels, dabs, dogfish (bull huss), flounders, mackerel, plaice, pollack, pouting, whiting, wrasse, and sometimes rays, skates and tope.

Rock fishing may yield worthwhile catches and give good sport at any time of day; the best bags of fish are frequently caught on a rising tide near dawn, or as dusk approaches.

TIPS

1. Stay well back from the edge of rocks a few metres above the sea – for safety reasons *and* so the fish don't see you!

2. Groundbait suspended in a fine mesh bag or scattered loose attracts fish to your baited hook.

3. Choose a bait the fish will recognise as a natural food familiar to them round the rocks, and present that bait in a place and manner which seems normal and "natural" to the fish.

4. Keep your line tight to prevent it snagging and snapping on submerged rocks.

5. Reel-in line immediately a bite is indicated. The hooked fish must be prevented from diving under or between rocks and severing your line.

6. You'll need a long handled landing net or drop net to lift fish from water a few metres below your rod tip. If you're fishing from a rock ledge many metres above the sea, you'll have to fish with extra strong line of at least 13.60kg (30 lb) breaking strain so that you are able to haul your catch up the rock face.

Safety Hints
* Never go rock fishing alone.
* Wear walking or climbing boots; never rubber boots – they slip on wet rock.
* Carry a watch and make sure you know the times and heights of local tides. Stay well above rising tide waves.
* Keep back from the edge of the rocks; avoid slippery weed covered sections; stick to safe positions you can quickly vacate if the weather and waves turn rough.
* NEVER run across rocks.
* Save up for a comfortable sea angler's flotation jacket and wear it – just in case!

Right methods and rigs for rock fishing include:
Sliding float; heavy float; expendable float; rotten bottom; spinning for bass, mackerel and pollack; driftlining; feathering for mackerel.

Tackle Notes: (see also Chapter 31)
Suitable rods: strong rods, from 2.74m (9 ft) to 3.65m (12 ft) in length.
Suitable reels: fixed spool or multiplier.
Suitable line strength: from about 5.44kg (12 lb) to 8.16kg (18 lb) breaking strain. See also ***TIP*** number 6 on page 261.
Suitable weights: from about 14g ($^1/_2$ oz) to 42g ($1^1/_2$ oz) depending on the distance you wish to cast and strength of current.

38

Ace Boat Fishing

Sea fishing from a dinghy accompanied by an *experienced* boat handler, or sea anglers' commercial charter boat, is an ace way to savour exciting angling over mysterious depths: there's the thrilling anticipation of turning up trumps and landing the BIG one!

Fish shoals often follow regular routes across the seabed to established feeding grounds, called MARKS. Known "marks" nearly always guarantee good results. Marks favoured by fish (see Chapter 30) may be areas of sand, sand/mud, shell-grit, underwater rocks and reefs, deep holes, hollows, gullies, troughs or wrecks.

To learn boat fishing properly and locate the local "magic" fishing marks, put to sea with a professional charter boat skipper. He'll show you fish-catching tricks taught him by fellow skippers and champion sea anglers. The most economical way to boat fish frequently is to join a sea angling club, and take advantage of the club's discount block booking scheme. Your club books a boat and skipper for a fishing expedition and off you go – all the joys and rewards of expertly supervised boat angling at low cost.

Inshore fishing
Sea angling from a boat within 4.82km (3 miles) of the shore is "inshore fishing". A dinghy (*close* inshore) or motor launch is normally adequate for this type of angling.

Inshore fishing near sand or sand/mud river estuaries produces fair-sized bass, dabs, flounders, mullet, plaice, thornback rays and occasionally turbot.

Rocky, rough inshore seabed is good hunting ground for coalfish, conger eels, dogfish (bull huss), pollack, pouting and wrasse.

Deep sea fishing
Once 4.82km (3 miles) or more away from the shore, you're

deep sea fishing – regardless of the depth of water beneath the boat. A purpose-built sea-going vessel is essential for deep sea fishing.

Among the larger fish caught from deep sea marks are: big cod, coalfish, conger eels, halibut, ling, pollack, rays, skates, tope and turbot.

TIPS

Especially for supervised charter boat anglers

1. Don't drink too much home-brewed beer the night before your boat trip! Grab a restful night's sleep; dress in warm clothes and eat a light breakfast.

2. Pack a hearty lunch and flask of hot soup.

3. Take a spare pullover and waterproofs or a sea angler's flotation suit.

4. Tackle ought to include: a heavy, blunt instrument to kill fish for the family's cook; a sharp filleting knife; protective leather gloves for handling rough-skinned or spiny fish, and a sea angler's hook disgorger or artery forceps. A sea angler's long handled, large frame landing net helps board big fish!

5. And don't forget to take plenty of bait; a board on which to cut the bait; spare hooks and weights.

6. After fishing's finished, clean and tidy the boat. Leave everything "ship shape and Bristol fashion" and you'll be welcomed back, next time.

Safety Hints

Especially for supervised charter boat anglers

* Wear an inflatable life jacket (either your own or one supplied by the boat's skipper). A sea angler's flotation suit is a wise investment. Your life is worth the price!

* Never wear thigh boots in a boat. Should you fall overboard, they'll fill with water and sink you like a stone. Wear rubber soled walking boots or calf high rubber boots, and kick them off as soon as possible if you should go over the side.

Right methods and rigs for boat fishing include:

Sliding float; 2 hook running leger; 2 boom paternoster; boat leger; spinning; driftlining; jigging; trolling; feathering; even fly-fishing inshore, using freshwater fly-fishing tackle, techniques, and large artificial flies – for fish feeding on the surface, especially bass, mackerel and mullet.

Tackle Notes (see also Chapter 31)

Suitable rods: powerful, stiff boat rods from 2.13m (7 ft) to 2.43m (8 ft) in length. Line class 9.07kg (20 lb) or 13.60kg (30 lb) – see page 230.

Suitable reel: multiplier.

Suitable line strength: from about 6.80kg (15 lb) to 11.33kg (25 lb) breaking strain for normal boat fishing with a 9.07kg (20 lb) line class boat rod; about 11.33kg (25 lb) to 15.87kg (35 lb) breaking strain with a 13.60kg (30 lb) line class boat rod, where particularly large and heavy fish are expected.

Suitable weights: from about 227g (8 oz) to 0.90kg (2 lb) depending on strength of current, depth and size of bait fished.

39
Knots, Rigs and Fishing Methods

This chapter is concerned with knots, rigs and sea fishing methods; some simple, others complicated, ingenious or plain weird!

Be warned: sea anglers DO become obsessed by the arrangement of hooks and weights at the end of line. I know sea anglers who spend more time designing and tying rigs than fishing!

Experienced anglers develop their own favourite super-successful rigs to suit specific localities and species of fish.

You'll soon devise your own winning rigs! And someone will sidle over to you, point inquisitively at your rig and say, "What about the angle of the dangle on your doodum? What do you call it? How do you tie that!? Please show me."

TIPS

To keep pace with the latest experiments and discoveries in "doodum" tackle rig construction, read sea angling newspapers and magazines.

KNOTS

Knots for sea anglers come into and pass out of fashion faster than ladies' hats. Learn a few good knots that work well for you; practise tying the knots to perfection, then stick with them until you need something different or stronger.

Meanwhile, the following knots – properly tied – won't let you down.

TIP

To tighten knots fully; spit on them and pull the ends tight with angler's pliers. Saliva moistens the knot, easing the turns of line together firmly under pressure. When you trim the knot with pliers or scissors, leave "ends" of about 4mm (⅛ inch).

Tucked half blood knot

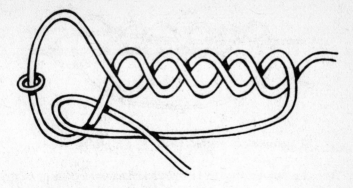

Fig. 128 Tucked half blood knot.

To tie line to a loop or any eyed item of tackle (hooks, swivels, split rings, weights etc.). This knot is usually adequate for sea fishing.

Palomar Knot

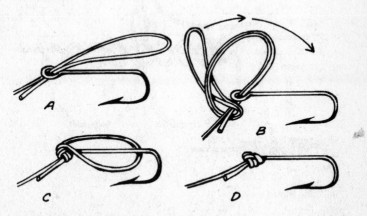

Fig. 129 Palomar knot.

The **palomar knot** is a slightly stronger knot, preferred by many sea anglers for tying line to hooks and/or swivels.

Universal or "grinner" knot

Fig. 130 Universal or "grinner" knot.

An extra-strong alternative to the tucked half blood knot (see fig 128).

Blood loop

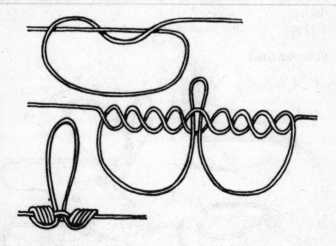

Fig. 131 Blood loop.

For tying a loop in main line. A short length of "stand off" line presenting the hook and bait is then tied to the blood loop. The short length of stand off line is commonly called a "snood" or "dropper" (see also page 271).

Double overhand loop knot

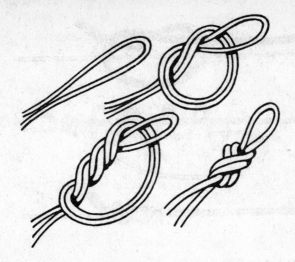

Fig. 132 Double overhand loop knot.

To tie a loop at the end of a length of line.

To join looped lines, traces, etc.

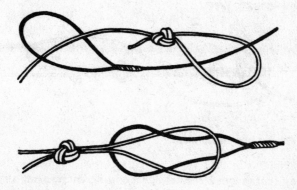

Fig. 133. To join looped lines, traces, etc.

Simple, strong and effective way to join loop knotted lines, looped trace, etc.

Leader knot

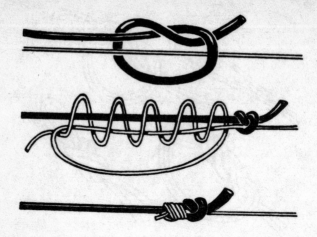

Fig. 134 Leader knot.

For tying beach casting "leader line" to main reel line (see Chapter 35 and page 254).

Double grinner knot

Fig. 135 Double grinner knot.

Strong knot to join 2 lines of equal or different breaking strain.

Stop knot
To stop a sliding float (see rig, page 273) at the required depth, and/or stop otherwise free-moving swivels, beads, weights etc. slipping unchecked along line.

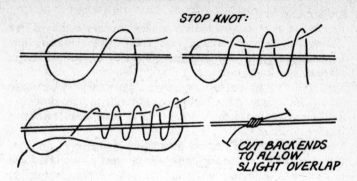

Fig. 136. Stop knot.

RIGS

The term "rig" refers to the planned arrangement of float (if any), swivels and/or split rings, beads (if any), knots, weights, hooks etc. along the end section of your line – the part of your tackle set up that *catches fish*.

Right rigs to use for best catches of big fish of different species are listed in Chapter 30 and Chapters 34 to 38. However, the rigs shown on the following pages are but a few of the many "right rigs" that consistently bring success when properly fished.

QUESTION: "When is a right rig wrong?"

ANSWER: "When it doesn't catch fish!"

About rigs

Rigs can be made in comfort at home; wound on a small line winder frame, or carefully coiled, and stored tangle-free until wanted.

Ready-made rigs are marketed and available from your local specialist tackle dealer. Of course, they're more costly than home made rigs, but time-saving and convenient if you don't mind paying the price. They show how professionally tied rigs look.

Doodum rig words

Your guide to some sea anglers' jargon.

Dropper: same as "snood", see below.

Snood: short length of line tied to hook.

Terminal tackle: same as "rig", see above.

Trace: length of line or wire tied between hook and main line.

Beads: act as protective buffers against abrasive action of free sliding weights, swivels or split rings on knots tied in main line.

Leger stops: angler's plastic leger stops may be used on line in place of stop knots (see page 270) tied to line.

Split rings: strong and less expensive alternative to swivels (see below) for attaching line and pieces of tackle to line. However, unlike swivels, split rings don't help prevent kinks, twists or tangles in line.

Swivels: "swivelling" action of rotating swivel eyes prevents twists and kinks in line and helps stop tangles! Also an easy and efficient way of joining lengths of line and/or linking weights to line.

To make the rigs illustrated in this book, you may choose to buy swivels and/or split rings, beads and leger stops from your tackle dealer, or put the rigs together using only simple knots and save money. They're *your* rigs!

RIG NOTES

The object of any rig is to present hookbait in a "natural" way to the species of fish you're hunting, without alarming the fish or making them suspicious.

If your rig fools fish into seizing the bait, it's a winning rig. Sketch your best fish-catching rig designs in an exercise book or "log" book.

Think about the place on or near the seabed, and/or the depth you want to present your hookbait to particular fish (refer to Chapter 30). Take a close look at rig designs and decide which one is more likely to catch fish. Then construct the rig.

Make a few different rigs at home and act the part of a wily big fish – see how the rigs look through your pretend fish's eye. Tug the hook and feel the resistance fish will be aware of as they examine the bait. *Think* about the rig *before* you use it.

The battle of wits with big fish is won at home in the comfy chair, before you go fishing!

TIPS

1. Keep rigs simple.
2. After use, check rigs for signs of damage – cuts, nicks, splits etc. and line strain (limpness). A damaged or strained rig loses fish! Replace parts where necessary. Expert sea anglers regularly re-tie rigs with new line.

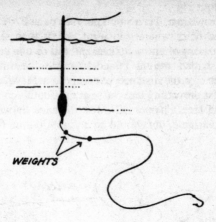

Fig. 137 Light float rig.

Light float rig

Use a slim float and small freshwater fishing weights – enough
to sink (cock) the float so that only its tip shows clearly above
the water. Adjust to present your baited hook at the depth you
expect fish to be feeding (see Chapter 30). Re-adjust when
necessary to allow for rise and fall of tide etc.

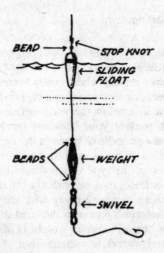

Fig. 138 Sliding float rig.

Sliding float rig

Use a narrow float. Tie a stop knot (see page 270) onto the main line at the point where you want the float to stop. Re-adjust when necessary to allow for rise and fall of tide etc. A "ball" or "barrel" shaped weight is ideal; attach the smallest weight required to cast the distance you want to achieve, and hold your bait against prevailing current(s) at the depth you expect fish to be feeding (see Chapter 30). The distance between hook and swivel is variable, but should be at least 304mm (1 ft).

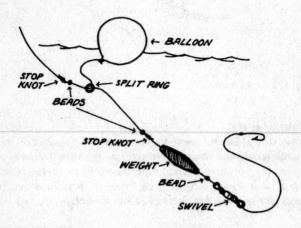

Fig. 139 Heavy float rig.

Heavy float rig

For float fishing large, "heavy" baits for big fish in deep water over rough or rocky ground where costly losses of conventional floats are probable, due to snagged and broken line. This rig also keeps most of the line below the water off sharp seabed rocks, if you decide to present your hookbait lying on the bottom. Remember to make periodic changes in the depth setting (when necessary) to allow for rise and fall of tide. Small, bright coloured balloons, of the type which would be around 102mm (4 inches) fully inflated, may be partially inflated to give lower resistance to a fish swimming away with the hookbait. Use a small split ring that won't pass over the bead and stop knot/leger stop. A "ball" or "barrel" shaped weight is ideal. The distance between hook and swivel is variable, but should be at least 304mm (1 ft).

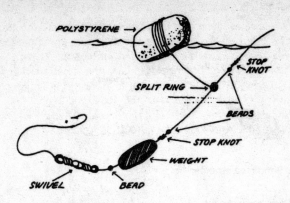

Fig. 140 Expendable float rig.

Expendable float rig

To fish over rough or rocky ground where costly float losses are probable. A chunk of polystyrene tile or packaging is usable, as are sealed and painted small plastic bottles; scraps of cork board or balsa wood etc. Anything that floats! A "ball" or "barrel" shaped weight is ideal. The distance between hook and swivel is variable, but should be at least 304mm (1 ft). Adjust depth setting of the "float" (if necessary) to allow for rise and fall of tide.

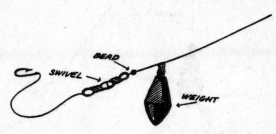

Fig. 141 Basic leger rig.

Basic leger rig

To lay hookbait on the seabed. The distance between hook and swivel is variable, but should be at least 304mm (1 ft). Because your line is free to pass through the weight's "eye", shy or suspicious fish can tug the bait without immediately feeling resistance.

275

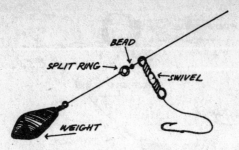

Fig. 142 Simple paternoster rig.

Simple paternoster rig

To present your bait above the seabed, moving with the current. The distance between weight and split ring is variable, but should be at least 304mm (1 ft). The distance between hook and swivel (free running on main line) is variable, but should be at least 152mm (6 inches).

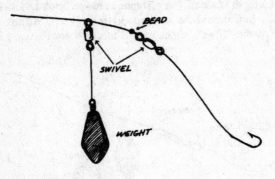

Fig. 143 Running paternoster rig.

Running paternoster rig

To offer your hookbait anchored above the seabed, and permit the fish to take the bait without immediately feeling resistance from the weight. The distance between hook and swivel is variable, but should be at least 152mm (6 inches). The distance between weight and swivel on connecting line is variable, but should normally be about 609mm (2 ft).

276

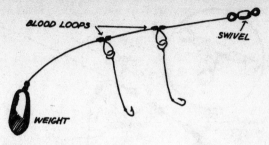

Fig. 144 2 hook paternoster rig.

2 hook paternoster rig

To present 2 baited hooks above the seabed. Two different hookbaits may be used if you wish. Some beach casting (see Chapter 35) anglers clip a small split ring onto the weight's "eye" and tie line to the split ring, thereby reducing seabed wear and tear on the knot. Alternatively, the line can be tied direct to the weight. 3 way swivels may be used in place of the blood loops. The distances between weight, 1st blood loop and 2nd blood loop and top swivel/or split ring, are variable but should each normally be 457mm (1½ ft). The distance between hook and blood loop is variable, but should be about 203mm (8 inches).

3 hook paternoster rig

To present three hooks and baits above the seabed at different depths. Three different baits may be used. The distance between each blood loop is variable, but should normally be at least 457mm (1½ ft). The lines connecting hooks to blood loops should be at least 203mm (8 inches).

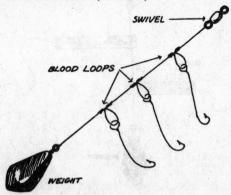

Fig. 145 3 hook paternoster rig.

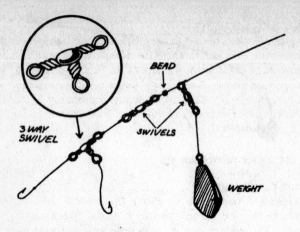

Fig. 146 2 hook running leger rig.

2 hook running leger rig

To present 2 hookbaits on or very near the seabed. Two different
baits may be fished. The distance between hooks and 3 way
swivel is variable, but should be at least 203mm (8 inches). To
fish the bait just above the seabed, attach the weight to a swivel
on the main line by a line about 1m (3 ft) long; or to lay the bait
on the seabed, fit the weight direct to the main line. The distance
between 3 way swivel and bead is variable, but should normally
be at least 304mm (1 ft).

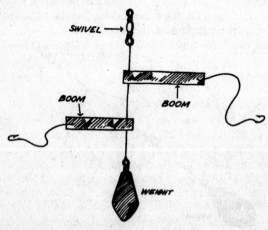

Fig. 147 2 boom paternoster rig.

2 boom paternoster rig

To present 2 baited hooks above the seabed, and moving freely in the current. Plastic booms rid the possibility of lines tangling and encourage vigorous movement of the baits in a current. Two different baits may be fished. The distance between weight and boom is variable, but each spacing should normally be at least 457mm (1¹/₂ ft). The hooks should be at least 203mm (8 inches) from the booms.

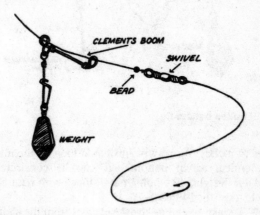

Fig. 148 Boat leger rig.

Boat leger rig

Simple and effective leger rig for boat anglers. The distance between hook and swivel is variable, but should normally be about 1m (3 ft). Your bait is presented on the seabed; line is free to move through the boom without jarring against the weight to alarm bait-biting fish.

Rotten bottom rigs

For use when fishing over reefs or rocks, where you're prepared to lose a trapped weight, but reluctant also to lose swivels, hooks and long lengths of line. If your weight is inextricably caught among rocks, steady pressure on your line by pulling with gloved hands (don't strain your rod) snaps the weaker "light" line attaching weight to main line. The lighter line should be ABOUT half the breaking strain of the main line. The distance between weight and swivel is variable, but should be at least 203mm (8 inches). The hook ought to be a minimum of

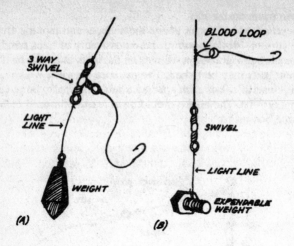

Fig. 149 Rotten bottom rig.

152mm (6 inches) from swivel or blood loop on the main line.

Economical rotten bottom rigs can be constructed with expendable weights like bolts, nuts, stones with naturally worn holes etc. (see fig 149 (B)).

DON'T make sweeping overhead casts from the shore with a rotten bottom rig. The weight could break loose and injure someone!

Spinning trace

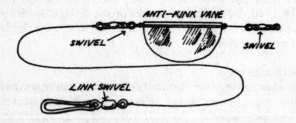

Fig. 150 Spinning trace.

To spin a bait, usually an artificial lure, simply cast your line and then reel-in. Raise and lower your rod tip; move the rod tip from side to side, and vary your reeling-in speed. These actions make the spinning bait/lure come "alive" to interested fish. The link swivel snaps onto the swivel-eye on lures; enabling fast change of lures when required. However, the trace line can be tied direct to the lure's swivel-eye or an eyed hook. The anti-kink vane helps prevent kinks, twists and tangles in line. A special anti-kink weight may be attached to the trace or main line in addition to, or instead of, the anti-kink vane. The attachment of an anti-kink weight gives potential for casting longer distances; sinks the bait/lure deeper in the water and slows the rate of "spin". The distance between link swivel and anti-kink vane is variable, but should normally be about 762mm ($2^1/_2$ ft) to 1.52m (5 ft) depending on the size of bait/lure you're using and depth of water you're spinning.

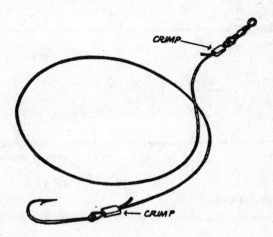

Fig. 151 Wire trace.

Wire trace

For attaching to line when hunting fish with strong jaws and sharp, line-cutting teeth. Angler's trace wire is marketed in strengths ranging from 4.53kg (10 lb) breaking strain to over 91kg (200 lb) breaking strain. Special ready-assembled wire traces and hooks suitable for conger eels, halibut, ling, skate and tope are stocked by specialist tackle dealers or you can make your own. You'll need angler's crimping pliers to "crimp" tight the securing metal crimps or "ferrules" (see fig 151). The length of wire traces is variable, but should normally be at least

457mm (1½ ft). One metre (3 ft) is a popular minimum length. For big fish use a wire trace of at least 36.28kg (80 lb) breaking strain).

MORE USEFUL METHODS

Driftlining
From shore or anchored boat; simply cast your line and let it "drift" with the current. The depth your bait is presented to fish depends on: a) length of line released from your reel; b) strength of current; and c) weight of bait and amount of additional weight (if any) attached to the line.

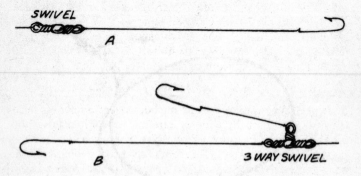

Fig. 152 Driftlines.

Rig: Driftline rigs may be fished with one or 2 baited hooks (see fig 152). In rigs "A" and "B" allow 1.5m (5 ft) between the hook at the end of your main line and swivel. With rig "B" the distance between second hook and 3 way swivel should be at least 305mm (1 ft).

TIPS
Attach little, if any, weight to the line. Driftline in places where your line won't snag on submerged obstacles. Gradually let out line from your reel, to a maximum length of roughly 20m (65½ ft). Occasionally reel-in and then release a metre or two of line; this action raises and waves your hookbait enticingly in the water.

Feathering

Fishing a hook or series of hooks wrapped around with feathers (real or imitation) and attached to your line. Commercially marketed feathering traces are available from sea angling tackle dealers. Once you see how they're put together, you can make your own!

The feathers, imitating a small shoal of tiny fish, may be trailed behind a boat, or cast out on line (which can be weighted) from pier, jetty, harbour wall or rock outcrop, and retrieved in a jerky manner to excite and attract hungry fish.

Feathering is sometimes an effective way to catch large numbers of small cod; mackerel or pollack.

Jigging

A method of fishing bait, often an artificial lure, from boat, pier, jetty or harbour wall. Cast the line (which may also be weighted) and reel-in line jerkily and very slowly. As you recover line, raise and lower the rod tip to give a "jigged" rise and sink motion to the lure or bait.

Trolling

Style of fishing from a slow moving boat. A basic spinning trace (see page 280), usually with an anti-kink weight in place of the anti-kink vane illustrated, is attached to your main line and trailed behind the boat. The depth your bait (commonly an artificial lure) is presented to fish depends on: a) speed of the boat and length of line released – normally about 50m (55 yds); and b) amount of weight attached to the line.

40

Cook Your Catch

Eat delicious meals prepared from freshly-caught fish and know that the highly nutritious flesh, which is low in fat, rich in protein and vitamins, is completely free of the chemical additives found in some commercially marketed fish.

Bumper catches of fish are easily cleaned and filleted or cut into chunky cutlets and frozen sea-fresh in your freezer. Frozen fish stays in excellent condition for at least 3 months.

Many exciting, mouth-watering fish dish recipes are widely available to enthusiastic chefs. The liberal use of inexpensive home made wine, beer or cider bestows a new zest to appetizing fish cookery.

Fish is easily digested, and, according to grandma, "good for the brain."

By the sea
Fish you decide to keep for cooking should be killed straight away. To kill a fish, strike it firmly across the back of its head with a heavy object. Conger eels are a special case, see page 198. Store the dead fish in a shady place out of sun and wind.

Gut fish as soon as convenient after killing them; simply slit open the stomach and remove insides. The liver plus any roe (eggs) may be kept and cooked.

Don't leave slippery fish guts lying about. Either put the guts in a plastic bag or covered container for use later the same day as groundbait, or throw the guts into the sea as a gift to the fish.

Cut off and dispose of spines or spurs (see spurdog, page 201). Removing the head from large fish is optional, but does save carrying extra weight on the journey home. Some chefs prefer to cook fish with the head left on. Rinse the gutted fish in salt water to get rid of blood and torn skin tissue.

At home
Scrape off fish scales in warm water. Remove fins and tail and

skin (if appropriate) with a sharp knife. Trim the fish flesh into slim fillets or slice into chunky cutlets.

FISH FOR THE FREEZER MUST BE FROZEN WITHIN 24 HOURS OF BEING CAUGHT.

Portions
227g (¹/₂ lb) fish per person satisfies the healthiest appetites!

TIP
Most of the flesh on rays and skates is found on the wings. Conger eels taste superb cooked and served in their skins.

Popular ways to cook fish
Baked fish: bass, cod, conger eels (skinning optional), dogfish, gurnard, halibut, john dory, ling, mackerel, rays (cut off and cook skinned wings only); skates (cut off and cook skinned wings only); soles (skinned), turbot, whiting.
Boiled or stewed fish: cod, conger eels (skinning optional), halibut, john dory, mackerel, skates (cut off and cook skinned wings only); soles (skinned), turbot.
Casseroled fish: angler fish, brill, coalfish, cod, conger eels (skinning optional), dogfish, halibut, ling, pollack, turbot.
Fried fish: bream, coalfish, cod, dabs, dogfish, flounders, garfish, halibut, john dory, ling, mackerel, plaice, pollack, rays (cut off and cook skinned wings only); skates (cut off and cook skinned wings only); soles (skinned), whiting.
Grilled fish: bass, bream, cod, conger eels (skinning optional), dabs, dogfish, halibut, john dory, ling, mackerel, plaice, rays (cut off and cook skinned wings only); skates (cut off and cook skinned wings only); soles (skinned), tope.

BON APPÉTIT!

Index